Living Beyond the "End of the World"

Living Beyond the "End of the World"

A Spirituality of Hope

MARGARET SWEDISH

ORBIS BOOKS

Maryknoll, New York 10545

Founded in 1970, Orbis Books endeavors to publish works that enlighten the mind, nourish the spirit, and challenge the conscience. The publishing arm of the Maryknoll Fathers and Brothers, Orbis seeks to explore the global dimensions of the Christian faith and mission, to invite dialogue with diverse cultures and religious traditions, and to serve the cause of reconciliation and peace. The books published reflect the views of their authors and do not represent the official position of the Maryknoll Society. To learn more about Maryknoll and Orbis Books, please visit our website at www.maryknoll.org.

Library of Congress Cataloging-in-Publication Data

Swedish, Margaret.
    Living beyond the end of the world : a spirituality of hope / Margaret Swedish.
        p. cm.
        ISBN-13: 978-1-57075-767-9
    1. Change—Religious aspects—Christianity. 2. Forecasting. 3. Hope—Religious aspects—Christianity. I. Title.
        BV4509.5.S94 2008
        261.8—dc22
                        2007039700

For my godson, Aidan Romero
Remember the time we stood on the bridge over
the river and you said to me: "Someday
I will bring my godson here."
We will always be together there.
It will be our bond, our special place.
It is written on my heart.

and for Maya
Earth's Friend, and mine.
You got here just in time.

and for Deanna
A light in my life.

Be strong.

Contents

Preface

No doubt every generation feels that it is born to exceptional times. Yet it is now apparent that we are indeed facing times unprecedented in the evolution of our species, if only because we face the prospect of our own extinction. Everywhere we turn there are fundamental challenges to our way of life and to how we think of ourselves—as human beings on this earth, as US Americans.

At the very least, we cannot go on as we have been. The changes we face are huge—and they are scary. Our way of life is dying—or perhaps to put it another way, it is killing us, killing life on our planet—and it can no longer be supported. Whatever denial mechanisms we choose to distance ourselves from this reality, we cannot make it go away.

Global climate change, wars for oil, looming conflicts over fresh-water sources, expectations of constant availability of an immense array of consumer goods, mobility that we claim as practically a birthright, adding house to house and field to field in an "ownership society" (the summer home, the winter home, the condo downtown, as well as the house in the suburbs)—these trends are crashing into one another in dramatic fashion. Until now, many battles that took shape around them had to do with basic questions of justice and moral values, issues related to vast inequities among people and nations, the concentration of wealth among the few, and the growing gap between rich and poor.

But we are now confronting an issue that is even more fundamental and that adds enormous weight to the issue of justice; that is, how we live, how we consume, the way in which we have exploited the earth since the dawn of the industrial revolution for our comfort and enrichment in this country is not sustainable. We are steadily accelerating toward the limits of this US way of life—in other words, toward a destructive, possibly fatal, future, unless we make some drastic changes now.

We are at the point where we as a society, connected deeply and intimately to a human community that spans the globe, must make some fundamental decisions about how we are going to proceed. The question of justice is intertwined with the question of human survival and the decisions we will make about our future.

We are shocked by the massive death tolls in earthquakes and hurricanes without recognizing what has happened to the global population in the past fifty years. Humans have spread across the globe, doubling, tripling our numbers in the space of a few generations. Many environmentalists argue that we have already overpopulated the earth—and the population is growing still. When disasters happen now, like those we have faced in recent years, they are likely to be accompanied by massive death tolls. When new viruses appear, and they always have and always will, they are far more likely to spread quickly across the globe. We have learned this lesson from the AIDS epidemic, the coming to the United States of the West Nile virus, the worldwide fear of an outbreak of the H5N1 avian flu virus, and the resurgence of a virulent strain of tuberculosis not responsive to treatment.

We are accelerating climate changes that increasing numbers of scientists believe can no longer be reversed. Melting permafrost in Siberia, summer melting of the Arctic Ocean, collapsing Antarctic ice sheets, receding glaciers, and warming ocean temperatures may indicate that we have already arrived at the tipping point where irreversible global warming will alter life as we know it across every part of our planet.

The news and warnings feel overwhelming at times, and it is normal to want to shut off the noise and go on about our lives as if environmental impacts are not true, not imminent, not here right now. We read that extinctions are happening at a dizzying pace, that desertification is threatening hundreds of millions of people, that rising ocean levels are threatening some of the world's largest urban centers, that we are reaching peak oil production with all that will mean for our oil-based economy, and on and on. Some say the earth will respond to the unprecedented stresses on its richly diverse ecosystems with mass die-offs of species, including our own.

As if this were not enough, we are also confronting an increasingly conflictive political environment around the world, including intensifying competition to grab control of natural resources; the rise of a fundamentalist global Islamic insurgency that the West seems too lazy or hubristic to understand; mass migrations of people who cannot survive in their homelands who are crossing borders in search of work; more traditional clashes of global powers competing for political, economic, or military advantage; and the same old ethnic and nationalist clashes that have taken place throughout our history. All of these stresses are intertwined in complex and bewildering ways.

In this country we are also confronted with the challenge that, just as we face this time of human transition that requires the best of all of us and our earnest participation in the decisions that need to be made, our democracy seems to have fallen apart, taken over by the very corporate powers in whose interest it is to maintain the status quo as long as possible or by ideologues with a grandiose notion of US supremacy that they are actively asserting around the world.

We have precious few leaders willing to talk honestly about any of these issues.

Many people are asking why fundamental change in this country seems so impossible, given the evidence we all have in front of us of a world reeling with change. Are we human beings really unable to alter self-destructive behaviors until we are faced with disaster? Are we really so disconnected from our fate and the fate of humanity that we are unaffected by the suffering, and imminent suffering, of the majority of people around the world because of how we live? Biological beings that we are, is there some fundamental flaw in our species that prevents us from adapting appropriately, no matter the changes going on all around us? And are we in the United States so full of ourselves and our grandiose sense of our national identity and purpose that we cling to the fantasies and myths no matter what the evidence to the contrary; for example, that we are the supreme power of the world, that we are hated because we are "good" or because of our "freedoms," or that we have a greater right to survival—our relative comfort intact—than others in the world?

Given the evidence, especially since 9/11, the question for me has changed from how to prevent a terribly destructive, turbulent, even disastrous time in human history to how we are going to live through it. It has become quite obvious that we cannot save ourselves from a very difficult future, though we could mitigate the worst impacts if we could wake ourselves up from our hypnotic, self-deluded state. What kind of human beings are we going to be—and I mean *we* as US Americans, people of *this* society—as these major trends unfold? What will we create in the midst of turbulence, fear, insecurity, "unnatural" natural phenomena, economic dislocations, and more?

It is apparent that our political, religious, moral, cultural, and certainly our economic leaders are either unable to grasp the magnitude of the challenges, or, if they can, to tell us the truth about them. As a result, they are unable or unwilling to issue a call to our nation to begin urgently implementing the fundamental changes in our personal, social, economic, and political lives that these times demand.

Alongside these extraordinarily difficult trends, something else is happening. We stand before a virtual revolution—not unlike the time of Copernicus—in how we perceive ourselves as human beings on this planet. Great scientific achievements, not least of which is the Hubble Space Telescope, have altered our understanding of the universe and our place within it. Hubble photos peer not only into distant space but also distant time, reorienting our sense of place and even of what we call home, a concept that enlarges with each new discovery. Scientific discoveries provide information that can lead to wonder or to dread in regard to the possible fate of humanity, the earth, the solar system, and the universe itself.

All of these changes we face as human beings, piled together in this moment, are indeed frightening, disorienting, and overwhelming.

How do we not become paralyzed and hopeless? How do we begin a dialogue on our situation in ways that do not bring people (myself included) to despair but instead to a desire for action based in compassion and exhilaration at the challenge and a new sense of purpose and mission for the human community?

These are some of the questions I have thought about much in recent years.

The question of change, conversion, and transformation is especially important for me in this era of the "red and blue" cultural divide. We seem to believe that few people are able to change their fundamental values and belief systems, that people are now basically close-minded and set in their ways, no matter what evidence might contradict those ways or beliefs. If that is so, we are doomed to a future of increasing dissolution of society, greater violence, fear, and upheaval.

But I don't believe this. I don't believe this in part because of my own history, in which I have seen what has happened in the lives of tens of thousands of US Americans because of their participation in the work of solidarity with poor peoples in Central America engaged in a struggle for liberation. I have seen lives turned upside down as the realities of war, repression, and injustice confronted US citizens with a different truth about their history. I have seen people who began to perceive privilege and affluence through the lens of the poor and changed their lives accordingly.

I believe human beings can deal with harsh realities and be changed. I believe it because I have seen it happen. It is not easy. Confronting the reality of the so-called Third World, along with the culpability of the United States in the tragic history of oppression in that region, was not easy for middle-class and upper-middle-class US Americans. Still, it happened. And that should give us all hope.

People change; people willingly undergo conversion. And we must change. It will be hardest in those societies that have the most to surrender in terms of consumer lifestyles, of power and control, and of identities based in these things.

But I have watched people throw all of that away when they discovered a reason to be alive and a purpose and meaning to the human journey and their own lives that made doing so far easier than one might think.

In the end, the longing for meaning seems a stronger motivation than selfish fear. And that is why I wrote this book, to begin a conversation, to share some of my own reflections on the major issues we now encounter as we evolve in our understanding of what it means to be a human being in the larger scheme of things and what it means to be a US American at this moment in history. Another writer might come up with another list of issues and other avenues to explore the nature of the challenges. These are the ones I think about and have talked about with many colleagues, friends, and family members.

In late July 2005 I began a journey I had wanted to do since my youth— to take a long solitary drive across this vast country, to have time to take in the incredible geography, the many cultures that go with the changing land- scapes and histories, to embrace my people and my country with all its warts, failings, character, and strengths.[1]

Times have changed. I undertook my trip in a time when there was no place I did not witness ecosystems in severe stress, polluted waters, disap- pearing glaciers, overpopulated and overdeveloped desert communities, gas- guzzling SUVs and giant pickup trucks with no apparent practical use, air pollution in places of spectacular natural beauty, radio preachers condemn- ing most of society to Armageddon, and right-wing radio talk-show hosts fomenting hatred toward feminists, gay and lesbian people, migrants and immigrants, non-Christian people, non-born-again Christians, Muslims, and always and forever *liberals*, as if the very word indicated some unmention- able, dreaded social disease.

At the same time, I saw much of what remains so good about this country and its people, from truck drivers to railroad workers to National Park rangers to motel managers to members of American Indian nations and more— generous hearts, heartfelt friendliness to a stranger, shared love of the na- ture I was exploring, pleasure in my joy at being in their part of the world, and in many cases, expressions of the same concerns I bore in my heart as I traveled highways from Takoma Park, Maryland, to Mukilteo, Washington, and from Oregon's Pacific Coast to Delaware's beaches.

I am sobered by the challenges we face, but I have not lost heart. We may not be able to avoid some of the harsher consequences of our human hubris and fear, but we have within us everything we need to create something new in the midst of the chaos, something redeeming, something that salvages our earth's human experiment toward greater, richer, more sacred life.

In the end the message regarding change must be one of hope. The alter- native is not acceptable—possible, but not acceptable.

Acknowledgments

A book can feel like such a solitary endeavor. Hours melt into days that melt into weeks and then into months in front of a computer wondering at times if you will ever reemerge in the world.

But, in reality, a book such as this one is never solitary. Without the example of others, the work of others, and the encouragement and support of family, friends, and community, it would never happen.

I thank all those who gave me places to write, access to wireless, and all the moral support I needed to stay with it. It was a huge work, and without your tangible contribution it would not have been completed. You know who you are.

Special thanks to Jane Blewett, Lou Niznik, and Dr. Gerald Barney. You have been mentors in more ways than you know.

Finally, my thanks to Robert Ellsberg of Orbis Books, who believed in this project and then helped make it better.

Permissions

Excerpts from *The Upside of Down* by Thomas Homer-Dixon. Copyright ©
Resource & Conflict Analysis Inc. 2006. Reproduced from the US edition
by permission of Island Press, Washington D.C.

Excerpts from *Ecosystems and Human Well-Being: Our Human Planet* by the
Millennium Ecosystem Assessment. Copyright © 2005 by the author. Reproduced by permission of Island Press, Washington D.C.

Excerpt by Erik Reece, first published in *Orion Magazine*, January/February
2006. Copyright © 2006 by Erik Reece, reprinted with permission of The
Wylie Agency, Inc.

Excerpts from "Corn Can't Solve Our Problem," by David Tilman and Jason Hill, *Washington Post*, March 25, 2007. Reprinted with permission of
author.

Excerpts from *Limits to Growth: The Thirty Year Update*, Donella Meadows,
Jorgen Randers, and Dennis Meadows, Chelsea Green Publishing, White
River Junction VT, 2004. Reprinted with permission of publisher.

Excerpt from "Can the Twilight of the Gods Be Prevented," Sven Burmeister,
in *Friday Morning Reflections at the World Bank: Essays on Values and Development*, Seven Locks Press, Santa Ana CA, 1991. Reprinted with permission
of publisher.

Excerpt from *The Poverty of Affluence: A Psychological Portrait of the American
Way of Life*, by Paul Wachtel, New Society Publishers, Philadelphia, 1989.
Reprinted with permission of author.

Excerpt from "Cosmic Theology: Ecofeminism and Panentheism," Ivone
Gebara, interview with Mary Judith Ress, originally published in *Creation
Spirituality* magazine, November/December 1993, Vol. IX: 6), found in *Read-
ings in Ecology and Feminist Theology*, ed. Mary Heather MacKinnon & Moni
McIntyre, Sheed & Ward, Kansas City, 1995

Excerpt from "Impasse and Dark Night," Constance Fitzgerald, O.C.D.,
from *Living with Apocalypse: Spiritual Resources for Social Compassion*, edited
by Tilden H. Edwards. Copyright © 1984 by Shalem Institute for Spiritual
Formation, Inc. Reprinted by permission of HarperCollins Publishers.

Introduction

Regarding Our Predicament

More than a decade ago I discovered a little book called *The Friday Morning Group*, a collection of reflections by World Bank staff members who gathered on Friday mornings to discuss the values that motivated their development work at the bank. One of the essays was by a deputy director from Sweden, Sven Burmeister, who reflected on the predicament posed by the limits of the earth's carrying capacity and the growing demands of human consumption that far surpass those limits.

What he said was this: the earth has the carrying capacity to support the per capita resource use of the United States indefinitely for about half a billion people. If US Americans lived as frugally as people do in Europe and Japan, the earth could support that level of resource use indefinitely for about one billion people. The current population of the earth is now 6.5 billion and will be more than 9 billion by the year 2050, just over four decades from now.

I could tell right away that the math didn't work out. By these calculations, it appeared that we could not continue to live as we do in this country unless we are willing to eliminate, oh, at least some eight billion people over the next forty years.

Clearly, we are in trouble.

I have shared this information in some of the talks and workshops I have given in recent years, and the reaction is usually the same. Silence. Not an indifferent silence, or the silence of resistance, but a heavy weight settling in as the repercussions begin to sink in. There is no escaping the discomfiting challenge to our way of life here in the United States, a challenge that is no longer one we can consign to some future generation, but one that will affect our lives right now.

Change is inevitable. We need to commit to deep and profound change within our culture and society and within our personal lives if the majority of human beings are to survive.

Nor can we escape the impact of the forces now at work that are altering human life across the globe. We know that we will not be exempt, that our own survival here in the United States is at stake as well, not just the lives of poor people in far-away places. We cannot live as if we are on an island isolated from the impact of natural and unnatural forces that will be wreaking havoc across our planet—global climate change, energy and fresh-water shortages, mass extinctions of species in the web of life on which we all depend, floods, drought, disease, violent conflict, collapsing economies—forces from which we cannot protect ourselves with stronger fences, homeland security, or bloated military budgets.

There are no gated communities that can protect us from the consequences of what we humans have done with our patterns of consumption and our belief that we could dominate and subdue the earth without the earth having something to say about it, a rebuke in the strongest terms.

Nor is it likely that those eight billion people will go quietly to their deaths without making a claim on us regarding their humanity, their dignity, their right to life.

The evidence has been clear for some time now that we humans, especially those of us with high levels of consumption, have created an environment that is increasingly hostile to human life. We have exploited the natural gifts of the earth and polluted our atmosphere by the way we have chosen to live. Predictions of worldwide calamity because of global climate change are becoming increasingly dire, and we seem unable either to grasp the seriousness of the threat or to make the changes required to lessen the impact of forces we can no longer reverse but only hope to mitigate.

The heavy silence that often follows when I share these views is reflective, I believe, of three things. One is the overwhelming nature of the information and, with that, an understandable sense of helplessness before the magnitude of the changes required to stave off disaster. Another is a tendency toward denial, a resistance to absorbing just how bad this news is, a cultural habit of wishful thinking deeply embedded in US American optimism. And the third is that, when faced with the crisis, there is still some desperate hope that the changes demanded of us by our situation will not upset our lives too much, that "something" will come along to save us. Yet, the trends are right in front of us, and once we know what we know, we cannot "un-know" it or pretend it isn't true. The changes will disrupt our lives—drastically.

How drastic depends upon whether we are willing to take on the challenge forthrightly, with a profound sense of connectedness to human beings as a species and to the earth's life systems of which we are an organic part, or instead, we continue to live in denial until the changes are forced on us by calamities, natural and otherwise, that are difficult even to contemplate.

One way or the other, the earth is going to teach us that we are an organic part of a whole. The earth is going to reveal to us just how profound our connections are to the whole of humanity and to the profoundly broken and abused webs of life. We can choose to cooperate with those systems in order to salvage human life, or the earth will be forced to adjust to the new reality we have presented it, finding a new equilibrium among these broken systems. Scientists tell us that this new equilibrium may or may not allow for the survival of the human species.

We are beginning to get a sense of what this will entail with the effects of global climate change already under way. The earth is certainly trying to tell us something as weather becomes a permanent fixture of news headlines—floods, drought, raging fires across forests and deserts, sand storms over newly desertified lands, hurricanes, tornados, and more. Meanwhile, predictions of the potential devastation are presented to us in a steady stream of troubling studies and computer models. A long list of books, powerful documentary films, and TV feature stories press home our predicament. The stress and distress of the human community increase. And still we remain resistant to change.

How people respond reflects the levels of fear, denial, and empowerment that are at work in their lives. One response is to cast suspicion on the science itself—suspect the messengers or disparage their expertise, deny that science is telling us anything real or factual, or consign science to the level of mere opinion. This argument has worked its way into our political discourse, impeding efforts to address the ecological crisis directly. Another response is to retreat into religion, to count on God to save us from ourselves. Still another is to embrace the disaster and count on a rapture for the righteous that will lift the saved out of the catastrophe and transport them into heaven, leaving the unrighteous to suffer through the calamities of Armageddon.

I am horrified by the image of such a God and frightened by the attraction of such a deity for hundreds of millions of people. This God is bent on destruction, and his worshipers seem entranced by what he is supposedly about to do to our world because of our sins. This response seems to me to be an expression of deep despair over the fate of humanity.

But these issues are not the only ones rocking our world.

Science crashes up against biblical belief

At the same time that we are dealing with ecological and economic issues of vast importance, we are also coming to a new understanding of the earth and universe from which we emerged. The Hubble Space Telescope is but one of the many scientific achievements of recent decades that have put the human experience in an entirely different context of space—life on a tiny planet orbiting an ordinary star swirling through the Milky Way galaxy in a universe of immense proportions. We have come to see our place in the universe in a wholly new way and, from the new perspective, we seem small indeed.

At the same time, the "new physics" reveals a cosmos of deeply interrelated energy and matter from which we cannot separate ourselves, along with multiple dimensions of space beyond our perception or comprehension. We are stupefied and knocked off balance by these discoveries for good reason, because they are disorienting indeed, challenging our comfortable understandings of our place in creation.

Some respond to these amazing discoveries with wonder, many others with dread. And I can assure you that there are many more astounding discoveries to come in our lifetime. This science is just getting started.

Meanwhile, right now US Americans live in a society in which more than half of the people do not believe in evolution. According to a *USA Today/* CNN/Gallup Poll conducted in September 2005, 53 percent of US Americans believe that human beings were created "exactly as described in the Bible."[1] How, then, do most people react to the science that tells us our universe was created out of a massive explosion of energy some fourteen billion years ago? What happens to a whole construct of literal biblical faith and our concept of God?

For many, the conflict is frightening and disorienting, and for this reason they greet the unfolding consciousness of our place in the universe—what has been dubbed the New Universe Story—with staunch resistance. It is undoubtedly a story that challenges many of the old frameworks of meaning and faith that are part of the Christian underpinnings of US society going back to the Puritans. From the new cosmology to the new physics, old gods are being toppled, though not without a tremendous struggle to keep them propped up on old altars with old orthodoxies.

Because of new scientific knowledge we find ourselves confronted with scenarios both chilling and exhilarating—from dealing with the real possibility that our universe is headed to a cold death to the possibility that there is purpose in this fourteen-billion-year evolution of a cosmos in which we are but one significant expression. The existence of a God standing over and above creation is being challenged by a sense of spirit that is within and at the very heart of the entire cosmological process of creation, manifested through us, not outside of us. On the other hand, the cold death version poses the question of whether there is a God or any meaning at all to the human journey.

Responses to these recent discoveries span the range of human reaction to stressful changes. Religious orthodoxy and fundamentalism are on the rise. Creationists insist that God put us on this earth as we are some thousands of years ago. Despite the science, they will not accept any challenge to the image of a powerful God creating this world, as it is, by simple command, acting from the outside, and all in a mere six days. Some also cling to the belief that there is a heaven outside the tribulation of this world in which the souls of the just, their identities intact, will exist in happy eternity; the fate of the earth, therefore, is of little consequence ultimately. This seems to me to be a response motivated by real internal distress, dread, and fear as our meaning constructs are profoundly threatened by the new understandings of our universe and our place within it.

But not everyone responds with fear. Many others embrace this moment in the evolution of consciousness with wonder, awe, and exhilaration, willing to confront their dread in order to be part of a process in which the act of creation is carrying us toward an unimaginable new understanding and perception of meaning and spirit.

The tension is increasingly apparent between the planetary crisis now facing us and this vastly expanded knowledge of our place in the universe. It is a tension between a destructive lifestyle that sees nature as mere resources to use for human benefit and a sense of wonder and awe about the place of this planet within a solar system within a galaxy within the vast expanse of the universe—and the miracle of life and consciousness on that planet, how unlikely that it occurred at all, what an amazing thing is this biosphere from which we emerged and that we are now in the process of destroying.

But this is not all; still more is going on to unsettle us.

Cultures and ethnicities come crashing into our space

As the world population grows; as the globalization of corporate capitalism continues to seep into every corner of the world, upsetting cultures and societies, continuing its relentless assault on the environment; as increasing millions of human beings are displaced by this form of economic globalization or environmental catastrophes, nation-state borders have become more porous than ever before. The United Nations estimates that on any given day some 175,000,000 migrants roam the earth looking for work, a number that has doubled since 1975.

As people flow from one country to another in search of survival, a new mix of cultures, languages, and ethnicity has reached virtually every corner of the United States and much of Europe. White Western identity is being challenged as never before, especially for those who believe that this is the identity of entitlement, intelligence, power, and privilege, the vanguard of progress and truth. While few proclaim this belief system openly, many of us are too embarrassed to admit that we harbor something of these sentiments in hidden recesses of our spirits, raised as we were in the atmosphere of such entitlement.

Population growth rates are also varied across cultures and geographies, and one thing appears certain—the domination of Western Caucasians is no longer tenable as the population of this planet becomes ever more rapidly a population of richly diverse colors, cultures, languages, and religions, overwhelming any desperate hope we might have to hang on to a geographically defined white Christian society.

Once again, responses to this demographic upheaval are mixed, from outright racism and fear and a resurgence of ethnic hatred and discrimination, to tolerance for those whose labor we need to harvest our food, clean our houses, and help raise our kids, to welcoming this diversity with open arms, along with all that it is possible to learn from this mix of cultures and life experiences.

But there is more yet, tectonic shifts in how we think about ourselves.

Founding myths clash with the real world

As US Americans, we grew up on the myths of early explorers, heroic settlers, founding fathers with ideals of democracy, endless frontiers, and the resulting sense of expansiveness that we cling to even to this day. But we reached the limits of expansion long ago. Unable to spread out, we are turning growth back in on ourselves through suburban and exurban sprawl, destroying more green spaces for developments that are increasingly dependent on oil-consuming life patterns. This growth is adding to the destructive life patterns that have us choking on toxic air, warming the globe at accelerated rates, creating communities that will not be sustainable beyond another generation (unless we organize them vastly differently), and using up dwindling energy supplies as we sit in ever-worsening traffic congestion. All these add to increased levels of stress throughout society.

As children in this society we were taught that the United States had a "manifest destiny" that justified its expansion into any space it desired. The new United States was, after all, such a marvel, so superior to anything that had come before, that it deserved always to expand, to grow, to be richer and more successful. There ought to be, therefore, no limit to our reach as long as it is enhancing our lifestyle. This is, after all, the American Dream.

Whether or not that dream was ever real for the majority of our people, it is certainly not real now. But if we think about the reality on which that dream was built, we see that it was always deeply flawed and morally suspect. As the original European settlers first spread across this land, they expected that the land and its peoples would simply fall at their feet, or fall into place, as they built a new empire. Indigenous peoples were conquered or slaughtered to make way for this new ideal. Wars with Mexico and Spain, and a few cash deals with France and others, expanded the empire. From this history grew the roots of what in our day is called US exceptionalism—a belief that the United States is qualitatively different from (that is, better than) other countries. It was repeated in other forms south of our borders through US domination over Latin America, propping up compliant dictatorships throughout much of the twentieth century, and in other parts of the world by way of military and political interventions too numerous to list here.

Two centuries of living this belief and we wonder why so many people hate us. Aren't we good? Aren't we free? Doesn't everyone want to be like us—except evildoers and those who hate freedom or come from backward cultures? Are we not the country that struck blows for freedom in two great World Wars and the Cold War that ended in the collapse of the Soviet Union? Aren't we the beacon of liberty for all the world's oppressed? American ideals have always rubbed up against political reality at the point where those ideals were turned on their head in the exercise of US power abroad, those moments when the United States betrayed its own proclaimed values by engaging in political repression and domination. The tension is old, and it continues.

Perhaps if we were more honest with this history, we would be less surprised by some of the tensions and conflicts in which we find ourselves today, both foreign and domestic. What is exceptionalism to us is hubris to others, an inability to be humble and to see ourselves as merely human, no greater or lesser than anyone else. Exceptionalism has allowed us to quiet our consciences and justify a great deal of evil, from Wounded Knee to Hiroshima to Guatemala to Abu Graib.

A deeply embedded religiosity runs through this history, going back to the Puritans, a belief that the United States is not only a morally superior nation but also the biblical chosen people, the city on the hill, a beacon of God's righteousness before the "heathen," a place where justice is not under law so much as under God, especially God's judgment, his sword being wielded in a world of sin. That thread of fundamentalist religiosity has come to dominate much of the right-wing political discourse in this country in recent decades, further distorting our sense of identity and proving to be a divisive influence in the nation's politics.

As I marched in the streets of Washington DC with 200,000 of my fellow citizens to protest the war in Iraq on September 24, 2005, I was struck by a small group of pro-war counter-demonstrators who carried signs that read: "God bless America. Kill the terrorists." Below the words was the painting of an automatic military rifle.

In expressions like these we see an intolerant brand of fundamentalism, with its righteous, wrathful God, still manifesting itself within the political discourse of US society. That it rose all the way to the White House and even into high levels of the US military in recent years is testament to its continuing power within the nation's self-identity.

This religiosity undergirds a framework of values that justifies actions such as the war in Iraq, the expansion of US influence into lands of "heathens" and "unbelievers," and efforts to coerce Congress and the courts to pass laws discriminating against and suppressing the rights of populations within the United States that are not Christian, not "saved."

The obsolescence of the nation-state

Finally, the example of the war in Iraq revealed yet another challenge to our cultural self-identity. The United States is hardly the only powerful actor in the world. In fact, its influence is likely to diminish over the next decades for reasons of history, economics, and shifting international dynamics. The 2003 debate in the United Nations Security Council that predated the war presented a new view for US citizens—finding ourselves part of a world that does not feel the need to take its lead from the United States. We are one part of the world, a powerful actor, no doubt, but one whose use of hubristic unilateral power is causing other nations to act, even to cooperate among themselves, to blunt that power.

Meanwhile, our economic dominance is being challenged by new actors, especially China and India, as well as certain Latin American countries, and we may soon find ourselves no longer the great economic superpower of the world. Economists anticipate that China will become the world's largest economy within a decade. At the same time, China is now one of our largest creditors, holding substantial portions of the US debt. How do we negotiate with China on issues such as human rights, global warming, and carbon emissions in the context of this new relationship? Are we ready to adjust to a new reality in which the United States is no longer the dominant superpower?

As we ponder all these human dilemmas and challenges, we will need to come to terms with something essential and obvious—that none of the most important questions about how we are going to survive on this planet can be answered nationally. Like it or not, we are now bound to a world in which the consequences of all our social, political, environmental, and economic actions are borderless. The radiation from a nuclear exchange anywhere in the world will not stop at the borders of the nations where that exchange takes place. The pollution from China's coal-fired power plants is already adding to the pollution in Seattle, Portland, and northern California. Global climate change is not something that a nation can build a wall of policies around to protect its borders. And the most stringent border-enforcement policies in the world will not keep desperately poor people from crossing borders in search of survival.

Whether all the righteous believe it or not, God does not prefer the survival of US people over the survival of other human beings in this world.

Unless we are willing to give up our national self-centeredness and become equal partners with other nations in reinventing how human societies live on the planet, prospects for our world will diminish indeed.

As I sat down to write this book, I felt enormous compassion for my people, this troubled culture that gave birth to me and of which I am a part. I felt compassion for the tumult that awaits us and the crisis of conscience it will entail. We seem ill-prepared for the times that are coming, and we will have difficulty rising to the challenge, in part because we have benefitted so lavishly from the present construct of our world. We have developed a deeply entrenched national religiosity that protects us from seeing the truth about ourselves and the situation we have created with our extravagant lifestyles.

However, not looking at the world won't help us either. It is time to bring the many dimensions of the crisis to bear on this society, and to do this from the perspective of *faith*, to give it, and us, a good look, and ask how we will face the "end of the world" that is surely coming. I can promise you that it will not be easy reading.

What I have done here is focus on several of the crises that will alter our world profoundly and imminently. I want to share what I have learned about them and how the interlocking nature of these multiple crises begs the need for immediate and radical change in how we live. Then, I want to offer some thoughts on how faith and religion can help or hinder us as we take up the challenges of our planetary crisis. In the end, I want to issue my own call in regard to those traditions and offer a word of hope and encouragement as we move forward in this great task of our generation.

In Chapter 1 we look at the disasters of recent years, like earthquakes and hurricanes, and pose questions about how we will deal with them as population grows, along with death tolls, and climate change ensures that there will be more of them. We examine what they tell us about how we have lived on the planet and open up the "Katrina metaphor," a reflection on what the destruction of New Orleans tells us about our relationship with the earth.

In Chapter 2 we address climate change and the threat it poses for the survival of human communities and other species around the world. Chapter 3 explores the coming energy crisis and how it will affect our way of life. It reflects on the non-sustainability of our suburban and exurban worlds as well as on how our refusal to plan actively for a world with diminishing fossil fuels will add to the coming chaos. It also examines the ecological damage we are inflicting in our quest to find enough fossil fuel, as well as biofuels, to stoke the engine of our economy and our mobile way of life for a while longer.

In Chapter 4 we address the gravest crisis we face for human survival— ecological overshoot, living beyond the means of the earth to replace what we consume or to absorb our waste. We already consume at a greater level than the earth can sustain, and conditions will only worsen as we add two to three billion people to the planet in the next forty years.

Chapter 5 describes our "world of trouble," how these many layers of crises are bound to create turbulence and violence in the human community.

We will need to decide how we are going to live through such a time. In Chapter 6 we take a special look at US society and the American Dream, the non-sustainability of an economic logic that claims that every generation can be more affluent than the last and that economic growth can solve all our problems. The following chapter then examines the deep spiritual roots of our ecological crisis, offering a reflection on the alienation from nature manifested in our lifestyles and our values and the religiosity that has helped give expression to that alienation.

In Chapter 8 we address the question of hope and where it exists in such a world. We posit the "end of the world," not an apocalypse but rather the end of a way of life, the industrial and post-industrial world that has brought us to the brink of catastrophe. We are urged to enlarge our sense of God beyond the human story to one that can embrace the magnitude of the crisis and of our discoveries about the universe and the place of the human within it.

The conclusion poses the most important question faced by this society as it faces the crisis and the turbulent transition through which we are about to pass: what kind of human beings will we be as we go through the crisis? We reflect on the role of faith and religion in answering that question.

Finally, as we begin this journey, I want to say this. Our identity as a people and as a nation truly is being shaken by all these trends, and we are only seeing the tip of the iceberg—a rapidly melting iceberg at that. An old identity is being upset or found to be actually destructive, and we have yet to find the new one. I suspect, and I hope, that the old nationalisms will soon be replaced by a new "species identity," one that can bind together the human world because of all that is happening to us, and because of what we need to do and to be in order for the human species to survive. Our sense of identity must enlarge, and we must begin to see not only the danger but also the necessity of altering rapidly the role of this society in creating that danger.

This is also a religious challenge. Most of our society remains deeply religious. What values from our faith traditions do we bring to this planetary crisis? Do they help inform it, provide a way forward, a framework of meaning and values, a vision that can work toward healing the broken and severely compromised life-support systems of the planet? Do they add to the alienation or help overcome it? Do they lead to despair that we can do anything to save life on the earth, or do they offer real and concrete hope that what we do now can indeed make a difference? Do they keep God separate from this great drama and task of our time or help us find God right in the midst of it?

Without doubt, what I am presenting here is a lot to absorb, and it is appropriate and healthy to feel fear. Like many people in our world, I am afraid, terrified, about the future. I love this earth, my home planet, and I sense deep within this story the possibility of a loss so vast I cannot take it in—nor can I accept it.

We have a lot to think about, but unfortunately not a lot of time—time is what we are definitely running out of if we are to soften the impact of the drastic changes descending upon us. We must decide whether we are going to try to protect ourselves from them, dam up our lives and our spirits in an attempt to hold them at bay, or cooperate with them, work with them, to create the new way of human survival on this planet. This survival will mean new ways of living, wholly new economic thinking, new political structures, all based on a set of values rooted in a radically new understanding of the place of the human within the life of the planet. It will mean seeing our role not as one of taking more and more pieces of the planet to possess and defend—the driving force behind manifest destiny and corporate capitalism—but rather one of healing, relinquishing ownership and attempts to control nature and seeing the various gifts of the earth as aspects of our own beings, our bodies, our spirits, to be protected in their integrity for their place within the life-giving systems that birthed us, nurture us, and ensure life for the next generation, and the next.

Dammed water creates enormous potential energy. When the dam breaks, the force of the flow takes out everything in its path. I believe the United States as a polity and society is engaged in desperate efforts to reinforce the dam, to hold back the forces that are ready to overwhelm it. But it won't work. The force of change is too great. We can be overwhelmed, even destroyed, by what is to come, or we can decide to take up the challenge with determination, solemnity, and even joy, believing we are up to the task.

We could look at the crisis from a very different perspective. We could see our awareness of it as an important moment in the evolution of consciousness, the one when this species became aware of its danger and survival instincts began to kick in. Perhaps then we could see this moment not as a great disaster but rather as a great adventure, indeed one of the greatest adventures in human history—to salvage the human prospect, to help our earth renew itself and heal from the damage we have caused. This is the time to take up a new way of life that honors our place in the scheme of our planet, to reinvent meaning and faith in the context of healing what has been broken, and to create a world hospitable to life in all its rich diversity, including the diversity of the human community.

I am not a scholar. I do not approach these issues from the vantage point of expertise in fields of science and research. I approach them as an activist, as a writer, and as someone who has long followed a path of spiritual seeking, from my Catholic Christian roots through social justice work and solidarity with the poor to an expansive new appreciation for the Gaia/earth life of which we are a part and a sense of the immense spiritual potential of the human person, especially when freed of the bonds of oppression, whether those bonds are economic, political, cultural, or religious.

And so I invite you to take this journey. My hope is that these reflections provoke a great deal of thought, intense conversations, and heartfelt spiritual struggle, with the goal of contributing to a new dynamism within this culture commensurate with the seriousness of the predicament in which we find ourselves. We have an immense challenge in front of us.

But while the conversation is essential, along with all the retreats, conferences, and workshops that inspire and empower us and that help build our communities and networks, there is more now that we need to do. It is time for us to work at this great task of our generation, to become consciously engaged in the work of reinventing the human presence on this planet. It is time for all of us to take our part in the unfolding story of our earth community. Right now, that story is reaching a climax, and the conclusion is uncertain. The earth will go on for millions of years beyond our lifetimes, but whether or not it will be able to hold human beings within its fabric of life, well, the answer to that question is now in our hands.

1

Of Earthquakes and Hurricanes

or,

Learning to Face Disaster

> *In time of crisis,*
> *we summon up our strength.*
> —MURIEL RUKEYSER[1]

There is no question that we are in a time of crisis. We will need all the strength we can muster. How else will we be able to look honestly at our situation? Aren't we already overwhelmed with disaster upon disaster, one horror after another? Are these, indeed, apocalyptic times or just the usual turbulence of human history, which each generation considers exceptional?

—The day after Christmas 2004, more than 250,000 people are killed in Indonesia, Thailand, and Sri Lanka by a tsunami that strikes islands and coastal areas without warning. On October 9, 2005, more than 85,000 people are killed in an earthquake in Northern Pakistan and India. Earlier in October, 1,300 Guatemalans are buried under a landslide after several days of rain—villages become instant cemeteries. On May 27, 2006, an earthquake strikes the Indonesian island of Java, killing 6,700 people and injuring 36,000.

—On August 29, 2005, a Category Four Hurricane strikes the southern Gulf Coast of the United States. More than 1,800 people are killed in its aftermath, a major US city is destroyed, half a million people are left home-less. In 2003, 26,000 thousand people are killed in a massive earthquake that destroys much of the Iranian city of Bam. In late October 1998, it begins to rain in Central America and does not stop for seven days. Several feet of rain fall on Honduras and parts of Nicaragua, El Salvador, and

Guatemala. Eighty percent of Honduras is affected. More than 9,000 people die, many of them washed away.

—In 2005 scientists and world health officials work urgently to prepare the world for a potential pandemic of an avian flu strain (H5N1) that could kill hundreds of millions of people, an estimated two million in the United States alone.

Add disasters to the list. There are, and will be, many more. There are many ways to interpret such events. Here's one version:

The signs and portents don't look very good. We are seeing signs in the sun and the moon and the stars, and on earth nations are indeed in agony, "bewildered by the clamor of the oceans and its waves" (Lk 21:25). The end times are surely upon us. The wrath of that old warrior God of the Old Testament has come over us. God is announcing to us that he has had enough of our earthly sinfulness, our corrupted souls, and our filthy ways, of homosexuality and feminism, of working women and abortionists, of sexuality and rock n' roll that sickens our children, of secularism and liberalism that oppress the people of God and drive God out of the public market-place. Nonbelievers, apostates, and "heathens" are striking out at the faithful with great violence, flying planes into tall buildings, blowing up commuter trains, be-heading captives, and spouting their hateful ideology over the Internet. The hand of God is no longer there to protect us; it has been withdrawn.

God has waited long enough for us to repent. We have been deaf to his com-mands, and now it is too late; his vengeance is upon us. First come the earthquakes, floods, and other natural disasters. These are the final warnings—get ready, the time comes soon.

Any minute now, the one next to you will be taken up—and when that person is taken and you are not, you will know you are in big trouble.

Living earth

Well, as I said, that's one version of events.
Here's another:

The earth is alive, constantly shifting, seething, creating, and destroying. There have always been earthquakes, floods, hurricanes, tornados, avalanches, and volca-nic explosions. What is different is that we have reproduced exponentially in the past one hundred years and our planet has gotten a bit crowded. In 1950 the world's population totaled two billion people; by 2000, we had reached 6.5 billion. We are headed for over 9 billion by 2050.

Masses of people now live in very dangerous places—on fault lines and along seacoasts, on fragile bluffs with an ocean view, in desert communities dry as tinder each summer—and when disasters strike, many people are likely to die and homes and businesses will be destroyed. Human beings have put enormous stresses on very vulnerable geography and have altered the climate of the planet in a way that is likely to increase the fury and unpredictability of these natural disasters.

Once upon a time the vast forests of Central America and the Yucatan put a brake on the power of a hurricane as it struck land. Much of the forest no longer exists. In Central America, as in many parts of the world, poor people have little choice about where to build their simple houses and grow subsistence crops. The safer lands, the more productive lands, are in the hands of the rich and the business classes. Poor people are forced up onto steep mountainsides or into ravines prone to flooding, living in housing of sticks, cardboard, dirt, and clay that cannot withstand a torrential downpour or the trembling of the earth. Lacking electricity or the ability to tap into existing energy sources, they are forced to cut down trees for wood to heat their stoves for cooking, adding to the pressure on forests already decimated by timber companies to supply the wood for our housing developments and our throw-away chopsticks, our brown paper grocery bags, and our corrugated cardboard boxes.

In August 2005 I was driving through southwestern Montana on highway 93, an area where more than two dozen fires were burning in the mountain wilderness. Brown smoke and haze wafted through the broad valley, and the smell of burning trees filled the air. I expressed my dismay and sorrow to the man behind the desk in the motel and asked about how this year compared to others. Oh, he said, this was actually not such a bad year, fewer fires than the last, fewer fires than usual.

The fires burn every year, and always have, set off by lightning storms during the dry late-summer months. The difference is that now many people have moved closer to the wilderness and so the fires come closer to populated areas, now they must be fought, now they are on the TV news.

He explained that the fire fighters fight the flames as they come close to human habitation, steering the fires toward the wilderness. At that point, they just let them burn.

Not God, just a sprawling population, just some folks wanting a summer home in the mountains, bringing attention to one of the many ways nature has controlled and replenished the forest over millennia.

Less than a decade after the big event, I traveled to Washington State to pay homage to Mt. St. Helens, which blew its top—literally—back on May 19, 1982. It is one of my favorite places in the United States, a place where one can get a glimpse of the power that boils and rumbles under our feet, deep down below the earth's surface. The explosion took thirteen hundred feet of elevation from the mountain's glorious cone. The first time I visited, it was largely a moonscape—except for the places where the wild flowers were growing across now-treeless mountain valleys, except in the newly formed lake brimming with life, except for the gentle reminder of abundant life as a deer strolled by, softly wading on the shoreline.

What to us looks like moonscape and disaster is just the earth still creating itself, replenishing, renewing.

Around the other side of the mountain is the site of Harry Truman's Spirit Lake Lodge. Born in 1896, Truman was by many accounts a cranky old man with a checkered past and few friends. He had lived long on the side of the volcano and, when the warnings came, he did not want to leave his property. He knew the mountain, he said, and the mountain would never hurt him. "When you live someplace for fifty years, you either know your country or you're stupid."

Truman and his lodge lie buried under some 150 feet of the rock and ash that came cascading toward the lake within seconds of the blast—his burial ground, his own private cemetery. I wonder if he had time to address the mountain in the instant before his death, a word of protest, perhaps, at the betrayal, or a word of defiance. Scientists say he may have had just enough time to turn his head.

A few years later I visited a second time and stopped by the brand-new Visitor Center. There I attended a talk given by one of the National Park rangers describing the geology and history of the volcanic Cascade Mountains. The Cascade Range, which stretches from Canada south across Washington and Oregon, has several active volcanoes; Mt. St. Helens is not the only one that rumbles and roars from time to time.

One of them is Mt. Rainier, which many seismologists believe will blow within the next fifty to one hundred years. The death toll will be different this time. St. Helens is away from densely populated areas; still, fifty-seven people were killed by blast, ash, and toxic gas. The blast created winds of three hundred miles per hour. It darkened the region for hundreds of miles.

But as anyone who has visited Seattle knows, Mt. Rainier is a near neighbor. It is—right there. As you drive around the Seattle area, you see signs all around—in case of evacuation, run *up*.

There is no way we humans can outrun, or drive fast enough to escape, the winds and rock flows that will come from the explosion of so much pent up gas and energy; therefore, go up. Schoolchildren are taught this.

So, back at the Mt. St. Helens Visitor Center, after the presentation, I asked the ranger more about the impact of a Mt. Rainier eruption. Which way would it go? Would there be lava? Would it be mostly gas, rock, and ash, like Mt. St. Helens?

He took out a geological map of the Seattle area and pointed out exactly where the flows would go, down which ravines and valleys, down which streets and highways.

And then, with an obvious frustration just below the surface, he pointed out exactly which of those spots are now prime real estate being built up by developers.

I wonder if these developers show prospective home buyers these geological maps. I wonder if they encourage them to go talk to a ranger.

How many of the Indonesian and Thai people who died in the 2004 tsunami were workers servicing a coastline tourist industry that exists for the pleasure of the affluent of other countries? How many who died were tourists? We love the coast, the warm waters. We want to live there, build vacation houses, escape the cold winters, tip the waiter for bringing us a drink on the beach. We don't think much about the impact this is having on the ecosystems of coastal lands or on their peoples. Won't they just welcome the jobs, the investment?

We don't think much about the natural disasters that will come, because they have always come and will come again. We can't imagine being limited by nature, or needing to consider the impact our lifestyles might have on notoriously volatile natural systems. Even though lava flows and tsunamis and earthquakes do not distinguish among peoples, will destroy what we build, will destroy lives and economies, will strike where they are intended to strike by the nature of this living planet—can't we still live wherever we want to? Can't we still build whatever we want, wherever a buck is to be made, wherever the view is wonderful? Can't we just pretend it will never happen—and buy insurance, just in case? And won't technology and human ingenuity make all things possible?

Are we really going to rebuild the areas around New Orleans that flooded when the levees broke?

New Orleans.

Navigation is a major foundation of the economies of thirty-three states along the Mississippi. The river provides the means for the commerce and recreation that sustain tens of millions of people. But it has an inherent problem; it is prone to flooding.

And so, to service this human activity and to secure the burgeoning communities being built along the river banks from these periodic natural disasters, early European settlers, and later the US Army Corps of Engineers, built levees along the river banks, redirected water flows, dammed and dredged, in order to beat this enormous natural waterway into submission—literally, to force it to submit to human will—thus supporting a thriving and critical economy through the heart of the nation.

And thus also helping to create the conditions that would destroy New Orleans.

It seems that one result of these monumental efforts, undergone over a couple of centuries, has been the slow erosion and destruction of the protective wetlands in the Mississippi delta that provided a buffer for storms like

Hurricane Katrina. The frequent flooding of the river brought down to the delta the sediment that replenished the large swath of wetlands that protected the coast. Because of the diminishment of sediment flow, the delta is disappearing. A part of Louisiana is now inexorably sinking. Meanwhile, New Orleans, which is also sinking, is a city surrounded by lakes, rivers, and marshes, built on land below sea level, protected by levees, an enormous act of faith and trust in the human power to tame and subdue the forces of nature.

Since it rains in New Orleans—often a lot—the city had to be protected not only from the waters of rivers, lakes, and the Gulf of Mexico, but also from the water that falls from the sky. So, besides the levees, enormous pumps were constructed to take out every drop of rain that falls into the "bowl" that holds the city.

This system failed in the wake of the hurricane.

Researching the topic on a variety of websites, I found revealing examples of the spiritual or relational divide around this question of how human beings approach the forces of nature, in this case, the Mississippi River and the issue of water.

Here is how the US Army Corps of Engineers approaches the challenge:

Without question America's greatest river, the Mississippi, has made major contributions to the physical and economic growth of the nation. It is a navigation artery of great importance to the nation's transportation system, carrying an ever-growing commerce. Coursing through the heart of America, it supplies water for the cities and industries that have located along its banks. More and more the Mississippi's importance is emphasized as America continues to grow. This great river is, truly, one of the nation's outstanding assets. *Uncontrolled, it would be just as great a liability.*

The Mississippi River always has been a threat to the security of the valley through which it flows [I am sure the poor river didn't know it was a security threat to the United States, and you know what we do to security threats]. Garciliaso de la Vega, in his history of the expedition begun by DeSoto, described the first recorded flood of the Mississippi as severe and of prolonged duration, beginning about March 10, 1543, and cresting about 40 days later. By the end of May the river had returned to its banks, having been in flood for about 80 days.

Since that time, explorers, traders, farmers, men of commerce, and engineers have known—sometimes too well—the Mississippi in flood.

The Mississippi River has the third largest drainage basin in the world, exceeded in size only by the watersheds of the Amazon and

Congo Rivers. It drains 41 percent of the 48 contiguous states of the United States. The basin covers more than 1,245,000 square miles, includes all or parts of 31 states and two Canadian provinces, and roughly resembles a funnel which has its spout at the Gulf of Mexico. Waters from as far east as New York and as far west as Montana contribute to flows in the lower river.

The lower alluvial valley of the Mississippi River is a relatively flat plain of about 35,000 square miles bordering on the river which *would be overflowed during time of high water if it were not for man-made protective works*. This valley begins just below Cape Girardeau, Missouri, is roughly 600 miles in length, varies in width from 25 to 125 miles, and includes parts of seven states—Missouri, Illinois, Tennessee, Kentucky, Arkansas, Mississippi, and Louisiana.

Floods of 1849 and 1850, which caused widespread damage in the Mississippi River Valley, revealed *the national interest in controlling the mighty river*.

By the year 1879, the need for *improvement* of the Mississippi River had become widely recognized. The necessity for coordination of engineering operations through a centralized organization had finally been accepted.

Accordingly, in that year, the Congress established the Mississippi River Commission and assigned it the duties . . . "to take into consideration and mature such a plan or plans and estimates as will correct, permanently locate, and deepen the channel and protect the banks of the Mississippi River, improve and give safety and ease to navigation thereof, prevent destructive floods, promote and facilitate commerce, trade, and the postal service." (emphasis added)[2]

And you thought, as you gazed upon Ol' Man River with awe, watching the barges float lazily along the channel, that you were gazing upon a natural wonder. It certainly was one, once.

What nature took hundreds of thousands of years to create was seen by European settlers, including us, as a *problem*, a problem to be solved by resolute human will and ingenuity.

No one can say we tried to tame the river out of ignorance. We knew what it could do. Is it possible that the river knew best how to protect its own banks, that it knew, innately, what it was doing, that the point would have been to live *with* it, rather than to alter it for our economic benefit?

But, it is true, commerce and the economy built around it would not have developed as it did, many cities would never have been built, the entire country would have developed differently, and New Orleans may never have existed as a large metropolitan area to be destroyed in 2005.

When humans try to outwit nature

So that's one view, powerfully anthropocentric, seeing the human project as something to which the earth is made to submit, whose forces are to be tamed for our use. And that is magnificent and wonderful, deserving of awe over our amazing ingenuity.

Here is another view. This one comes from a report in September 2002 by Daniel Zwerdling for National Public Radio.[3]

"Right now, an entire region of the United States is crumbling and sinking into the sea. Scientists say it's causing one of the worst and least-publicized environmental disasters in America's history. . . . There's a moral to this story: when humans try to outwit nature, it can strike back with a vengeance."

As he flew over Louisiana's wetlands with biologist Bill Good three years before Katrina struck, Zwerdling described what he was seeing: "Coastal wetlands are lands that get flooded by tides. They're bursting with life, like rainforests, and these are some of the greatest wetlands on Earth. They sprawl 300 miles along the Gulf of Mexico, and they go up to 50 miles inland. They're the heart of the Mississippi Delta; and this astonishing landscape is vanishing." Good says, "If we'd taken this helicopter trip 50 years ago, it would have looked like the Great Plains . . . like the prairies in the Midwest, solid, vast expanses of grass . . . verdant green from horizon to horizon." Now it is "a ragged patchwork," with "thousands of streams and lakes and canals eating away at the grasslands like cancer."

Pointing toward the fishing boats in a nearby bay, Good noted that in the 1980s the area was "solid ground."

"That scale is monumental and the significance is really hard to put into words. . . . It's very hard to get your mind wrapped around how large and important and productive and unique all of this is. To see it simply dying is a tragedy, a tragedy of immense proportions."

(In February 2005 National Geographic News was reporting that chunks of land the size of a football field were being lost *every thirty-five minutes*.[4])

To get to the source of the wetlands disaster, Zwerdling went off to view the levee system along the banks of the Mississippi River with Oliver Houck, head of the environment program at Tulane University's Law School. Houck said, "There is no place in the world that has a levee system that is as extensive as this one—it's a monster system."

"The banks here are about 20 feet high," Houck explained, as they stood atop a grassy embankment. "When we cross the banks, you'll see on the other side [that] if these levees were not here, that water would be at about eaves' level across the houses behind us"—a bit like what happened in August 2005.

"I always wondered what 'levees' meant," said Zwerdling. "A levee is a wall. A levee is a wall to keep the river out of your living room."

To keep the water out of the living rooms of Louisiana coastal residents, engineers built two thousand miles of levees along the Mississippi and its branches. All of this was to prevent the floods that are a natural part of the river's long history, floods that come frequently, and sometimes disastrously, in terms of lives and property.

The system was also intended to protect the city of New Orleans as these floods washed down to the delta. That was the disaster for which they had prepared. Engineers pretty much ignored the other possibility, the disaster that could come from the south.

"Before people built these walls," said Zwerdling, "the giant Mississippi [and its tributaries] helped build America, washing millions of pounds of soil from all over the country down to the Gulf of Mexico."

"That's what built south Louisiana," added Houck. "The Mississippi built five million acres of land."

Under the weight of this heavy, rich soil, the marshland is always sinking, but before the dams and levees stopped the flow, the river always brought more, and the marshes provided a protective barrier to New Orleans and nearby communities from the full brunt force of tropical storms. When hurricanes strike land, they begin to lose strength. While the coast is hit with fury, much of the punch of the storm then begins to abate, like taking a steaming kettle off the burner. As the wetlands disappear, the Gulf of Mexico is growing inexorably closer to the city of New Orleans.

Houck reflects on how the Army Corps of Engineers persistently fought the river with more dams, more dredging, and always more levees. "And every time they thought they'd conquered nature, the river proved them wrong," said Zwerdling. "So the army built more walls and they built them higher." Houck says, "The army has finally won the war—they've tamed the Mississippi."

But the victory was pyrrhic, to say the least. Soon after building the system, the delta region began to sink. The wetlands are now sinking into the sea, or, as Zwerdling put it, "The Gulf of Mexico is essentially drowning them." What had once been marshland prairie that could support giant oak trees is now riddled with ponds and mud, a sign that it is coming apart. As the land sinks and the water levels rise, the marsh grasses can no longer hold the soil. "The plants die," said scientist Denise Reed, whom Zwerdling interviewed for this report, "and when plants die, there's nothing to hold it together."

How much land is Louisiana losing? Zwerdling reports that right now, the state's coast accounts for 80 percent of the land loss in the United States. Louisiana's Department of Resources Office of Coastal Restoration and Management reports that, at the current rate, the state will have lost 527,000

acres of coastal lands by the year 2050, along with the rich biodiversity that
it once harbored. The Gulf of Mexico will have moved thirty miles north,
and New Orleans will be still more exposed to the full force of a hurricane—
or any tropical storm, for that matter.

As evidence of the loss of resilience, S. Jeffress Williams, a coastal scientist with the US Geological Survey, told Congress at a hearing in fall 2005
that some of the marshes lying east of the river lost more than 25 percent of
their land area during Katrina.[5] They were simply too deteriorated to hold
together.

But there is still more to this story, other ways that humans managed to
beat up on the delta. Zwerdling's report points out that thousands of canals
have been dug through the marshland by energy companies like Shell and
Texaco since the 1950s, when they found vast amounts of oil and gas buried
there. Aerial views reveal these waterways crisscrossing the delta, dredged
and straightened to make way for drilling holes to extract oil and gas. "There
are thousands and thousands and thousands of these across coastal Louisiana," said Reed.

The energy industry is Louisiana's largest, which means there are powerful economic interests at work here. And those interests span everything
from the power and influence of the oil industry itself to the economy of a
relatively poor state that needs jobs and a tax base, to politicians who want to
be elected to office, to gas the people need to drive their cars, to the heating
oil and natural gas necessary to cool or warm homes. A confluence of economic interests, a fossil-fuel-based consumer society, and human hubris have
conspired to destroy the wetlands of Louisiana's coast, bringing disaster ever
closer to the city of New Orleans and other coastal communities.

"This marsh cannot survive in this state much longer. It's like the edge of
a blanket starting to fray. Once it starts, it goes very rapidly," warns Reed.

Next, Zwerdling went off on a boat with Rick Eddy, who runs a bait-and-
tackle shop in the town of Leeville, to visit a nearby cemetery, "because this
is the only way you can see it." Headstones stick up out of the water when
the tide is low and virtually disappear when it is high.

"The cemetery's all under water," Eddy says. "It's eroded right away. I've
been in this area for 15 years. When I first came into this area, there was all
land there. It's very heartbreaking. And to have something like this come
along—and erosion. Some of the headstones are all busted up. The mauso-
leums, it's just a pile of rubble really. Kinda hard to put it in words."

Right—he did pretty well.

Writer Anna Quindlen, in an essay entitled "Don't Mess with Mother,"
reflected on the deeper meaning of Hurricane Katrina:

New Orleans lived for 80 years with the granddaddy of all environmentally misguided plans, the project that straightened out the mighty

Mississippi so its banks would be more hospitable to homes and businesses. Little by little the seductive city at the river's mouth became like one of those denuded developments built after clear-cutting. It was left with no natural protection, girded with a jerry-built belt of walled-off water, its marshland and barrier islands gone, a sitting duck for a big storm.[6]

Another Mississippi anecdote, because it is important for this story: In 1993, spring deluges that fell on states adjoining the river caused the greatest floods in centuries. In the areas where the levees were built to protect river harbors and commerce, they worked. The damage was minimal. However, the levees also concentrated the flow of the water, increasing the pressure and the violence of the water flow. When the water passed the levees, it burst out into the unprotected farmlands and small towns, increasing the extent of devastation in those areas.

Water has to go somewhere, after all.

The disaster resulted in billions of dollars in economic damage alone.

The mighty Mississippi. In our human attempts to tame it, to put it to use for our commerce and our enjoyment, we had the hubris to believe we had beaten it into submission. We changed its behavior, all right. But it remains mightier than we and will at times break out of these constraints, reminding us of the earth's power, the power of water, and what it means when the earth, which took millions of years to create the delicate balance of its rich ecosystems, is put out of balance. The Mississippi was feeding the delta, the Mississippi had created its own flood plain to absorb the water, until we built on it, then leveed, dammed, and dredged it. The Mississippi needs vastly more space than it now has to be the river it was created to be. We have squeezed it into the dimensions that fit our human plans. It was bound to rebel. And this won't be the last time.

As Hurricane Katrina passed by New Orleans, a disaster predicted over two decades unfolded exactly as was inevitable, a disaster for which the ground had been long prepared.

Now the river is a way of life, it is river views and commerce, fishing industries, riverboat gambling, jobs for millions, economic life for cities and small towns. For now, our economic life depends on a faulty model of development, built on a faulty sense of the human as over and above nature, more powerful than it, following a religious mandate to dominate and subdue and put it at the service of "man"—with this result.

This disaster is a fine mixture of the forces of nature, mis-thought development, and global warming. They combined to destroy a major US city.

And what now for New Orleans? As the debate raged on about its future, as people insisted that they be allowed to rebuild their destroyed neighborhoods, those on the other side of the grassy embankments holding back the water, there is another topic that no one wants to talk about, the elephant in the room that everyone still chooses to walk around rather than acknowledge—the disaster they did *not* prepare for.

Hurricane Katrina did not hit New Orleans directly. The eye hit nearly sixty miles to the south and east in the small community of Buras-Triumph. By then, it had diminished to a Category Three storm. The city has not yet experienced the bigger disaster long feared—a Category Four or Five storm making a direct hit from the south. New Orleans was flooded not by a storm surge from the Gulf of Mexico but from the collapse of levees after the storm had passed by, when people were breathing a sigh of relief that the city had been spared the worst.

So while scientists, meteorologists, and others had been trying to warn the city for decades about a potential disaster, this was not even the one they were most concerned about. The one that causes them to lose sleep is what would happen if a Category Four or Five hurricane hits New Orleans dead on.

In another Zwerdling report, Houck presented the concern: "It was always thought that the big threat of flooding in New Orleans was the river—and it was—because it flooded regularly. So we beat flooding by taming the river. The irony of history is that we—like one of those old citadels in an adventure story—defended ourselves against the enemy that we knew, which was the river, but to the rear and to the flank was this other threat, which we are only now beginning to appreciate, and it may be too late to prevent."[7]

Poignant reading three years *before* Katrina, isn't it? We didn't prepare well for the disaster we thought we had prepared for—floods from the river and lakes. What about the one still to come—what will it entail?

The fear is this: a Category Five hurricane makes a direct hit on the city. Now, before Katrina, which depopulated much of the city, there were half a million people in the metropolitan area, plus thousands more in nearby coastal communities. As of this writing, the city's population stands at 150,000, and is growing.

In studying this bigger threat to the former population, the examples scientists looked at are Hurricane Camille (1969), the largest storm ever to hit the United States (it missed New Orleans by one hundred miles), and Hurricane Andrew (1992). These were monster storms. They would have crushed the city. When Hurricane Georges approached in 1998, officials, aware of the studies, decided to play it safe and evacuate the city. What happened was not comforting. Roads were quickly clogged with traffic and, had the storm hit, tens of thousands of people would have been completely vulnerable, trapped on the highways in their cars. The other problem is that those very same roads would have probably flooded. Not only can people not get out, but rescuers cannot get in.

Now, back to the problem of the disappearing wetlands. With less protective buffer, a storm surge could put much of the "bowl" containing New Orleans under twenty to thirty feet of water. That water will be full of debris that will sweep over everything in its path. And because of the levee system, the water that gets in will not be able to get out; the pumps will be under water and not functioning.

Walter Maestri, working at the emergency command center in Jefferson Parish, told Zwerdling that the city will "look like a massive shipwreck. Everything that the water has carried in is going to be there. It's going to have to be cleaned out—alligators, moccasins, and God knows what that lives in the surrounding swamps, have now been flushed, literally, into the metropolitan area. And they can't get out, because they're inside the bowl now. No water to drink, no water to use for sanitation purposes. All of the sanitation plants are under water and, of course, the material is floating free in the community. The petrochemicals that are produced up and down the Mississippi River—much of that has floated into this bowl. . . . The biggest toxic waste dump in the world now is the city of New Orleans because of what has happened."

Army Corps of Engineer officials talk about the difficulty of rescue and recovery—neighborhoods and streets obliterated, no street signs to help them find their way, no medical facilities to take the sick and injured, no morgues for the dead.

Okay, what death toll were they anticipating back in 2002? Some estimated twenty thousand to forty thousand. An Army Corps researcher said more like one hundred thousand.

Maybe Katrina was as much a blessing as a curse. Maybe by cleaning out the city—although at the cost of more than 1,000 lives and 300,000 displaced—it saved the lives of tens of thousands more, depending on what we do now. Again, the portends are not favorable. We didn't listen to them before Katrina. Are we listening now? Yet the warnings are increasingly dire, more costly.

Some say the city should be abandoned and relocated farther inland, at least those sections below sea level. Many displaced residents still want to go home. Business owners have recreated a French Quarter playground. It's hard to give up on a city with such a rich history, such a deep impression on the soul of this nation. And it is utterly "un-American."

Houck thinks they could ring the major towns, but "if we aren't going to draw a line and try to protect every little town, we would have to do some serious people relocation, and that would humanely require compensation."[8] We couldn't even get the federal government to fund fully the temporary housing needs of the displaced in the immediate aftermath of the disaster. How can we realistically expect a commitment to "humane compensation" for permanent relocation?

In 2002 Houck was saying that it's time to "stop the foolishness of permitting yet more residential development. We are granting permits every week for new subdivisions right in the path of where this stuff is going to go. We're still covering those people with flood insurance."[9]

Maybe Houck and the park ranger should get together—for some consolation. It's hard to be the canary singing in the mine when everyone else wants to drown out the song.

Some people want to create a system of pipelines, pumps, and canals along the Mississippi to capture the river sediment and send it to the delta. Though many scientists believe this would work, it would take many years and billions of dollars. The coastal area probably does not have that kind of time.

Meanwhile, the displaced, mostly the poor of the city, still feel pretty much abandoned by their government at all levels.

Oh, a final anecdote for what I like to call the Katrina metaphor: Because of the drain on federal funds for the war in Iraq and the new Homeland Security Department, along with the infamous Bush administration tax cuts, the annual federal budget for levee restoration, pumping stations, and flood control for the Louisiana coast had been slashed in 2003 and 2004. There were several critical projects under way in the New Orleans area at the time, particularly to shore up levees around Lake Pontchartrain. The levees around the city, like everything else, are sinking. The levees need to be raised, but that cut-off of federal funds stopped the work in its tracks. Following the dreadful 2004 hurricane season (four struck Florida that year), the federal government proposed the steepest reductions ever for hurricane-and-flood control. Even an important research project to study the potential impacts of a Category Four or Five storm could not be completed.

Now, you tell me what we should do about New Orleans. And tell me, from this story, the message here about the human relationship with the forces of nature.

There are stories like these all along the coasts of the United States.

Investing in disaster

On October 10, 2005, the *New York Times* carried a story on its front page that reveals another kind of response along the spectrum of human reaction to dire situations. For some years scientists have been trying to draw our attention to the extent of the melting of the polar ice cap at the North Pole during the summer months. They predict that within a few short decades the Arctic Ocean will be totally liquid for several months of the year. In 2005 the ice cap had shrunk to the smallest size ever recorded by humans.

The article even reflected on how our familiar image of the earth from outer space will be altered—how the brilliant white that wraps the North

Pole will turn a seasonal blue. Imagine that! In our lifetime the image of the planet from outer space will be dramatically altered.

This is alarming for a couple of reasons. For one, it is another sign of global warming, another bit of evidence that shows us that the phenomenon is real. In fact, scientists are surprised that it is occurring this rapidly; they knew this would happen, but not so soon.

The other reason for alarm has to do with what the melt of the polar ice cap will mean for our coasts and for the warming problem itself. It is another indication of the melting that is going on around the earth, the receding of glaciers, the collapse of ice shelves in remote northern and southern climes. Scientists predict that this will raise sea levels around the world dramatically, threatening cities like New York and London with inundation. Forget New Orleans, or the million-dollar houses built on stilts in South Bethany, Delaware, or the high-rise hotels built smack on the sand beaches of Ocean City, Maryland, or the sweet summer beach houses on the Outer Banks of North Carolina.

This could all begin to happen in our lifetimes.

The ice melt is also likely to accelerate the warming of the earth. Ice reflects sunlight back into the sky. Water absorbs it. The more the water absorbs light, the warmer the earth gets.

Much has been written about global warming in recent years, and I will have more to say about this in the next chapter. But the story in the *New York Times* was about something else; it was about how some people are dealing with this looming crisis—by investing in it.

The story begins with Pat Broe from Denver, who is betting on the disaster to come, having recently purchased a Hudson Bay port that may one day soon be at the epicenter of an old seafarer's dream come true—a northwest passage to the Far East. Seems Broe bought the port from the Canadian government for seven bucks. Apparently it isn't worth much—until the ice melts.

Some individual and corporate investors look at the looming crisis and see before them a great opportunity to make some money—a lot of money. Not only will there be a shorter passage for trade in goods from North America to Asia, but there is something else that lies under all that ice and permafrost—oil, once again oil, always oil.

Here's how the *New York Times* described it:

> By Mr. Broe's calculations, Churchill could bring in as much as $100 million a year as a port on Arctic shipping lanes shorter by thousands of miles than routes to the south, and traffic would only increase as the retreat of ice in the region clears the way for a longer shipping season.
>
> With major companies and nations large and small adopting similar logic, the Arctic is undergoing nothing less than a great rush for virgin territory and natural resources worth hundreds of billions of dollars.[10]

Scientists have found "hints" of oil within two hundred miles of the North Pole, the article says.

I love this, too: clever entrepreneurs see possibilities for new tourist cruise destinations, great fishing opportunities, and more.

Ports will be built, fragile terrain covered over with roads for oil-drilling rigs and pipelines, and soon, I imagine, the local Wal-Mart will appear.

There are human beings that will cash in on just about anything, I guess.

But my question is this: are we learning nothing from our predicament? While investors dream of fortunes (we always do, it is how and why we settled the frontier, after all), what do they think will be happening down south where once arable lands will be turning to deserts, where billions of lives will be threatened by the ramifications of drastic climate change, where major cities will be in crisis, where mass migrations from once-habitable areas will be part of the human landscape everywhere?

It would seem that we tend to adapt to these looming crises by wishful thinking and a heavy dose of denial, or by avoiding as much as possible any worry and stress (the culture treats these as bad things rather than as symptoms appropriate to our condition), or by hoping they will not upset our lives too drastically (trust me, recycling bottles and cans will not quite do it). We continue along, supporting a way of life from which we simply do not seem able to wrench ourselves.

Am I being too harsh? Let me share a couple more examples of what I mean.

Remember the Mississippi floods of 1993? Here is a tidbit from an Associated Press article dated February 18, 2006, while Katrina, one would think, was still a vivid memory. "Around St. Louis, where the Mississippi River lapped at the steps of the Gateway Arch during the 1993 flood, more than 14,000 acres of flood plain have been developed since then. That has reduced the region's ability to store water during future floods and potentially put more people in harm's way. . . . Similar development has occurred around Dallas; Kansas City, Missouri; Los Angeles; Omaha, Nebraska; and Sacramento, California."[11]

Nor did Katrina alter development plans in any way. Gerald Galloway, professor of engineering at the University of Maryland, cited in the article, said, "The half-life memory of a flood is very short."

One presumes all these property owners were able to obtain flood insurance.

Eighty-five percent of the Mississippi River that flows by St. Louis is contained behind levees. The Associated Press was told by Nicholas Pinter, professor of geology at Southern Illinois University, that these levees "have raised flood levels 10 feet to 12 feet higher than they were just a century ago." He noted the similarity with the levees in New Orleans.

Oh, and by the way, Missouri is also the site of the epicenter of four of the largest earthquakes ever recorded in the continental United States, occurring in 1811–12. The area that includes Missouri and surrounding states is called the New Madrid Seismic Zone, and its center lies along the southern border of Missouri, where it abuts Tennessee and Arkansas, and joins the southern tip of Illinois. Seismologists have been warning that the area may be ripe for another temblor soon, a high probability of a major earthquake within the next three decades—this time with a vast population sitting on top the moving plates, many of them living behind the levees.

Floods and earthquakes in the heartland of the nation. I wonder how many quake-proof buildings, or perhaps stricter building codes, have been or are being developed in areas around this ancient fault line. I wonder what happens to the levees when this temblor strikes. I wonder if restricting development in dangerous areas has been considered.

Sadly, since this would be costly and objectionable to developers and would-be property owners, and would hamper economic activity, what local jurisdictions are doing instead is getting better prepared for the disasters that inevitably will come.[12] At least that lesson is being learned from the sad story of the Gulf Coast. But have we added this cost into the price of the property, into the taxes on developers and home owners? Have developers and officials considered the human lives that will be lost? One can be warned, perhaps, of a flood, but an earthquake?

Another example: New Orleans is not the only metropolitan area in the United States that levees have made possible. East of San Francisco lies the delta of the Sacramento and San Joaquin Rivers, which receives runoff water from about 40 percent of California. The story may have a familiar ring. The land is below sea level, and one thousand miles of levees hold the water at bay. The area includes the city of Stockton. Its population is booming.

Jeffrey Mount, geology professor at the University of California-Davis, said, "We are reinventing Katrina all over again." He estimates "a two-in-three probability over the next 50 years of a catastrophic levee failure."[13] A large failure, say as result of an earthquake, would inundate the entire region.

Mount told the Associated Press that there are two kinds of levees in California, "Those that have failed, and those that will fail."

Irony abounds. As the Associated Press reports, "In California, the modest investment required to shore up a levee protecting farmland can result in dramatic increase in the value of that land, Mount said. That, in turn, increases the likelihood a farmer will sell out to developers, ushering in the construction of houses on what had been flood plain. 'You actually spur development. It's a self-fulfilling process,' Mount said."

You gotta love the free market as it plays its vital role in this dynamic of disaster. All investors are doing is meeting demand. They are not responsible. And God forbid we should ever stop developers from doing their business, even if it ultimately means saving untold numbers of lives and more hundreds of billions of dollars in economic loss. There is an ideology at work here, and it says this is a rational way to do business.

Anna Quindlen writes:

> How many times do we have to watch homes cantilevered over canyons surrender to a river of mud or beach houses on stilts slide into the surf to know that when we do high-stakes battle with Mother Nature, Mother takes all? Once I heard a businessman at a zoning board meeting say, "Well, a person can do what he wants with his land." Actually, that's not true; that's why zoning exists. Is any city, town, or state brave enough to just say no to waterfront development that destroys dunes, despoils water and creates the conditions that will, when a storm strikes, create destruction?[14]

Yes? No? Anybody?

A final word from Nicholas Pinter: "If you want to look at what probably—unfortunately—will happen in New Orleans in the next 10 years, look at what has happened in St. Louis in the last decade."[15]

And this added note: a warming climate is likely to increase the severity of storms and therefore the frequency of extreme flooding. Expect more days ahead glued to your TV screens watching the horror of human beings killed, injured, their lives destroyed by the disasters to come. And for those who still do not believe that it will happen to them, or happen in their lifetime—whole cities destroyed, hundreds of thousands of people displaced, thousands dead here in this country—I give you Katrina.

It's about a relationship

Ben Franklin, in his inimitable wisdom, once said that "the definition of insanity is doing the same thing over and over and expecting a different result." In our case, we not only do the same thing, but more and more of it—from more housing developments in diminishing green spaces, on flood plains and fault lines, to more shoreline development and mountain homes, to increased oil-based mobility of humans and products, to consumption of what we believe are endlessly replaceable goods, and on and on. As we lose the natural beauty that once surrounded us and become saturated with consumer goods in this country, we try to force more and more cultures and economies to open up their markets and follow our example, trying to coerce or entice them into living just like us. By Franklin's standard, we have truly gone insane.

As we crowd this planet, more disasters will affect more people. Some of these will be forces of nature, like earthquakes, tsunamis, and hurricanes. Some of these will be human made, natural disasters grown more unnatural because of the heavy human footprint on the planet. We have lived as if the earth would never move under our feet, or our nearby volcanoes would never explode, or the ocean would never send a killer wave to our coasts in our lifetime.

What happened on the day after Christmas in 2004 was *necessary* for life. That may be hard to hear, but the kind of earthquake that created the tsunami is, literally, something the earth needs to do so that there is life. That earthquake was the result of one tectonic plate slipping underneath another. It is a form of recycling. The oceans and continents drift on the earth's crust, moving inches every year. The crust recycles, creating mountains and volcanoes, enriching soils, maintaining the chemical balance of the oceans. This recycling makes the planet habitable. If the earth doesn't do this, life as we know it dies.

It is hard to grasp the renewing nature of what in human terms was such an enormous disaster. But it may tell us something about our planet that we need to know, what we are a part of, the meaning of the regenerating nature of life and death and life and death, and how we might learn to live more humbly, more appropriately, more tuned in to the forces of nature as they create and re-create life through the churning, teeming, often violent forces of this uniquely amazing planet.

At the same time, because we humans are everywhere, we had also best search deep within ourselves for the values and meaning, the deeply rooted spirituality, that will carry us through these disasters, horrific as they are in human terms, until we can achieve in future generations a better balance of human population with the forces and energies of the earth.

We will need all our spiritual and moral strength to bear the costs. We will need neither to be crushed by the death and suffering nor to turn away from it. We will need a whole lot more compassion that doesn't diminish with the passage of time. We will need to decide as a society what kind of people we are, what we are willing to let go and let be, as we face more of these crises.

The story of the Mississippi delta is in the end about a relationship, the relationship between humanity and the environment that surrounds us, forms us, is us. One could take an example from the therapeutic world as yet another metaphor—we are in an abusive relationship with an intimate other. We have created a dysfunctional relational dynamic, and now we don't know how to stop it. It is destroying both of us—one from the physical abuse, the other from loss of soul. And deeply embedded in the dynamic of the abuser is the dynamic of power.

Comparing the relationship between the river and the Army Corps of Engineers with that of Rick Eddy at the tackle shop in Leeville, or scientists like Reed and Houck, those who feel the loss because it is a part of them, we begin to get a better sense of the choices before us. And none is more essential than the choice we make about the kind of relationship that will guide us now. More than anything else, this will determine what comes next and whether there is hope in the decisions we make about how to proceed. Those decisions will be very hard ones indeed. But if we choose to go on as we have been, then we had best prepare ourselves for the disasters to come. They will represent without doubt a culture that has truly gone insane.

2

Climate Change

or,

Facing Human Extinction

*It's like going up to the edge of a cliff, not
really knowing where it is. Common sense
says you shouldn't discover where the edge is
by passing over it.*
—Thomas E. Lovejoy[1]

We are all contributing to the death of the living systems of our planet.
We are participating inexorably in the process of creating the conditions for
the extinction of our species, along with millions upon millions of other
species already lost, irreversibly fated to disappear, or on their way or approaching the point of no return. We contribute each day to the death of
the lush rich nature that has formed the context for wonder and spiritual
meaning for humans for tens of thousands of years. We are in the process of
destroying that which gave birth to us and sustains us.

Do I have your attention? How does it feel to read that? Or have you
never entertained the thought? It's a tough one, for sure.

This is not about guilt. I imagine none of us deliberately chooses to participate in this death. There are those who know it is happening, and for
reasons having to do with both power and wealth, are doing their best to
keep this information from others or to deceive them. I leave them to their
own consciences; this isn't really addressed to them (though the work we
need to do *will* be).

It is hard to be born in the first generation that has to deal with this
looming possibility, that has seen it become real. But we need to decide what
we are going to do. The first time the threat of extinction became real in my
life, an actual possibility, was the year I turned thirteen. One day my family

21

gathered around the radio, listening to President John F. Kennedy tell us that the Soviet Union had placed nuclear missiles on the island of Cuba and that we were on the brink of atomic war. In grade school we had received ID bracelets that we were to wear 24/7 "just in case" (those of a certain age and above know what I am talking about). I still have it in a box of memorabilia in my desk drawer—a reminder of how early the "big fear" stalked my life. Much later, I would wonder what made them think that if I were evaporated in an atomic explosion my little metal bracelet would survive, lying there intact in the ashes, or the little pile of dust, or the shadow on the sidewalk, saying "this is who she was."

What made them think there would be anyone around to read it?

Kennedy was not of the mind to allow that to happen, and it didn't. Over the years we reached a certain chilly peace with the Eastern Bloc. The threat of mutual annihilation and a modicum of sanity on the part of world leaders kept us from falling over the precipice.

Maybe we became complacent then, though President Ronald Reagan, wrongfully credited with the demise of the Soviet Union and the end of the Cold War, brought us near one more time. I remember losing sleep some of those nights back in the early 1980s. The fear ignited outrage and a power-ful peace movement, however brief its expression. In 1982 I marched in the streets of Manhattan with over a million people to say no one more time to this possibility. The march was led by Japanese survivors of Hiroshima and Nagasaki. I walked with them for a while that day and still have the little gifts, medals, and cards they gave me as we bowed over and over again to one another. They are precious reminders of how human beings can reach over the most monumental chasms of bitterness, hatred, and war—bridges usually created by those who suffered the consequences rather than by those who caused them.

The difference now, perhaps, is that what we face is not some sudden dramatic turn of events that can be held at bay, or made to go away, through some hard negotiating and deal-making that ends the stand-off, and then life goes on, the tensions lowered. There is no clear enemy, an "other" from whom we can defend ourselves or to whom we can talk and resolve the crisis. It is something that has come upon us, bit by bit, while we weren't paying much attention, something of which we are so intimately a part that we cannot see it clearly, though it is accelerating with unsettling speed now and affecting all of our lives.

We have altered the climate and the ecosystems of our planet; we have thrown the earth's atmosphere out of balance. The changes are already mani-festing themselves, and many of them will get worse quickly now. No world summit, no gathering of world leaders, however large and grand, can come to a decision that will make this go away. We cannot sit down with nature to negotiate, to ask it to change its mind and restore the old balance.

I don't mean to imply that human extinction is right around the corner, as some doomsayers posit. Actually, I don't think we're going to get off that easy. There will be a road to take us there, for sure, and it will not be a pleasant one. Will we look for another path while there is still time to change course (not much time, but a little)? Will we be willing to take it?

We are in big trouble, and our efforts now must be geared toward avoiding the worst and living—equitably, compassionately, justly, humbly, lovingly, *differently*—through the difficult times ahead.

To what extent are we willing to alter our lives, the way we live here on our home planet, in order to save ourselves, much less leave a viable planet, one capable of offering a rich life, for our children and grandchildren—or, in my case, my nieces and nephew (Deanna, Jessica, Rachel, Stephen, Elizabeth), my grand-niece and grand-nephew (precious Francesca and her baby brother Elliot), my nine-year-old godson Aidan and his brother and three sisters, Jane and John with whom I lived for ten of their growing-up years, my friend Maya, whose Bat Mitzvah, her coming of age just shy of thirteen, was celebrated by her loving friends and family in June 2006, and sweet Maura, young daughter of two old and dear friends. The upcoming generations will begin to feel the real brunt of the coming changes. We are leaving them an extraordinary burden for which they did not ask.

Here's an idea. Grab some photos of your favorite young people and put them in front of you as you read this chapter, or write down their names and use the paper as a bookmark. Keep them in sight as we ponder these things. We need the motivation for the great work that lies ahead.

It's happening

So, climate change. What do we know? What don't we know? How long do we want to wait to find out?

I am not a scientist, and so much has been written about global warming and climate change that I don't feel the need to present the research one more time. Even the media has begun to figure out that this is a big story, with far more coverage of the looming crisis in newspapers and on TV in the past few years, along with voluminous material on the Internet, and powerful documentary films, such as Al Gore's much-acclaimed *An Inconvenient Truth*. With this wealth of information available, I will only summarize some of the major trends for the purpose of this reflection, and then urge you to go to those sources.

First of all, we must lay to rest any doubt that the globe is warming in ways not explained by the cycles of nature. It is—more rapidly than many had predicted—and the largest factor in this unprecedented warming is human impact. There are still nay-sayers, but behind many of them are institutions funded by people with a vested financial interest in the issue, like the fossil-fuel industry. So be sure when you are researching the topic that you examine the source of the funding for research studies.

A great effort has been under way to monitor and to respond quickly—and, if possible, preemptively—to the reports of scientists and environmental groups regarding global warming and the resulting climate disruption, to cast a cloud of uncertainty over the conclusions of studies done by thousands and thousands of scientists, research institutes, the United Nations, and nongovernmental organizations (NGOs) around the world. The idea is to bring uncertainty into the discussion, as if there is a debate with two different sides of equal stature and weight. This is simply not true.

What I am finding instead is that some of the most skeptical independent scientists are losing their doubts about whether or not the earth is warming and about the human contribution to this alarming trend.

One of the more compelling examples is Dr. Rajendra Pachauri, current chair of the influential Intergovernmental Panel on Climate Change (IPCC). The IPCC was created in 1988 under the auspices of the United Nations and comprises two thousand scientists and other experts from across the globe. Their peer-reviewed studies make up an overwhelming body of science on climate change and the impacts to come if nothing substantial is done to reduce the human impact on the atmosphere.

Through the years their reports have grown increasingly dire—from seeking to prove the potential for human contribution to warming to acknowledging that it has already begun, much sooner than anticipated. In 2007 the IPCC issued a series of new reports indicating that we will face severe consequences in this century if temperatures continue to rise.

The Bush administration, which consistently downplays the threat of global warming and works in the international community largely for the purpose of trying to make the issue go away, dismissed from its first days the work of the IPCC. The previous chair, Dr. Robert Watson, chief scientist at the World Bank, was a particular annoyance to the energy industry, which had supported Bush's 2000 presidential campaign, because of Watson's repeated calls for urgent action.

A report from the IPCC in 2001, the first year of Bush's first term in office, indicated that human-caused global warming was already well under way and that the disruptions to come would be many and difficult.

Early that same year Exxon executives sent a memorandum to the White House asking that Watson be replaced "at the request of the United States." Get rid of the messenger was their approach. (Remember those secret meetings on energy policy headed by Vice President Dick Cheney back in 2001? Wouldn't you like to know more about them now?)

Dr. Pachauri was the choice of the White House (Al Gore described him as a "let's drag our feet" candidate),[2] and the administration successfully lobbied other countries to support him.

So what happened once Dr. Pachauri had all those reports in front of him, after he listened to scientists day after day? In January 2005 at a conference in Mauritius attended by representatives of 114 countries he told the assembled gathering: "Climate change is for real. We have just a small window of opportunity and it is closing rather rapidly. There is not a moment to lose." In case anyone missed his point: "We are risking the ability of the human race to survive."[3]

Oops.

Because of the warming

So, then, what's going on? What do we need to know? A few salient facts:

The temperature around the globe is rising, and the rate of rise correlates nicely with the rise of carbon (CO_2) emissions and other so-called greenhouse gases in the atmosphere since the beginning of the industrial revolution, in other words, with human impact. These emissions have been increasing exponentially with the rapid pace of population growth and economic expansion since World War II.

They are called greenhouse gases for exactly the reason one builds a greenhouse to grow plants—to trap heat in a limited space. And, as you know, it can get uncomfortably steamy in a greenhouse.

Because of the warming ice all over the world, ice that has been in place for thousands upon thousands of years, is melting. This is causing ocean levels to rise worldwide, a steadily increasing threat to low-lying coastal communities (a few examples: most of Bangladesh, large swaths of Florida, the Atlantic Ocean barrier islands), several major metropolitan areas (London, Shanghai, Boston,[4] and Manhattan, for example—oh, and New Orleans), and entire island nations (the Maldives, Tuvalu, and Kiribati in the South Pacific), what some have dubbed "the Atlantis scenario."

The warming is also disrupting habitats in extreme northern and southern latitudes, threatening mass extinctions of wildlife, including such legendary creatures as polar bears, walrus, and penguins

A report on global warming that aired on *60 Minutes* on February 19, 2006, included the startling fact that 98 percent of the glaciers on earth are melting. So is the Arctic Ocean's polar ice cap, which has shrunk by 20 percent in the past thirty years, and the Antarctica and Greenland ice sheets, something scientists did not expect to see happen in our lifetime.

During my drive across the country in 2005, I visited Montana's Glacier National Park, a place I had long wanted to see. But I came a bit late for ideal glacier viewing. Of the park's 150 glaciers, only thirty-five remained. These are expected to be pretty much melted within the next two decades.

A week or so later I was at Paradise in Mt. Rainier National Park. I hiked with my brother and sister-in-law up to the Glacier View viewing point, a spot where one can stand before the glorious volcanic mountain peak and its magnificent glaciers—and it was obvious how much they had receded since I was last there. The same at Mt. Hood in Oregon. At both parks rangers spoke of the changes they had seen over the past ten to twenty years—receding glaciers, warmer winters, changes in the flora and fauna. The thing about global warming is that you can not only feel it, but see it if you venture out to these places. It is dramatic.

On Trail Ridge Road in Colorado's Rocky Mountain National Park, one of my favorite places in the world, I hiked a lovely trail along a mountainside through the forest just below timberline. I passed two people on this hike, so I had nature pretty much to myself, which is always best for encountering wildlife. Along the way up the mountain, not more than twenty yards from me, I came upon a yellow-bellied marmot. It was very busy, but, startled to attention, kept a wary eye on me at first. I stood perfectly still for a while until it grew more comfortable, more relaxed and natural, and then went back about its business. The marmot even "posed" for a photo. It was one of those very sweet gratuitous encounters that come for the patient nature lover.

So you can imagine my sorrow when I read not long ago that the yellow-bellied marmot is one of the animals whose future is in jeopardy because of climate change, which is disrupting its habitat.[5] The marmot hibernates in the winter, but recent observations show that it is waking up too early now, emerging from its hole a month earlier than expected. What rouses the animal is the sense each spring that the earth is warming. Now the marmot awakens while there is still deep winter snowpack and it cannot get to food. It then starves.

These are US stories, but they are mirrored all over the world. The magnificent glaciers near Banff, in Canada's Alberta Province, are receding. The glaciers in the Andes that provide water for millions of people in Peru and Bolivia are disappearing. This sets the stage for a monumental challenge to find other water sources and the potential of a huge flood of environmental refugees out of these areas in the next generation.

In Tanzania, the twelve-thousand-year-old glaciers atop Mount Kilimanjaro are crumbling, melting, and falling apart. They have been there since the end of the last ice age. If current conditions persist, they are expected to disappear by 2020. The melt is due to changing climate conditions related to global warming, as well as to forest reduction brought about by human activity, such as clearing for agriculture, forest fires, and the honey collectors who smoke bees out of their hives. Forest loss has caused a drop in precipitation, meaning less snow and ice to replenish what melts each year. In addition, the remaining older snow is darker and dirtier, absorbing more sunlight than fresh white snow. The result is even more warming.[6]

"The loss of foliage causes less moisture to be pumped into the atmosphere, leading to reduced cloud cover and precipitation and increased solar radiation and glacial evaporation," according to Douglas R. Hardy, climatologist at the University of Massachusetts in Amherst.[7]

This is a good example of how multiple forces rooted in human activity combine to break down an old ecosystem—global warming plus unsustainable patterns of human production.

Even the world's highest mountain is not immune. Mt. Everest is reported to have shrunk by four feet, probably due to glacier melt. Sherpas in Nepal, who have been climbing the mountain for generations, say they are "seeing widespread evidence of snowlines receding. . . . In 2002, a team of climbers sponsored by the United Nations Environment Program found signs that the landscape of Mount Everest had changed significantly since Sir Edmund Hillary and Tenzing Norgay first conquered the peak in 1953. The team found that the glacier that once came close to Hillary and Norgay's first camp had retreated three miles, and a series of ponds near Island Peak—so-called because it was then an island in a sea of ice—had merged into a long lake."[8]

The list goes on. In the past couple of decades, scientists have measured "a 5.5 percent shrinkage by volume in China's 46,298 glaciers, a loss equivalent to 3,000 sq. km. (1,158 sq. miles) of ice: there has been a noticeable acceleration in recent years. . . . If the climate continued to change at the current pace, [Chinese scientist] Yao Tandong predicted that two-thirds of China's glaciers would disappear by the end of the 2050s, and almost all would have melted by 2100."[9]

The possibility of Greenland's massive ice cap melting entirely is a threat that really keeps climate scientists awake at night. Should the worst happen, ocean levels could rise twenty feet over the next few centuries, something that would surely mark the end of life as we know it. Giant glaciers are already slipping away from the ice cap, accelerated by melting ice that slips through holes in the glacier, forming a layer between the ice and the rock, which then acts as a "conveyor belt" sending ice flows down to the sea. As the glaciers break away, the ice cap is more exposed to the warming effects of the sunlight and air.

All of this ice melt is fresh water pouring into the salty seas. Part of the scary Greenland scenario is this: through the world's oceans runs a current called the Gulf Stream. It is this current that moderates the climate of Europe. Ever wonder why England and Ireland, which have the same latitude as Labrador, do not freeze like the dickens in winter? It is the current, and many fear it is already slowing and could ultimately break down. Remember the heat wave of 2004 that killed over thirty thousand people in Europe? They could expect a lot more of that, along with profound changes in the land itself, with more weather extremes, drought, floods, blizzards, and altered landscapes threatening agriculture, among other things. This might help explain why several European governments are nagging the

United States endlessly about the need for action to slow the warming—now.

It may be difficult for many of us to *experience*, to *see*, the reality of a warming globe and resulting climate disruptions from the vantage point of our busy daily lives, especially in urban and suburban communities where unfortunately we are so cut off from direct experience of the natural world. It is even more difficult if we are economically stretched, working hard to pay the bills, raising our families, just trying to keep up. These melting geographies may still seem remote. But the evidence is not hard to find. And the closer we are to the edge economically, the harder it will be to absorb the impacts of the deleterious changes to come.

In addition, part of the bad news is that by the time we begin to feel the worst impacts, it may well be too late. And since so much that we need to know is being kept from us, is not deemed newsworthy, despite the mounting evidence, or is not discussed by government leaders because of fear of voter backlash, or by religious leaders because of fear of congregation backlash, many of us are going to be taken completely by surprise when it comes crashing into our neck of the woods.

But, for some people, there is no surprise at all, and we should be paying attention to them.

Because of the warming the permafrost is thawing in Alaska, Siberia, Canada, and all around earth's northernmost climes. Permafrost is land permanently frozen—or so we thought. Communities have lived on it for thousands of years.

In Alaska it is not only the ice that is melting, it is also the land. And the impact of both is already devastating for many local communities. Here is another area where the evidence of a warming globe is visible and dramatic.

In the past thirty years the temperature of the soil in parts of Alaska has risen about 3 percent. "That might not seem like much," writes British reporter Andrew Buncombe, "until you consider the average global increase in surface temperatures over the last 100 years has been 0.6C." Buncombe describes the impact: "Around Fairbanks the implications are considerable. Roads and cycle paths have twisted and buckled, buildings have cracked and across the town there are large 'sink holes' where the land has simply fallen in on itself. Residents say the local authority has stopped repairing the damage to roads in anything other than a temporary fashion, knowing that each spring the land will likely melt and sink again."[10]

The impact of the melting land is compounded by the melting seas. Less ice and more liquid water along the shoreline means more erosion. The water freezes for the winter, and in summer the ice drifts offshore, protecting the land from the ocean waves. But now the melt comes sooner, lasts longer, while the summer ice has thinned and drifts farther out. "Now we have no cushion," said Barrow resident Mike Aamodt. "When the waves hit they can crack the ground. It's enough to topple it. The ground disappears."[11]

For the Inuit, who have lived in these cold regions for thousands of years, the changes threaten a way of life, an entire culture, that is tied to this geography. Some communities have already been forced to relocate away from the coast. Those living on remote islands will have little choice but to move to the mainland.

Aamodt told Buncombe that the city of Barrow, too, may have to relocate soon, because of the erosion. "Asked when the situation might become critical, he said, 'This month! It could happen any time. The storm in 2002 flooded right up to the edge of town.'"[12]

Just in this part of the world alone the cost of relocation will be huge. The remote Inupiat island community of Shishmaref voted to move to the mainland in 2002 at an estimated cost of $180 million. That's just one; there will be many more. Imagine whole cities.

If Alaska seems far away from most of us, let's at least remember that these communities are in the United States, part of us, part of our national reality. These are our fellow citizens, and all of us have added our measure to the forces that created this crisis, knowingly or not.

In Alaska and northern Canada indigenous communities with deep cultural and spiritual roots in the geography of the Arctic, whose voices seldom break through to the forefront of the political culture, are beginning to live a nightmare not of their making. Their sense of urgency is not being reflected in the larger culture at all. Those who live closest to the land and its rhythms, who are in profound relationship with their geography and the spirituality that emerges from it, simply know more than those of us who do not. They are first to hear what nature is saying, are first to feel the impact of subtle and then not-so-subtle changes, like changes in the behavior patterns of birds and animals or seeing the forests receding. Insects have appeared in Alaska for which there are no words in the language of the Inuit.

The land around the Arctic is that part of the globe that will feel the first dramatic impacts of climate change, the area most vulnerable initially. The Inuit are like the park ranger and the owner of the bait-and-tackle shop in Leeville, Louisiana; they are down there singing in the mine. It's beginning to get crowded down there.

At a hearing before the US Senate Commerce Committee in 2005, Sheila Watt-Cloutier, elected chair of the Inuit Circumpolar Conference, pleaded: "We find ourselves at the very cusp of a defining event in the history of this planet. . . . The Earth is literally melting. Use us as your early warning system. Use the Inuit story as a vehicle to reconnect us all so that we can understand the people and the planet are one."[13]

Now, at the risk of overwhelming you with more bad news from the world that is melting, I want to add one more tidbit of information about these thawing lands and what this could mean for our planet. In 2005, climatologists discovered to their alarm that "an area of permafrost spanning a million square kilometers—the size of France and Germany combined—has started to melt for the first time since it was formed . . . at the end of the last ice age. That area, which covers the entire sub-Arctic region of Western Siberia, is the world's largest frozen peat bog and they fear that as it thaws, it will release billions of tons of methane, a greenhouse gas 20 times more potent than carbon dioxide, into the atmosphere."[14]

The permafrost trapped the methane; the thawing is about to let it go. Western Siberia is warming more rapidly than any place in the world, according to the research. It is in a feedback loop; that is, the more the land melts, the more bare earth is uncovered, and therefore the more heat the land absorbs, warming it even more, melting it even faster, and so on. Scientists have noticed that so much methane is being released already that warm bubbles of gas can be seen in some spots even in the dead of winter.[15]

The release will continue steadily over time, and quicken exponentially because of the feedback loop—the point being that the longer we wait to slow down global warming, the more likely that we could reach a point of runaway warming that will be completely beyond our ability to influence by any changes we make.

"The most that can be expected, some climate scientists say, is to limit the human contribution to warming enough to forestall the one truly calamitous, if slow motion, threat in the far north: the melting of the Greenland ice cap,"[16] something we have seen may already have begun.

As for the melting Arctic Ocean, it is doing more than threatening ecosystems, wildlife, and nearby communities. It, too, is adding to the global warming problem. Ice and snow reflect sunlight back into the atmosphere. Water absorbs it. Well, like Siberia, you get the idea.

Computer studies show that one result of forces now at play could be the almost total disappearance of the Arctic tundra. A simulation that projected the increased concentration of CO_2 emissions in the atmosphere at slightly below its current rate of rise (0.45 percent instead of 0.5) indicated that "the concentration of carbon dioxide would double from pre-industrial levels by 2070, triple by 2120 and quadruple by 2160."[17]

Let's see, that's double during the lifetime of Francesca and Elliot, my godson Aidan, and my young friends Maura and Maya, and triple during the lifetime of their children. That feels pretty darn close.

The study shows that temperatures in these regions could rise as much as 25 degrees Fahrenheit by 2100. The Antarctic will warm more slowly, turning sharply upward by 2200.

In the simulation, the scrubby Arctic tundra largely vanishes as climate zones shift hundreds of miles north. [The US southeast is predicted to become a dry grassland, by the way, and the southwest will be really dried up.] Tundra would decline to 1.8 percent of the world's land area from about 8 percent. In the model, Alaska loses almost all of its evergreen boreal forests and becomes a largely temperate state.

Vast stretches of land would open up [which means more warming]. The area beneath the ice would diminish to 4.8 percent of the planet's total land area, from 13.3 percent.[18]

One of the authors of the study, Dr. Kenneth Caldeira, said it is no longer a matter of whether or not we need to address this problem, but when. "We can either address it now, before we severely and irreversibly damage our climate, or we can wait until irreversible damage manifests itself strongly. If all we do is try to adapt, things will get worse and worse."[19]

Those words, "manifests itself strongly," send a bit of a chill down my spine.

Remember, however—these are projections based on what happens if we do nothing, or not enough, to reduce the concentration of greenhouse gases. Even these scientists say that the message here is not to give up; rather, "the message should be the longer we wait to do something, the worse the consequences."[20]

Scared yet? It's okay. I'm terrified. The point is not to get paralyzed by the fear. It's to understand what's happening and then get busy with what we need to do. Fear is fine as long as we don't stall there, as long as it is a motivator, a wake-up call. Fear is our bodies telling us to pay attention, something is wrong. The worst thing is to let it settle in some dark corner of our spirits, or try to ignore it—it doesn't go away, it just festers, causing all kinds of other problems to our emotional, physical, and spiritual well-being. The best thing to do with fear is to greet it, see what it is trying to tell us, then take action to remove or heal the source. This book does not end with fear, so let's press on.

Because of the warming what happened to the Gulf Coast in 2005 and to Florida in 2004 is likely to happen again. And again.

In 2005, we ran out of letters in the alphabet for the names of tropical storms forming over the Atlantic Ocean—a record year. The last one formed in the month of December, an extremely rare occurrence. In 2004, four major hurricanes hit the state of Florida, inflicting tens of billions of dollars in damage. This, too, had never happened before.

Two of the most infamous of the 2005 storms, Hurricanes Katrina and Rita, were relatively modest (Katrina hit Florida as a mere Category One) until they passed over the Gulf of Mexico, reaching catastrophic Category Five levels rapidly, literally exploding over the warm waters before striking land.

A debate rages over whether or not the warming of the oceans will increase the *number* of hurricanes. There appears to be a natural cyclical pattern to the rate of hurricane formation, and we may simply be in one of the busier periods in that cycle. But there is less debate about this: the warming waters are likely to increase the storms' intensity. The temperature of the Gulf of Mexico has risen by several degrees in recent decades, averaging 85 degrees (it takes water temperatures of at least 82 degrees to make hurricanes). During the hurricane season, Gulf water temperatures now surpass 90 degrees, and some currents within it reach the mid-90s. Heat is energy. Heat creates more energy. Heat can really stir up the weather (like those late afternoon thunderstorms on a hot and humid summer day).

When Hurricane Katrina passed over those waters, after a brief visit to Florida as a Category One storm, it fired up to Category Five over the next two days. It became huge, covering practically the entire Gulf. Rita followed that September, firing up to a Category Five in less than twenty-four hours. Meteorologists were very impressed.

Because of this warming, come mid-summer through early autumn every year now, any hurricane that makes it into the Gulf has a very good chance of intensifying rapidly and dangerously, once more threatening the coast, and we will inevitably see more devastation come to the south of the United States.

But let's not forget the rest of the coast, the Atlantic Coast, where hurricanes have a long history of bringing tragedy to coastal communities. With rising ocean levels and more erosion of protective dunes and barrier islands as a result, combined with all that inappropriate development that has caused more damage to natural buffers, hurricanes and their resulting storm surges are also likely to wreak more havoc. As climate warms, and so the ocean, the threat of hurricane hits on places like New York City and Boston will also rise.

But, even as alarming as all this hurricane news, an additional event in 2004 frightened scientists even more. That year a hurricane formed over the southern Atlantic, something meteorologists had never seen before, in an area where the conditions for hurricanes were thought not to exist.

Named Catarina for the place it landed, the storm formed over the southern Atlantic and became a hurricane on March 28, 2004, coming ashore in southern Brazil. This is yet more evidence that something strange is happening over the Atlantic Ocean waters.

Because of the warming of earth's climate, its atmosphere has gone out of balance, has been disrupted. Earth has lost its old equilibrium and is trying to find a new one. This will lead to disruptive weather patterns and more frequent and deadlier weather extremes. While it is impossible to explain any single weather event by the sole factor of global warming, we can't help but notice the weather is simply in the news more often these days. Unprecedented events, one after the other, keep occurring, records continue to be broken.

Another example of this: the year 2005 saw a record number of tornados, following the record-breaking year of 2004. New England had record rainfall in spring 2006, fifteen to eighteen inches in southern New Hampshire and Massachusetts. And in the Washington DC area a foot of rain fell over a period of several days in June 2006, causing widespread flooding.

October 2005 saw the beginning of the longest period without measurable precipitation in recorded history in Phoenix, Arizona—142 days. Meanwhile, California endured weeks of heavy rains up and down the coast, leaving rivers swollen and causing mudslides and all sorts of mayhem. Seattle nearly broke a record for consecutive days of rainfall, not Seattle's usual persistent light rain either, but torrents. My brother who has lived in the area for fifteen years said he had never seen anything like it. One day in early January the Sea-Tac airport broke a record high temperature and rainfall total for that day. Landslides stopped some commuter rail service, and many rural areas were left under water.

On February 3, 2006, St. Petersburg, Florida, situated on the Gulf Coast, received a record twelve inches of rain in 3½ hours. Some roofs collapsed under the weight of the water, and streets flooded. Local officials said they couldn't see fifty feet in front of them as the rain poured down.

Meanwhile, in Texas, brush fires scarred the state, one outbreak burning an area the size of Rhode Island. Many homes were destroyed, and some people literally fled for their lives as the flames roared through. By July 2006, more than thirty wildfires were burning in the West, unusually early, and some scientists were beginning to report that global warming was one of the reasons—earlier springs, earlier mountain snow melt, more evaporation, leaving forests and deserts vulnerable to sudden ignition. Firefighters noted that the blazes were unusually ferocious and hard to get under control.

And this is just a sample from the United States. In the same period of time, an unprecedented drought had affected the Amazon River, drying its usual swollen riverbed, leaving boats stranded on dry land, and elevating the fire danger to an already seriously diminished rainforest. Scientists say the most likely culprit is global warming, another effect of the warmer Atlantic Ocean water temperatures, the same conditions that caused Hurricanes Katrina and Rita. "They . . . worry that if global warming is involved, as some of them suspect, it may be the beginning of a new era of more severe and frequent droughts in the region that accounts for nearly a quarter of the world's fresh water."[21]

Climate specialist Luiz Gylvan Meira, from the Institute for Advanced Studies at the University of São Paulo, explained, "A warmer Atlantic not only helps give more energy to hurricanes, it also aids in evaporating air." When air rises in one place, "it eventually has to come down somewhere else, thousands of miles away. In this case, it came down in the western Amazon, blocking the formation of clouds that would bring rain to the headwaters of the rivers that feed the Amazon."[22]

The earth is a magnificent system, energies interconnected, one affecting the other. That's why there is no escape. That's why what is happening in the Arctic and along the Amazon matters. It actually matters to all of us.

The drought in Brazil has been greatly assisted by the burning of forests, much of this illegal, by settlers seeking scarce available land in the country. Deforestation has also contributed. Again, much of the logging is illegal, though the government has been ineffective or indifferent about stopping it. All of this has contributed to the evaporation of moisture and prevention of cloud formation, and hence fewer rains. Tens of thousand of people are threatened by lack of water and the collapse of small economies based on things like fishing (imagine millions of fish baking in the sun along the dried-up river beds). Communities dependent on river transport for vital supplies have had to rely on Brazil's military to bring food, water, medicines, and other necessities.

One more point about the Amazon: there is lots of carbon dioxide resting in the earth there, and the release of this carbon dioxide because of the drought will lead to more . . . well, you know the drill.

Carbon dioxide, of course, is in the ground everywhere. It is part of what makes up the soil. Now scientists are discovering that climate change is causing the soil to release even more gas into the atmosphere. A study in England showed that an estimated thirteen million extra tons of carbon dioxide have been released into the air since 1978, exceeding the levels that were cut by cleaning up industrial pollution. This surprised scientists who thought that soil would keep the gas stored, even act as a buffer—what they call carbon sinks—to absorb some of our excess, one of the options that has been considered in international talks on climate change. Now they find that warmer soil will release still more greenhouse gases.

On February 18, 2006, the same day that the *New York Times* carried a lengthy story about the prolonged drought in the Sahara, bringing the threat of starvation to millions of Africans, it also reported the devastating mudslide in the Philippines that claimed more than fifteen hundred lives. The mountain collapsed under torrents of rain.

And then there's this, from the *New York Times*, February 19, 2006: "For the first time that anyone in Put-in-Bay [Ohio] could remember, the Great Lakes were ice-free in the middle of winter. Even Lake Erie, the shallowest of the five lakes and usually the first to freeze over, was clear. 'There's essentially no ice at all,' said George Leshkevich, a scientist who has studied Great Lakes ice for the National Oceanic and Atmospheric Administration, or NOAA, since 1973. 'I've never seen that.'"

Result of global warming? Can't say. Just more strange weather.

Or this: In January, while Seattle was being soaked, on the other side of the ocean, for the first time in decades, there was frost in New Delhi. Japan had its most severe blizzards ever, up to ten feet of snow, pretty much overwhelming local authorities. Calling the snow unprecedented, the army had to be called in to clear roads. A brutal winter descended on Kashmir, affecting the areas hit by the previous year's devastating earthquake, leaving hundreds of thousands of people without adequate shelter. For many in the hot climes of India, the unusual cold was lethal. Few people in places like New Delhi are prepared for near-freezing temperatures. Many people were reported to have died in the cold nights across Asia in January.

Because of the warming wildlife, the creatures with whom we share this planet are becoming confused, extinct, endangered. In North America scientists are already seeing many animals in distress. They predict vast changes in the landscape and among those who depend on it. Much of the wildlife we know, animals, birds, forests, will migrate steadily north or to higher altitudes as the earth warms. Some may survive and thrive; others will diminish or disappear.

This is another case, too, where development will accelerate the crisis. Many animals will find, as they try to migrate, that their paths northward and upward are blocked by cities and suburbs, vast treeless farmlands, or multi-lane freeways.

Waterfowl will have trouble finding rapidly disappearing wetlands. If birds and insects migrate, plants cannot be pollinated and may die off. If birds fly off in search of survival, they won't be around to eat the insects that attack trees, leaving forests more vulnerable to disease.

According to a report from the Wildlife Society, a collection of wildlife experts, scientists, and educators:

> Entire forests will migrate over time. . . . Sugar maples could abandon the northeastern United States, perhaps replaced by pine and hardwood forests of the southeast. Deer, bear, and other animals that inhabit them would move on also.
>
> The effect of rising temperatures has fallen unequally across North America. Nights have warmed more than days, while land surfaces have heated up more than ocean surfaces. Winters have warmed more than summers . . . and temperatures and precipitation in northern latitudes

have grown more than in the tropics. . . . Wetlands in the Midwest and central Canada are expected to dry up, causing some duck species to decline by as much as 69 percent over the next 75 years. . . .

Old weather patterns may no longer hold, and extreme events such as 100-year floods could become more common, affecting fish runs and waterfowl habitat.[23]

Okay, I don't want to type anymore of that. I grew up in Wisconsin and in recent years have spent a lot of time in Vermont, New Hampshire, and the eastern mountains of New York State. So let's move on. Please stay with me a bit longer here.

Global warming may also kill off plankton, the microscopic plant life that is the foundation of all life in the oceans. Scientists say that warmer waters could starve the oceans of nutrients, endangering "the entire marine habitat, which ultimately relies on plankton at the base of the food chain. . . . Without phytoplankton, the oceans would soon become marine deserts."[24]

And in British Columbia a mountain pine beetle is devouring the lodgepole pine forests, an unbroken swath of protected wilderness. The beetle has been part of the ecosystem there for a very long time, so why is this happening now? Because the winters are no longer cold enough to kill off the year's crop of beetles. Now they just reproduce like crazy, hatching their eggs by the millions and flying from tree to tree. Canada's Forest Service is calling this outbreak "the largest known insect infestation in North American history."[25]

Average temperatures in the region rose four degrees during the last century, according to the article, which was accompanied by an aerial photo showing a large section of the forest, its pine trees turning a dull red as they die. "Surveys show the beetle has infested 21 million acres and killed 411 million cubic feet of trees—double the annual take by all the loggers in Canada. In seven years or sooner, the Forest Service predicts, that kill will nearly triple and 80 percent of the pines in the central British Colombia forest will be dead."[26]

It is okay to grieve. It is appropriate to grieve.

The beetle is moving eastward now. "It has breached the natural wall of the Rocky Mountains in places, threatening the tourist treasures of national forest near Banff, Alberta, and is within striking distance of the vast Northern Boreal Forest that reaches to the eastern seaboard."[27] They may also move southward, tearing through Washington, Oregon, and right into Yellowstone National Park.

Yes, it is fine to grieve.

Experts say that more than one million animal and plant species could be on their way to extinction by 2050. If nothing changes, it is only going to get warmer after that, at an even faster rate.

I really have your attention by now, or you have thrown this book away, or you are very depressed. The sad thing is that there is so much more that I could add—the inevitable rise in infectious diseases and mosquito-borne illnesses (I came down with West Nile virus in 2003, a disease that will increase as warmer winters mean more mosquitoes), deaths from extreme heat and cold, threats of starvation for many vulnerable populations. The poor will be hit hardest, of course, having fewer protections, fewer resources for survival. Environmental refugees will number in the tens of millions, and then we will really find out how far human compassion and faith-based moral values stretch.

I don't know what to write to make this any easier. We live in an altered world, and what we decide now will determine how much more altered it is going to be.

Still skeptical? I have in front of me and surrounding me right now several inches of files with articles, research reports, news stories from hundreds of sources in England, the United States, the United Nations, scientific institutes, a growing pile of books on my book shelves, and computer disks full of even more articles and studies, along with a long list of websites bookmarked for quick updates. And much of this is just from the last several years.

The scientific consensus is so solid now that some say 95 percent of scientists believe that warming is real and largely human caused, though they still may argue about how fast it will occur and how much time we have—from none to ten or twenty years, meaning in any case doing something drastic *immediately.* Naomi Oreskes, a science historian at the University of California–San Diego, analyzed a random sample of one thousand research papers published between 1993 and 2003 and found that not one rejected the notion that human beings are causing the earth to warm.[28]

Another science historian, Spencer Weart, director of the Center for History of Physics, said, "The most important thing to realize is that most scientists didn't originally believe in global warming. They were dragged—reluctant step by step—by the facts."[29]

And here's a final sobering tidbit before some closing reflections on this chapter: The Norwegian government, undoubtedly feeling the early effects of a warming globe by virtue of its northern clime, and also being a nation far more conscious of such things and socially aware, has made an awesome and somber decision. Deep in a frozen mountain on a remote island, it is burying a vault, and in the vault will rest two million seeds, representing "the entire agricultural diversity of the planet."[30] The intention is to save this genetic memory for future generations in the event of a cataclysm, such as nuclear war or ecological collapse due to global warming. The hope is that survivors would be able to reestablish agriculture.

This is doom and gloom indeed—and a government is doing this.

So just how hot is it going to get? New computer models are not encouraging. Most say disaster will come with a rise of two degrees Celsius, which will become inevitable once we reach a CO_2 threshold of 400ppm (parts per million). At that point melting of the Greenland ice cap will become irreversible. Right now, the atmosphere holds 379ppm of CO_2 and the annual rate of increase is 2ppm—meaning we could cross the threshold in 2017. Other studies suggest that if we add methane and nitrous oxide to the calculation, two powerful greenhouse gases, we are already at 425ppm, past the threshold.

The 2007 IPCC report shows that a doubling of CO_2 in the atmosphere, predicted to happen by 2070, would cause a temperature rise of between 2 and 4.5C. This would be calamitous.

There is no way to soften this message. It is an old axiom of social justice work that we shouldn't scare people too much. But we need to face this full on if we are to rouse ourselves to the action needed to salvage life on this planet. If even *Fortune Magazine* is publishing doom-and-gloom stories about this, then perhaps it is time we all grow up and see the real world:

> The consensus on climate change has solidified to rival the medical consensus on the dangers of smoking—but in the matter of climate, public perception has yet to catch up. Like the tourists on Phuket beaches who stood and gazed at an oncoming tsunami because it was outside their experience, society is reacting to the coming wave of climate change without urgency. People still believe that the science is controversial and the threat of climate change far off in the future; and while a few businesses, notably major insurers, have begun to adapt, governments are responding only slowly.[31]

And I have to tell you that, right now, in this country, given the political culture, this will continue to be true until we the people wake up our government.

Right now, the earth is trying to adjust to us and to the damage we have done with our pollution and our waste, our unsustainable, exploitative, extractive way of life. The earth is trying to find a new equilibrium, and we must assist this process in the hopes that the earth does not need to throw us off in order to find it—because the new equilibrium could involve a temperature that we cannot survive.

Warming will happen no matter what we do now. The question is how much, and the answer to that is still up to us. But it *will* happen, and our lives, nature, will be changed forever. We need to find the inner resources—emotional, psychological, and spiritual—that will make it possible for us to face this, not with resignation and despair, or with anger and bitterness, or with destructive denial and defeatism, but with acceptance of our reality and what we have done to bring it about, a spirituality of grief and mourning that can only come about if we reconnect ourselves to the earth, allow ourselves to feel what it, and we with it, are going through, a spirituality that rejects despair, that sees the task at hand, and that commits to preserving the chance for a rich and sustaining life for our children and our children's children.

3

The End of "Cheap Oil"

or,

The Imminent Upset of Our Way of Life

Global warming is not an "environmental"
problem. . . . It is an energy problem.
—Michael Klare[1]

The dirty secret of the US economy . . . is
that it has come to be based on the ceaseless
elaboration of a car-dependent suburban
infrastructure—McHousing estates, eight-
lane highways, big box chain stores, ham-
burger stands—that has no future as a
living arrangement in an oil-short future.
—James Howard Kunstler[2]

We thought it would never end. But a whole economy, an entire way of
life based on the availability of cheap oil, is running into its inevitable limits.
Since we have constructed much of the functioning of our society around
it—even to the most basic necessities of life—we are in for a painful and
difficult transition. This post-industrial US way of life is going to become
increasingly expensive, harder to maintain, more vulnerable to international
conflict, ecologically unsustainable, and ultimately impossible, whether we
like it or not.

There is a lot of debate about how soon this is going to happen, but the
phenomenon known as peak oil looms somewhere in our not-too-distant
future.[3] That is the point at which the world will have reached peak production, the point at which we have pumped out half of the earth's supply
of oil and that most easily obtainable, after which the supply begins a steady

decline. This will occur as demand soars, especially in developing countries such as China and India, and as the inevitable result of adding another two to three billion people to our planet over the next forty years.

Fossil fuels are, after all, a finite resource, and we are bound to reach the limits at some point. Some geologists say that we have already burned nearly half the oil that it took the earth millions of years to create—in just the past 150 years—and the rate of burning is only going to rise.

Fossil fuels are just that—fuels from fossils, remains of creatures, organic matter, that lived on the earth millions of years ago. In centuries past, human beings discovered that this organic "goo" was perfect for slow burning—in oil lamps, for example, to light streets at night or rooms inside houses. This changed daily life, making it possible for people to do things at night. Lifestyles changed—and oil kept making more and more new things possible. Now we are flying around the world and speeding along super-highways; making plastic grocery bags and bottles, styrofoam cups and synthetic fabrics like polyester and nylon; farming with big machines and transporting food and goods across the globe; powering cars and trucks and lawn mowers and leaf blowers; and driving the kids to school and to soccer games. Life just gets easier and easier.

Oil is about to change our lifestyles again—because now we will have to learn both how to pay a whole lot more for it and how to live with a lot less of it.

The energy conundrum

Global warming is an energy problem. That is, more than anything else, exactly what it is. It is a direct result of burning fossil fuels, not the *only* factor, but the one that is caused by humans and most responsible for speeding up the heating process right now. The two biggest sources and worst offenders are oil and coal, fuels that provide the energy we need to drive our economy and our cars, to heat and cool our homes, to produce and bring food to our grocery stores, to make cars and plastics and toys, to power our factories and our milking barns, to move our goods in trucks, trains, and cargo planes, to keep the lights on, in fact, for just about everything we consume.

As Michael Klare points out, "Almost 90 percent of the world's energy is supplied through the combustion of fossil fuels."[4] This is what makes energy and global warming problems on a scale never experienced before by the human species.

These fuels create a waste product, and among the worst of the pollutants is carbon dioxide (CO_2). It lingers in the atmosphere; what is there now will take a century to dissipate, and we are adding more each day. These fuels we need for life are also driving up the temperature of our atmosphere to levels that are melting our glaciers and polar ice caps, altering our climate, and driving our planet toward a new atmospheric balance to which the human species may or may not be able to adapt.

It is true that CO_2 is needed for life itself, part of the chemical balance of the earth's atmosphere, developed over billions of years, that made the evolution of life possible. But we are now spewing more carbon dioxide at a faster rate than that balance can maintain—and so it is changing, becoming unstable, and the climate is changing accordingly in ways we still do not completely understand. And since we are still burning fossil fuels at ever greater rates, we do not know exactly where we are headed in what some scientists have called a grand unplanned scientific experiment whose results are largely unpredictable, though we have some scary hints about that.

So, this fuel for our post-industrial way of life, which is itself a chemical needed for life, now puts life itself, at least the life we know, in danger. Quite a conundrum, isn't it? Our energy lifeline is becoming one of the biggest threats to life.

What are we going to do about it? This is not just a technology question, or a policy question, or an environmental question. It is also a moral question, because few issues will have greater impact on the lives of human beings and the ecosystems within which we live and move and have our being.

Just as I am not a climate scientist, I am also not an energy expert. So I read, *a lot*. I prefer sources whose economic interests are not in the fossil-fuel industry, whose concerns are for the people of this earth, not profits, for other living creatures, indeed, for all life. So that is the orientation of this chapter. My concern is not what form of fuel will fill our gas tanks so that we can go on about our lives without disruption, one of today's grand illusions, or what environmental destruction will be required or worse, acceptable, to continue the functioning of this global economy. My concern is with what is required to alter the course that is leading us toward ecological disaster.

Global warming is an energy problem. The way we have produced and used energy, the fossil-fuel industrial age, is precisely what has brought us to the predicament outlined in the previous chapter. We cannot, therefore, slow and ultimately reverse those drivers that are super-heating our planet unless we figure out how to make the transition from fossil fuels to energy sources that do no harm, or at least do a lot less harm. There is no easy way to do this; there are not renewables out there just waiting for a little investment to magically replace fossil fuels and keep all the lights on and the gas tanks full, to keep our houses nice and cool as our summers get hotter and longer, or to keep us flying around the globe for our vacations and business meetings, or crammed onto our highways or stuck in rush hour traffic jams in the vehicles of our choice, no matter the gas mileage. There is nothing that exists now or in the near future that will replace oil, coal, and natural gas and continue the status quo of our consumption-oriented lifestyles beyond this generation.

A lesson shelved

We actually squandered one of our best windows of opportunity back in the 1970s when an oil crisis clobbered the US economy, bringing about the fifty-five mile per hour speed limit, dimming lights at the Empire State Building, and offering up forever the image of Jimmy Carter wearing a cardigan sweater as he asked the nation to turn down its thermostats and save energy.

After taking office in 1977, President Carter commissioned a group of scientists to study the "economic, demographic, resource and environmental future of the country," a three-year study that resulted in the *Global 2000 Report to the President*. It outlined many of the crises this world would be encountering by the end of the millennium, energy crunches, population issues, resource issues. In retrospect, the study was prescient. In a publication revisiting this study two decades later, the project director, Dr. Gerald O. Barney, who has a Ph.D. in physics and is an expert in computer simulation models for sustainable living, wrote that "most of its trends are still disconcertingly accurate."[5]

This is just one example, but an important one for us, because this study had for a short while the attention of the US government, of the president of the United States. In other words, it would not be correct to say that we did not have the information in time to begin making the necessary changes to soften the impact of the looming energy crunch.

That would have been a good time to initiate the post–oil energy future. But, alas, in 1980 Ronald Reagan pronounced amid the gloom, "It's morning in America," and the nation elected him president. Government copies of the report were destroyed, and by the 1990s we were entering the SUV era. Suburban sprawl was evolving into exurban sprawl, and we went about paving over farmlands and woods with subdivisions, strip malls, big box stores, and ever wider multi-lane highways. Folks with money for real estate wanted green space, and so more green space was carved up for them. Houses began growing into giant versions of themselves, with energy-wasting vaulted ceilings, as our automobile-dependent economy spread farther and farther away from urban centers. Commutes became longer, and no one in those subdivisions lived within walking distance of just about anywhere. Oil was cheap again, thank God, and it would be forever, wouldn't it? Wouldn't morning be forever and ever—as in Peter Pan, a *Neverland* of eternal childhood and innocence? And like kids balking at the limits imposed on them, we would never have to grow up.

Along came Bill Clinton and the good times really rolled. More people were getting richer, and the development boom proceeded apace. Soon mortgage rates were tumbling, more people were buying homes, and real estate boomed, meaning more people had equity to spend on bigger houses and more than one house and more vacations and more consumer goods and the family SUV—or two or three.

Meanwhile, the atmosphere just kept getting warmer and warmer, and the air more foul, and natural habitats more and more compromised and deteriorated, and more and more natural wonders were being destroyed to feed our insatiable thirst for fossil fuels.

As if there were no limits, ever, to which we Western humans, we superior beings, would ever have to submit.

Which is why the global warming problem, which is an energy problem, is also a moral problem, and perhaps, above all now, a spiritual problem.

Because we have squandered the time, because we let the oil and gas industry, which has contributed lavishly to politicians making energy policy over the years, snooker us into believing there was an endless supply of fossil fuels, because we let them do what the tobacco industry did with nicotine—create an addiction knowing that it could ultimately harm us—we will not, I repeat, we will not have in time the kinds of fuels that can simply or cheaply replace those that now fuel our cars and airplanes and trucks, or fuel the world's massive food production as now constructed, or bring our produce to the supermarket from faraway places, or fill all those orders for plastic goods. We are headed for a severe jolt.

The technology for alternative energy sources to begin to power us toward a different energy economy and way of life exists, but the economic rules have been rigged toward the oil, gas, and coal industries. To have replaced them with the least amount of disruption—well, it would have been good to start back in the 1970s, before it was "morning in America."

What is required now is a massive restructuring of the energy base of the economy, but the political will is still not there. There are promising initiatives popping up in many places but still not the required political commitment to flip the energy base. We are being told that we must not do anything too precipitous because it could threaten economic growth, but it is becoming abundantly clear that not taking stronger action now will ultimately cause the global economy to collapse. Those economies that have not prepared are not expected to fare particularly well.

At the very least, we will continue to see prices for fossil fuels rise dramatically, as the cost of extracting these fuels rises and as they become scarcer, affecting every part of the economy, including the economy of the family. Before the decline, energy will become increasingly unaffordable for a growing number of poor. Prices will rise for things like food as transportation costs rise. In addition, if we continue on the current course—developing as much of these fuels as possible to hold off the inevitable, or to buy time—the price we pay in ecological destruction to mine and drill and produce these fuels will become increasingly intolerable. In fact, it already is. And that ecological damage will bear the lion's share of responsibility for the breakdown of ecosystems where it occurs, the destruction of human communities, and, of course, the continuing pollution of the atmosphere with greenhouse gases.

How we deal with this energy conundrum will determine what kind of future human beings will have within the balance of all life on the planet, how violent the future will be, how many wars will be fought and where, how many millions will go hungry, how much suffering our children and our children's children will have to endure.

I wish I was over-dramatizing. It would make me feel better if I were using drama as a device to get your attention. Alas, that is not the case.

The reality is that, not far in the future, within a few decades at most, oil, natural gas, and even uranium for our so-called clean nuclear power plants will all be scarce, meaning not enough supply for demand, and that at an ever-widening ratio. This is not just an oil problem. Geologists report that US natural-gas production is approaching peak and could fall off suddenly over the next few decades, one reason prices have risen so steeply in recent years. Some people are using the energy crunch to make a major push for more nuclear energy, but nuclear power comes laden with issues regarding disposal of radioactive waste, international issues of proliferation in a world marked by terrorism, the energy and funds it takes for construction, and local opposition to having one "in my back yard."

The life of coal is longer—some say the United States has enough for 180 years or more—but, as we will discuss farther on, the environmental damage being done to get the coal has long passed the point of being morally and ecologically acceptable. In fact, it has already caused irreparable ecological damage—as in, *permanent and forever*—and in some cases destroyed local communities and sickened and killed residents in the vicinity of the coal mines.

So we have a problem. That upon which we depend for our entire way of life, fossil-fuel-based energy, is also bringing our lives, all life, into jeopardy and setting the course for a miserable future. What made possible this industrial and post-industrial way of life—our air conditioning and central heat, our suburbs and exurbs, our vacations in Europe, our NGO conferences around the globe, our winter vegetables and cheap consumer goods at Wal-Mart—will also destroy our way of life in the not-too-distant future.

That's it. That's our dilemma. Whatever else we hear about it, however we debate alternative fuels and technology, whatever controversy goes on around the exact point at which peak oil will occur, this is a key challenge for us as we consider how the human race will proceed with its life on this planet.

We have to face this question. It is inevitable, a sure thing, an inescapable fact of our twenty-first century lives. It is not a future question. It is immediate, right here and now.

If we wait until the crisis is upon us, if we don't begin the transition now, well, let's not think about that just yet (though if you live in a completely car-dependent suburb, you might take a moment to pause and consider). Let's just acknowledge that we are the generation that will begin to be affected by this and that this is the generation that must prepare for and begin the transition.

Because the transition is exactly that—a transition in our way of life. The sooner we stop fooling ourselves about this, the sooner we can get about the business of the transition—hopefully before we have crossed too many tipping points in our complex set of ecological crises.

It doesn't take much imagination to see what I mean. All we have to do is think our way through our day, how almost everything we do has some function related to the availability of oil, coal, or natural gas.

But oil is the key. It is not the only fossil fuel on which our life depends, but it is the one that has created a convenience of life we cannot imagine being without. In fact, we consider what oil provides as necessities for life now, not just added comforts, and have affirmed that by building a world that makes it so.

So now, when we are approaching peak oil, that point of maximum production and availability, we face one of the biggest transitions since humans evolved—a transition away from the cheap-oil-based way of life to something else, something that will not be *this* way of life. And we must make that transition as we reach another frightening peak, a peak in the human population of the planet. We must make this transition away from fossil-fuel energy sources at the same time that demand—and *need*—for them will rise as never before.

Our energy predicament

So let's look at some of the facts about our energy predicament, just to get a sense of how dependent we really are. Then we will look at why some of the proposed solutions, like corn ethanol or more coal-fired power plants, are no solutions at all.

First, 40 percent of US energy use comes from oil, but more sobering, 90 percent of transportation depends on oil. Think about that when surrounded, for example, by semi-tractor trailers on the Pennsylvania Turnpike bearing company logos from Wal-Mart, Safeway, Toys R Us, Piggly Wiggly, Deer Park, or Budweiser. The cost of everything inside those trucks will be affected by rising oil prices. Then consider this—the produce in your salad has traveled an average of approximately two thousand miles to get to your table, fueled by gas-powered ships, cargo planes, and/or trucks. And you probably drove to the grocery store to get these ingredients.

To put it another way, transportation accounts for two-thirds of this country's oil demand—*two-thirds*. A 2005 *New York Times* article relates: "America's fleet of more than 200 million cars guzzles 11 percent of the world's daily output of oil. Gasoline consumption has risen 35 percent since 1973, compared with a 19 percent increase in overall crude oil consumption." The article goes on to note that this growth in consumption comes mainly from the increased sales of light trucks, mostly SUVs, which in 2005 accounted for half the vehicles sold in the United States.[6]

There is something wrong with this picture, with living like this as scarcity waits out there for us in the not-too-distant future. But let's enlarge the picture.

Twenty-three percent of our energy use comes from natural gas, mostly as a source of electricity to heat and cool our homes, or to put those little flames under our stir-fry pans. Nuclear energy accounts for about 7 percent of energy use, small but significant, and because of the expense, the extended time it takes to get a nuclear plant on line, and the heated opposition that each proposed plant attracts, it is not expected to account for a more significant percentage any time soon, if ever.

A small amount of our energy comes from renewables like solar, wind, and hydrological sources, accounting for around 5 percent, a percentage that will grow considerably, one hopes, over the near future. We've all seen those amazing wind turbines popping up across the landscape in many parts of the country, or the solar panels that power lights along highways or at city bus stops. This is part of the new face of our energy base.

The United States was once a major oil producer, but US production peaked in the 1970s, exactly as predicted by Marion King Hubbert back in that decade, falling off steadily as a share of what we consume. The United States became a net importer of oil in 1970, and the percentage of foreign oil in our supply has grown ever since, from one-third in the mid-1970s to two-thirds now. Our biggest sources are Canada, Mexico, and the Middle East. And, as has become abundantly clear in recent years, the largest remaining reserves are in the Middle East. Mexico's oil fields are aging rapidly, leaking like crazy, and are likely to be tapped out in the next ten years, which means it will lose one of the biggest income sources for its economy (30 percent), and the United States will lose one of its suppliers. And so our dependence on foreign oil will continue to increase, and the growing proportion of that dependency will be on the volatile region of the Persian Gulf nations—Saudi Arabia, Iran, Kuwait, the United Arab Emirates, and Iraq.

The United States once had abundant sources of natural gas, but these supplies are rapidly being depleted. According to one oft-cited expert, Daniel

Yergin, chair of Cambridge Energy Research Associates: "North American supply has flattened out. Yet large amounts of new natural-gas-fired electric power generation have been added over the last decade, which means that demand will increase. Natural gas is also used in the making of ethanol, adding to the demand growth. This means growing imports of liquified natural gas—LNG—rising from 3 percent of our current demand to more than 25 percent by 2020."[7] More demand for energy meeting the limits of domestic production, meaning more dependence on imports for the energy base of our lives. Not just an oil problem.

Unlike oil, natural gas cannot easily be transported across vast distances. It must first be liquified, then shipped through pipelines or on specially designed refrigerated tankers destined for specially designed LNG ports, then regassified for distribution. This process is very expensive and ecologically dangerous. In a world where small groups of terrorists can do a lot of damage, the potential consequences of an explosion at an LNG port is sobering, to say the least, hence the mounting local resistance. Insurance costs alone make these prospects financially daunting.

For all these reasons, natural gas has become a very expensive commodity, and prices will only rise, permanently. Anyone who heats a home with natural gas already knows what this means, as prices have skyrocketed in recent years. Problems with natural-gas shortages and high prices will be persistent because we in the United States now depend upon it for 24 percent of our overall energy needs, and more than half of our energy to heat our homes.

But LNG is costly in other ways. The estimated energy loss of LNG production is between 15 and 30 percent. And, of course, the energy loss consists largely of the oil used in transport; it is itself an oil-dependent energy industry. Meanwhile, the whole process contributes to greenhouse gas emissions. And, finally, natural gas cannot easily be stored, like oil or coal, so we have no strategic reserve to protect us from sudden shocks, as we do with oil.

Energy investment banker Matt Simmons wrote in 2000: "North American natural gas has no excess capacity. It disappeared several years ago. What we do have is extremely aggressive decline rates in almost every key production basin making it harder each season to keep current production flat."[8]

In another article I found on the Internet from back in 2001 Brian J. Fleahy declared:

Consumption [of natural gas] has exceeded US production since 1985 and Canadian imports now supply 15 percent of US consumption. However, US production has declined since 1997 with new gas wells unable to offset a doubling of production well decline rates in the 1990s.

A similar pattern has emerged in Canada. Running faster just to stand still! There is no way US production and imports from Canada can grow at 2.6 percent annum [what would be required to meet rising demand].[9]

Many geologists believe the United States is at or near not so much a natural-gas peak as a cliff, thus explaining the spiking prices of recent years and the huge battles around opening up more off-shore and other ecologically sensitive areas to drilling. In the winter of 2005–6, folks across the country saw their heating bills rise as never before, the average rising to $1,000 or more for the first time in history.

It is going to get expensive to stay warm if we continue this energy route.

The higher prices also help explain the new interest in the extremely expensive proposals for liquified gas pipeline projects that are popping up in parts of the world where gas is plentiful—like Russia and Central Asia. This will have geopolitical implications, to add to the oil ones that plague global tensions.

The good news is that natural gas burns cleanly. It is not the burning that is the problem; it is everything that happens on the way to the furnace. That process is energy intensive, adds to our greenhouse-gas problem and other ecological destruction, embroils us further in international tensions and conflicts, and has in any case a very limited future. We cannot eliminate natural gas right now, but neither can we count on it for the future. I think about this when visiting a home with those vaulted ceilings, thinking about all that warmth rising to those ceilings and then just sitting there, wasted energy.

Dirty coal and the death of mountains

So let's turn to coal and see how it fares in our energy scenario. With oil and natural gas approaching peak and prices rising rapidly, while nuclear power remains caught in controversy, the world is turning its voracious energy appetite toward coal. We have lots of it here in the United States. In fact, if we think in terms of what we need for electric power supply, we have all the energy we need for, well, for a few more generations.

The United States is undoubtedly the world's King Coal. We have 25 percent of the world's coal reserves, and nearly 79 percent of the world's fossil-fuel reserves are represented by coal. So with this lion's share of fossil fuel right here in the United States, we should be in great shape for the future, right?

But here is the problem: coal is the dirtiest, most environmentally destructive energy source in the world. There is no energy source that emits more greenhouse gases or destroys more local ecosystems (rising competitors in this race, however, are tar sands and shale being exploited for oil, along with corn ethanol). Coal-fired power plants account for three-fifths of sulphur dioxide, the gas that causes acid rain, and one-third of mercury emissions. Coal is the most carbon-intensive fuel that exists, responsible for 40 percent of US carbon-dioxide emissions.

In 2005 nearly half of our electricity was supplied by coal-fired power plants. According to Jeff Goodell, who wrote the distressing book *Big Coal: The Dirty Secret Behind America's Energy Future*, each person in the United States uses an average of twenty pounds of coal per day. That's what our electricity usage represents. Every two seconds, approximately one hundred tons of coal is extracted from the ground.[10]

As executive editor for *Discover* magazine, Corey S. Powell, put it in his review of Goodell's book, "Despite its outdated image, coal generates half of our electricity, far more than any other source. Demand keeps rising, thanks in part to our appetite for new electronic gadgets and appliances; with nuclear power on hold and natural gas supplies tightening, coal's importance is only going to increase."[11]

The attraction is obvious. Powell writes: "A pile of coal containing one million B.T.U.'s worth of energy costs $1.70. The equivalent amount of natural gas runs about $9." Hey, don't we all like cheap energy, low home heating and air conditioning bills? Isn't this how we prime the pump for economic growth?

Of course, one of the dirty secrets of this pricing business is what is left out of it—the cost in human lives and ecological destruction. If those costs were added in, if we were made to pay the true price of coal, it would become unaffordable very quickly.

Here we are again with our conundrum: what we need for life, at least in the context of our current lifestyles and the way our societies and economies are organized, is what is also endangering life. And this danger is expected to grow in leaps and bounds under the most likely scenario, the path laid out by nation-states and the coal industry at this point in time.

According to 2007 estimates from the US Department of Energy, 153 new coal-fired power plants will be built in the United States by 2025, the majority of them with the old technology that spews carbon dioxide in vast amounts into the atmosphere, rather than with the more expensive, experimental new technology that captures CO_2 in production so that it can be buried underground. That's bad enough. At the same time, China is planning to build 562 such plants over the next several years. Both China and India intend to fuel their exponential economic growth with coal. The average life span of a coal-fired plant is fifty years, so these new plants will be with us for a very long time.

Keep in mind that China's smog is already killing Chinese, causing millions to be sickened with asthma and other respiratory diseases, and adding to the air pollution in Taiwan, Japan, and all the way across the ocean to Vancouver and Seattle.

How are we going to get the Chinese or the Indians to change their plans, or to pay for more expensive technology, especially as the energy needs and demands of their populations grow exponentially, if we are not willing to do the same thing? This country is the largest contributor of greenhouse gases in the world.

President Bush and his energy-industry supporters, those who have controlled policy for decades, promote voluntary measures and market incentives for the coal companies to invest in capture-and-store technology. We see how well this has worked. It is true that coal production is now cleaner than it was before, but emissions are still rising because demand has outgrown these pollution reductions. Coal remains the biggest CO_2 emitter of all the fossil fuels.

Erik Reece, who has written passionately about the damage caused by the coal industry in Appalachia, summed it up this way: "The sulphur dioxide that escapes from coal-burning power plants is responsible for acid rain, smog, respiratory infections, asthma, and lung disease. Due to acid rain and mine runoff, there is so much mercury in Kentucky streams that any pregnant woman who eats fish from them risks serious, lifelong harm to the fetus she carries."[12]

And then there's the exorbitant contribution all this makes to our global warming crisis. "If all the coal-burning power plants that are scheduled to be built over the next 25 years are built, the lifetime carbon dioxide emissions from those power plants will equal all the emissions from coal burning in all of human history to date," says John Holdren, a professor of environmental policy at Harvard University's Kennedy School of Government.[13] Wow. I feel the fear rising again, don't you?

Tim Folger writes:

Holdren and many others are especially concerned about the carbon dioxide, which unlike coal's other emissions is completely unregulated in the United States. By 2012, the new coal plants in the United States, China, and India will send 2.7 billion tons of carbon dioxide into the atmosphere each year. According to leading climate models, all the added CO_2 could trigger an average global temperature rise of up to 10 degrees Fahrenheit by 2100. That much warming could raise sea levels several feet, flooding the world's coastlines and shifting global weather patterns in ways that could cause massive recurring crop failures.[14]

Now, as we said, new technology is being developed that can capture the carbon produced in production and bury it underground. But it is expensive and a bit uncertain. Some scientists express concern about what would happen if huge amounts of buried CO_2 managed to escape into the atmosphere. But in any case coal companies do not have the incentives or a regulatory regimen right now that would force them to use it. Holdren says that, if all these power plants are to be built, it is crucial that they use this new capture-and-store technology. "If all those coal plants are built without carbon control," he says, "the amount of carbon dioxide added to the atmosphere would make it virtually impossible to stabilize atmospheric carbon dioxide concentrations at a moderate level."[15]

Sounds like a call to action to me—a call to *political* action. It seems to me that the debate about mandatory versus voluntary regulations should be about over.

But with coal, the problems go beyond the need to cap emissions. Another problem is how we go about getting the coal in the first place. Unfortunately, this means that even if we were to have mandatory regulations that force coal companies to capture and store carbon dioxide, and even if storage could be done safely, we would still have an unacceptable ecological problem.[16]

Here's the situation. Once upon a time coal companies dug deep tunnels and hired thousands of coal miners to go down into them to get the coal. That is what we are most familiar with, and it is still the way some of our coal is extracted. Coal mining has a terrible history in human terms, as we all know. Here is one startling fact from Corey Powell's review of Goodell's *Big Coal*: "More than 104,000 Americans died digging out coal between 1900 and 2005; twice as many may have died from black lung. The fatality rate in coal mining is almost 60 percent higher than it is in oil and gas extraction." That is the cost in human lives of the electric power we all take for granted. With each death there is the story of a family who has lost income, who lives in poverty, who must deal with this heavy human toll. This exploitation of the human is part of what has kept our coal-powered energy so cheap. We don't have priced into our bills things like a decent wage and benefits, much less a family's grief.

But in recent years companies have found a simpler and cheaper way to get the coal in Appalachia, one that doesn't need so many workers. Now they simply blast away the tops of mountains that lie over the coal seams; they blow them up, then with huge machines they bulldoze the detritus, take the coal, and dump the rest into the valleys. It may sound horrific, and it is, but it is certainly more economical. Faster, less payroll, fewer benefits to pay out—very sweet for the companies.

Really, there is no way to describe this unless you look at it. I don't know if there is any single act of ecological destruction that breaks my heart or gives me mind-numbing grief more than this, especially as I have lived near the Appalachian Mountains for nearly thirty years. They have become part of my soul.

As of this writing, more than 470 mountaintops in the Appalachian Mountains have been destroyed, blown to bits, crushed, bulldozed so that I can keep the lights on or stay cool enough to get some sleep on sweltering July nights in the state of Maryland.

With the benefit of new technologies, powerful explosives, and enormous earth-moving equipment, coal companies shear off the tops of the mountains and dump all the non-coal debris in the valleys, making new piles of earth, many of them laced with toxic chemicals, where rivers and creeks once flowed. Water sources for the poor communities in these mountain areas have been contaminated, and many people have been sickened.

Erik Reece calls this "ecological violence," a term we should put into our daily lexicon. Here's how he describes what you would see from a small prop plane flying over the "spine" of the Appalachian Mountains in Kentucky, West Virginia, and Virginia:

> You would be struck not by the beauty of a densely forested range older than the Himalayas, but rather by inescapable images of ecological violence. Near Pine Mountain, Ky., you'd see an unfolding series of staggered green hills quickly give way to a wide expanse of gray plateaus pocked with dark craters and huge black ponds filled with a toxic byproduct called coal slurry. The desolation stretches like a long scar up the Kentucky-Virginia line, before eating its way across southern West Virginia.[17]

Reece reports that from 1985 to 2001 governments approved sixty-seven hundred "valley fills" in central Appalachia. According to estimates from the US Environmental Protection Agency (a true oxymoron during the Bush years), Reece continues:

> Over 700 miles of healthy streams have been completely buried by mountaintop removal and thousands more have been damaged. Where there once flowed a highly braided system of headwater streams, now a vast circuitry of haul roads winds through the rubble. From the air, it looks like someone had tried to plot a highway system on the moon.[18]

The contamination of the land and human communities is taking a toll on the people's health, especially on children. Reece reports:

> An Eastern Kentucky University study found that children in Letcher County, Kentucky, suffer from an alarmingly high rate of nausea,

diarrhea, vomiting, and shortness of breath—symptoms of something called blue baby syndrome—that can all be traced back to sedimentation and dissolved minerals that have drained from mine sites into nearby streams. Long-term effects may include liver, kidney, and spleen failure, bone damage, and cancers of the digestive tract.[19]

What a business this is indeed—to change technology that allows you to shed your work force and then to pour toxins into the water sources and communities of the newly unemployed. It is hard to escape the moral challenge of this reality.

As you can probably guess, most of this type of coal mining goes on in relatively remote areas, off the interstate, out of view of most people. Some church and environmental groups are bringing delegations to view these sites, often in a cat-and-mouse game with the companies, who don't want them there. But people do go, and it is one reason why this story is finally making it into the light of day. If you can, go see it for yourself. Sit with a view of the devastation, sit quietly and listen to the landscape, to the forests and the streams, to the gaping wounds of the mountains. Just take it in. This is what our lifestyles are bringing about; and it is to support the energy requirements of those lifestyles that corporations are doing this, and politicians are allowing them to do it, often with generous tax breaks, which means with our money.

"Distance negates responsibility," said Reece's friend Guy Davenport, quoted in the article. It does indeed—and nearness hits us with responsibility right between the eyes. Think of it as a mirror put up before us, a reflection of our society. This is hard, I know. We hate feeling guilty. But guilt is not what I'm going for here, though there is plenty of guilt to go around. However, responsibility *is*.

The United States has a huge supply of coal, good news for our energy needs. It is dirty, but it is cheap and abundant. Even better, technology now exists that can turn coal into liquid, which means it could become a rising source of diesel for our cars and trucks. Jeff Goodell notes that we could do as good a job of weaning ourselves from oil by raising fuel efficiency standards. Right. Or we can give in to the auto and trucking industries and to Big Coal and gouge out more of our land for our gas and send global temperatures soaring toward the tipping point.

The stories from Appalachia are unforgettable. The pictures are haunting. Some 20 percent of coal production now comes from "mountain-topping," and some 65 percent from strip mining. Demand for energy is going to soar. What are we doing to this earth?

Having viewed the devastation, I'm afraid that, if you are like me, you will never again think the same way about turning on your lights.

Food or fuel?

Bad choice, isn't it? Who wants to have to think about that when gassing up the car? So, farmers across the country have been furiously planting corn for the burgeoning corn ethanol industry. Biofuels will help us break our dependence on foreign energy sources and are a renewable resource, or so we are told. But not all biofuels are equal, and corn, it turns out, is a very bad bet for our energy future. Despite that, the United States is betting on corn anyway to help fill our gas tanks.

There is no space here to go into the multiple complexities regarding ethanol and biodiesel, two strategies for replacing oil with energy from something we can grow on our farms or harvest from weeds, field waste, or prairie grass. Besides the fact that it is unrealistic to think that ethanol can be produced in anything near the amounts that would replace our oil and gas consumption, we must also wrestle with environmental issues that are hugely costly and in some cases disastrous.

Because this topic requires more attention than we can give it here, I urge you to become as well-informed as possible, since we will be debating these issues now and in the future. You can search the Internet using search strings like, "corn ethanol environmental problems," or "Brazil sugarcane ethanol environmental labor problems," or "biodiesel palm oil environmental disaster southeast Asia," and come up with articles that outline the dangers of many biofuels.

And the dangers are serious indeed. I will summarize some of them here in order to lead us to some concluding reflections for this chapter.

Some time ago I came upon this little tidbit in the *New York Times* business section in a column entitled "What's Offline?" It was a summary of information found in the online publication *Wired* that lays out some of the problems: "One acre of soybeans can produce 50 gallons of biodiesel fuel. There are 427 million arable acres in the United States. The average American driver uses 464 gallons of gasoline a year and there are 198 million drivers in the United States. All of which means: 'arable acres needed to make enough biodiesel: 1.8 billion.'"[20]

You see the problem?

Here in the United States, the crop we are turning to for ethanol is corn, mandated by our federal government, with big tax-payer subsidies to go along. Farmers in the chronically challenged farm states are jumping on the bandwagon because, at least as I write this, the switch is putting pressure on corn prices, which have risen steadily since the corn ethanol craze hit, which means real profits—again, at least for now.

So, right away we hit the agricultural land-use issue: how much land are we willing to take out of food production for biofuels, and does this help achieve our end of replacing our oil dependency? One oft-cited expert on this topic, David Pimentel, professor in the College of Agriculture and Life Sciences at Cornell University, wrote in 2001:

> The average US automobile, traveling 10,000 miles a year on pure ethanol (not a gasoline-ethanol mix), would need about 852 gallons of corn-based fuel. This would take 11 acres to grow, based on net ethanol production. This is the same amount of cropland required to feed seven Americans. If all the automobiles in the United States were fueled with 100 percent ethanol, a total of about 97 percent of US land area would be needed to grow the corn feedstock. Corn would cover nearly the total land area of the United States.[21]

Yup, a problem.

Pimentel says, too, that making ethanol requires—you can guess—fossil fuels. And because these fuels are still much cheaper than ethanol, ethanol producers use them to produce ethanol rather than the ethanol they are producing. To make this even less impressive in cost terms, this whole project is being generously subsidized with our tax dollars, which means the federal government is providing subsidies for a fuel that is raising the price of corn, which means raising the price of feed for livestock and putting pressure on foods that use corn and corn syrup, all of which means higher prices for things like cereals, milk, eggs, meat, and a lot of our processed foods.

Said Pimentel, "Abusing our precious croplands to grow corn for an energy-inefficient process that yields low-grade automobile fuel amounts to an unsustainable, subsidized food burning."[22]

Okay, but there is a potential here for high profits, no? Let's keep our priorities straight, or for the purpose of our moral considerations, *clear*.

Among the moral problems posed by the industry is the fact that the United States remains the world's largest exporter of corn to developing countries. The United States actually accounts for 70 percent of global corn exports. Beyond economic worries around the potential collapse of this export market is the impact it could have—if we proceed with massive corn-ethanol production—on food availability in poor countries, especially those where agriculture is already a marginal prospect because of poor land or climate change.

Lester Brown, president of the Earth Policy Institute in Washington DC, put the quandary this way: "We need to be concerned that we aren't creating an image of reducing grain exports in order to fill the gas tanks of our sports utility vehicles."[23] Ouch!

Our moral quandary, however, does not stop there. Since it is obviously not practical to put all our agricultural land under production for energy, we are likely to increase our imports of other biofuels, like sugarcane ethanol and soy-based biofuel from Brazil, or palm oil–based biodiesel fuel, the favorite in Europe right now, from Southeast Asia—at the cost of the Amazon rainforest, or the forests of Malaysia and Indonesia, vital ecological areas of our world that are being destroyed for agricultural production to fuel the trucks and automobiles of the rich Western countries.

All this is pretty bad, but there's more. All this environmental destruction and biofuel industrial production is going to increase carbon emissions by a lot—far more than the savings at the clean-burning end of our automobiles, that is, if the industry is allowed to develop as it is right now, without proper caution and government regulation. And what crops we choose to supplement our energy use (and supplement, not replace, is all we will be able to do) will make all the difference.

David Tilman, an ecologist at the University of Minnesota and member of the National Academy of Sciences, and Jason Hill, a research associate in the Department of Applied Economics at the same school, explain:

> Because of how corn ethanol currently is made, only about 20 percent of each gallon is "new" energy. That's because it takes a lot of "old" fossil energy to make it: diesel to run tractors, natural gas to make fertilizer and, of course, fuel to run the refineries that convert corn to ethanol.[24]

So, it takes a lot of oil and gas to make corn ethanol.

"If every one of the 70 million acres on which corn is grown in 2006 was used for ethanol, the amount produced would displace only 12 percent of the US gasoline market." And, I love this, the "non-fossil energy gained" is so small that "car tune-ups and proper air pressure [in tires] would save more energy."[25]

Yikes! No profits to be made there, except for some gas stations and mechanics.

Just to emphasize this point, one of the biggest corn-ethanol interests is the agribusiness giant Archer Daniels Midland (ADM), the largest ethanol producer in the United States. You have undoubtedly seen its "green" commercials on PBS and other TV channels. It is the big power behind the Renewable Fuels Association, an industry lobby, and has donated to both Republicans and Democrats. It also happens to operate coal-fired power plants in Illinois and Iowa. In 2006 it was constructing a coal-fired power plant to power its ethanol production plant in Clinton, Iowa.[26]

We are getting the picture here, right? Environmental groups, such as Greenpeace International, have also accused ADM (along with Cargill and Bunge, two other agribusiness giants) of financing soy production in Brazil that is illegally destroying the rainforest. The Environmental Protection Agency has charged ADM with violations of the Clean Air Act "in hundreds of processing units, covering 52 plants in 16 states." It has been fined by the Department of Justice and the state of Illinois "for pollution related to ethanol production and distribution."[27] It also has some problems with the feds under the Superfund clean-up laws for leftover contamination at numerous other sites.

Remember that thing Jesus said about being as wise as serpents? ADM and other corporate giants are appealing to our desire for a cleaner environment to address things like global warming and foreign oil dependency. But we must be very, very careful about who and what we believe, and that's where the wise as serpents part comes in. There are things we need to know so that decisions that are represented as "green" aren't decisions that actually further the destruction of our planet.

Now, back to Tilman and Hill. They point out that soybean production, used to make biodiesel, is headed in this same direction as corn. Scores of biodiesel plants were under construction as I wrote this. Are soybeans better than corn? Meanwhile, sugarcane ethanol, the kind being produced in Brazil, "produces about twice as much ethanol per acre as corn." Also, much of the energy to produce the ethanol comes "from burning cane residue." When grown on "established soils [it] releases 80 percent less greenhouse gases than gasoline."[28]

This is all very good. However, to feed this rapidly growing market, Brazil's production of sugarcane and soybeans is not just happening on those established soils. In fact, more of Brazil's precious Amazon rainforest and vast savannas are being cleared and put under monoculture crop production for biofuel—at an incalculable loss to this planet. But even beyond the loss of the forest and grasslands is this little problem—as the land is cleared, huge amounts of carbon dioxide held in those soils and plant materials for millions of years are being released into the atmosphere.

Tilman and Hill explain:

> Plants and soil contain three times more carbon than the atmosphere. The trees and soil of an acre of rainforest—which, once cleared, is suitable for growing soybeans—contain about 120 tons of organic carbon. An acre of tropical woodland or savanna, suitable for sugarcane, contains about half this amount. About a fourth of the carbon in an ecosystem is released into the atmosphere as carbon dioxide when trees are clear-cut, brush and branches are burned or rot, and roots decay. Even more is lost during the first 20 to 50 years of farming, as soil carbon decomposes into carbon dioxide and as wood products are burned or decay. This means that when tropical woodland is cleared to produce sugarcane for ethanol, the greenhouse gas released is about 50 percent greater than what occurs from the production

and use of the same amount of gasoline. And that statistic holds for at least two decades.[29]

Renewable does not necessarily mean better, and we best get educated and quickly before we find ourselves making huge miscalculations that could accelerate our path toward ecological tipping points from which there is no return.

A quick word about palm oil. Palm oil is ubiquitous. It is hard to get through a day without consuming it in some form. It is a key ingredient in much of our processed foods, though it is not necessarily good for us as it is high in cholesterol. But palm plantations are most unkind to this planet, in fact, an egregious hurt in many places—huge swaths of land (where poor campesinos often once lived until forced off by the palm oil corporations and their government backers) cleared for the trees.

Europe more and more is running its cars on biodiesel, and palm oil is a leading source. "Green" folks in Europe saw it as a sustainable energy option—from their point of view at filling stations in Europe. Meanwhile, in Southeast Asia palm plantations have brought about massive deforestation and contamination from chemical fertilizers. As the plantations spread over the land, the peatland where they grow best was drained and burned, sending enormous amounts of carbon dioxide into the atmosphere.[30] Draining peatland is especially dangerous as the soggy soil stores vast quantities of CO_2. One of the most stunning impacts of this is that Indonesia has now become the third leading emitter of carbon dioxide, after the United States and China.

Europe lacks the foodstuffs needed to meet fuel supply demands, and Europe is thinking "greener" than we are here in the states—with this result somewhere else. But isn't that how the Western countries have long related to poor countries that have what we need? Get the stuff with little thought to the consequences—over there. Except now we cannot separate the fate over there from our fate over here.

The consequences in two tropical countries far from home provide dramatic examples. Elisabeth Rosenthal reports that "Friends of the Earth estimates that 87 percent of the deforestation in Malaysia from 1985 to 2000 was caused by new palm oil plantations. In Indonesia, the amount of land devoted to palm oil has increased 118 percent in the last eight years."[31]

In addition to our global warming concerns, just think about what this means for the long-term viability of these two countries? As George Monbiot, who writes often on environmental and economic issues for *The Guardian*, describes it, "The entire region is being turned into a gigantic vegetable oil field."[32]

But there is still more bad news on the ethanol front, back here where we think corn will make us feel better about driving our cars. Genetically modified seeds. Of course, this would follow. The whole point is to create a corn crop with higher yields so that it can produce more each harvest through intensive monoculture row-cropping—and this kind of super-intensive farming requires massive amounts of fertilizers, herbicides, and pesticides (all of which require large amounts of oil and other fossil fuels, by the way). So one way to save money is to genetically modify the seeds to increase yields and make them immune to herbicides (Round-Up being one notorious example). Then farmers can spray the fields like crazy and everything dies but the corn. We already do this. Corporations like Monsanto have already compromised the natural genetic makeup of many crops by genetically engineering new seeds.

But agribusiness corporations have even bigger things in mind. "Developing energy crops [like switchgrass, an ubiquitous prairie weed] could mean new applications of genetic engineering, which for years has been aimed at making plants resistant to insects and herbicides, but now would include altering their fundamental structure. One goal, for example, is to reduce the amount of lignin, a substance that gives plants the stiffness to stand upright but interferes with turning a plant's cellulose into ethanol."[33] Are we crazy? Kind of brings to mind the Army Corps of Engineers back in Chapter 1—if nature gives us problems, we'll just change nature.

Some environmentalists believe that this is how corporations finally hope to cash in on the investments they have made in developing GMOs (genetically modified organisms), which the world has been rather reluctant to accept in its food. If you can't get the dog to bark, whip it a little harder—or create a new dog.

The fear here, of course, is that these crops will inevitably cross-pollinate with other plants in the woods and fields and that we could find our forests drooping for want of lignin. GMO enthusiasts say this won't happen, but it has already happened in areas where GMO crops have been planted (right now, GMO corn is threatening the native corn of Mexico and its forty varieties).

Meanwhile, there is the food factor. In January 2007, protests and riots broke out in Mexico when the government raised prices for corn and, therefore, tortillas, a staple of the Mexican diet. What caused the increase was the sharp rise in the price of corn because of the amount of production switching from corn for food to corn for fuel. This is only the beginning of the conflicts that will result from this kind of tradeoff. As Tilman and Hill point out: "Three of our most fundamental needs—food, energy, and a livable and sustainable environment—are now in direct conflict."[34]

Again, keep in mind that other troubling demographic—the additional two billion to three billion people who will live on this planet in this next generation, all of them with needs for food, energy, and a livable, sustainable environment.

Farewell to the energy pipe dream

So there we are—another energy pipe dream smashed. It is not that biofuels have no role at all in our energy future. They do. But the role is small, and it must be done with great care. Before anything else, decisions about the future must be taken out of the hands of profit-making corporations, and a great deal of consumer education needs to be done so that people know exactly what they are choosing.

Food, energy, and a livable and sustainable environment are now in conflict. This is sobering and very real. Lester Brown points out that "the grain it takes to fill a 25-gallon tank with ethanol just once would feed one person for a whole year. Converting the entire US grain harvest to ethanol would satisfy only 16 percent of US auto fuel needs."[35] How far are we willing to go to satisfy that 16 percent? How far are we willing to go to supplement that supply with biodiesel from the rainforests of Brazil, Indonesia, and Malaysia?

I could not resist singling out this one example of the moral quandary, represented in the story of a US consumer included in a *New York Times* article in March 2007:

> Veronica Burgos, a 39-year-old bookkeeper, says she is not about to give up her aging gas-guzzling navy blue Ford Explorer to commute to work and shuttle her children around, even though gasoline prices in the Los Angeles area where she lives are now "ridiculous." "With this S.U.V., you really feel it, but I have two kids so I *need* it," she said. "In reality my husband would probably rather that I don't drive the S.U.V. so much, but I still do and I drive quite a bit. With work and two kids and all their activities, especially on the weekend, we're more comfortable in the S.U.V. So what are you going to do?" (emphasis added)[36]

"What are you going to do," indeed? I have seldom seen a more illuminating example of how wants and desires in a consumer culture are turned into *need*. How in the world did large families manage all those childhood road trips in the old station wagon back in the 1950s? What is wrong with a well-built car with child seats and seat belts that might get twenty or thirty more miles to the gallon? Or even better, a hybrid? Or even better, an electric car?

Companies like ExxonMobil say that the oil industry is providing what consumers want, supporting the lifestyles they want, the vehicle choices they make—and we keep on proving them right.

This isn't even the end of the story of how energy demand is destroying parts of our planet. In Canada massive amounts of land acreage have been cleared to get to oil sands—a hugely wasteful process that squeezes oil out of the sands, using massive amounts of energy to do it. With oil prices high, this has suddenly become economical, and the big oil companies, like Shell, ExxonMobil, and Chevron, are investing. The Canadian projects have wreaked habitat death, threatening old boreal forests, driving wildlife away, using vast amounts of water that threaten fish in local rivers, and causing sharp increases in acid rain.[37]

High oil prices also have investors looking again at oil shale, once considered too costly to put into production. The states with the misfortune of having oil shale to extract are Colorado, Wyoming, and Utah, much of it on federal land. Extracting oil shale involves large open pit mining and disposal of enormous amounts of waste rock.

I could go on. That's the sad part. I have not even covered all the ground here to be considered. We are going to have to make choices, and they are heavily weighted with moral and ethical content.

And we hate that. As a culture, we keep saying that we hate that—we hate being told that conscience needs to be part of our calculations in the things we buy and the lifestyles we choose. We hate being told that we may actually have to change how we live because of the impact on other human beings or on the natural wonders of the world. We hate being told that we are reaching the limits of economic growth, on what we can acquire, now, in *this* generation. It is much more convenient to keep our religion private, about personal behavior, about "me and God," and my personal sinfulness. It is hard to expand that religiosity back to the world, the poor, the community, the care for creation, that is a rockbed of our Judeo-Christian traditions.

But this isn't just a moral or spiritual issue that comes from our human constructs. It is now a message direct from the earth to one of its species: live within the limits, reestablish a balance among the human and the rest of the biosphere, or face unimaginable catastrophe. *The moral and ethical choices are not about whether or not this is true, they are about what we are going to do in the face of it.*

According to the Environment News Service, in 2002 the US Energy Information Administration reported that "world demand for energy is expected to rise by 60 percent over the next two decades. . . . The agency says the increased energy consumption, led largely by oil, will boost releases of carbon dioxide by as much as 3.8 billion metric tons per year in 2020. Oil will continue to command 40 percent of the world's energy consumption."[38]

Meanwhile, "a detailed analysis for the Danish Energy Agency calculates that to supply 9.3 billion people—which may well be the global population in 2050—with all their basic energy needs would require six times as much delivered (end-use) energy as the world supplied in 2000."[39]

It's okay to get depressed, to feel overwhelmed. As I look at these figures and then at the ravaging of the earth that is going on to meet current energy needs already, I can get very depressed. It looks quite impossible. That's why these challenges of our times, moral, ethical, yes, are also challenges of the spirit, because we have to find what we need within ourselves to turn this in another direction. And this is not going to be easy.

One of the tragedies of the wasted time is that the US government knows more about this than it cares to share with its citizens. In 2005, an expert in the energy world issued a report from a study sponsored by the National Energy Technology Laboratory of the Department of Energy entitled *Peaking of World Oil Production: Impacts, Mitigation, and Risk Management.*[40] The leader of the research team was Robert L. Hirsch, senior energy program advisor for Science Applications International Corporation (SAIC), with a long history of work with the US Atomic Energy Commission, the US Energy Research and Development Administration, Exxon, ARCO, EPRI—a long list of credentials. His Ph.D. is in engineering and physics.

The report begins:

> The peaking of world oil production presents the US and the world with an unprecedented risk management problem. As peaking is approached, liquid fuel prices and price volatility will increase dramatically, and, without timely mitigation, the economic, social, and political costs will be unprecedented. Viable mitigation options exist on both the supply and demand sides, but to have substantial impact, they must be initiated more than a decade in advance of peaking.

Now, as we said at the start, there is some debate about when peak will occur. Some think it has already happened, others that it will be around 2010, others give a somewhat later date. As the report says, many say the day is "soon," and soon is defined as within twenty years. But there has not exactly been a clarion call going out from our political leaders to alter our energy consumption patterns to prepare for peak.

Some of the initiatives Hirsch and his team recommend as mitigation options include some of the very projects we have found above to be ecologically destructive—such as liquified coal or extracting oil from oil sands— or woefully inadequate to meet growing demand, such as ethanol and biofuels.

As the Hirsch reports indicates:

> The problems associated with world oil production peaking will not be temporary. . . . The challenge of oil peaking deserves immediate,

serious attention, if risks are to be fully understood and mitigation begun on a timely basis. . . . Peaking will result in dramatically higher oil prices, which will cause protracted economic hardship in the United States and the world.

The report calls the problem of the coming peak in conventional oil production "unlike any yet faced by modern industrial society."

If this is so, should we not be preparing for it? Shouldn't there be a national call going out for all of us to start changing how we live, to reduce consumption, to restructure economies and the energy base of societies, to do all we can to get us through this transitional crisis? Shouldn't our religious leaders, perhaps, be at the forefront of that call? What are they waiting for?

Maybe this—in 2006, an Anglican bishop in London, the Rt. Reverend Richard Chartres, was blistered when he suggested that our energy-guzzling ways might actually be sinful. "Making selfish choices such as flying on holiday or buying a large car are a symptom of sin. Sin is not just a restricted list of moral mistakes. It is living a life turned in on itself where people ignore the consequences of their actions."[41] Again, ouch! His comments drew a great deal of criticism, with lovers of sports vehicles basically saying that the good bishop should not be "pointing the finger." Why not? Jesus did. Anyway, imagine what would happen in our congregations if this message was preached at our weekly services with all those SUVs parked out in the church parking lot.

By the way, you'll be interested to know that the DOE tried for a time to suppress the Hirsch report.

I conclude this chapter with this last example of our conundrum. While I was writing it, the New York Times published a front page article entitled "Oil Innovations Pump New Life Into Old Wells."[42] It reports on how new technology is making it possible to pump more oil out of our depleted wells, injecting high-powered steam and gas to force the stubborn stuff out of the ground. High oil prices are making this economically feasible. In the article Daniel Yergin voiced the "good news," saying that many times in the past we have thought we were running out of oil, but then it doesn't happen. The New York Times went on to consign the notion that oil production has peaked a "minority view, held largely by a small band of retired petroleum geologists and some members of Congress." Whew, that's harsh. "As the industry improves its ability to draw new life from old wells and expands its forays into ever-deeper corners of the globe, it is providing strong rebuttal in the long-running debate over when the world might run out of oil."

The article does mention the concerns of environmentalists, noting the oil industry's insistence that there "are few alternatives to fossil fuels" to meet global demand. "Inevitably, this means that global carbon emissions used in the transportation sector will continue to increase, and so will their contribution to global warming."

I got pretty depressed reading this, wondering how many others would see this information as exceedingly bad news. At least an imminent oil shortage crisis would get our attention, make us realize that our oil days are numbered. If we won't help save the atmosphere by cutting our carbon emissions, maybe we will be willing to adjust knowing that peak oil is coming.

I am not an energy expert. I don't know what this means in the medium to long term about peak oil, whether this means we really do not have near-term supply problems, only solvable technology problems, or if this kind of pumping is really the sign of arriving at the last gasp in these fields, as some have predicted. But if we do not have an immediate supply problem, that means we must choose to change our lives to reduce our oil consumption and our carbon footprint drastically, for the sake of the planet.

Will we make such a choice?

I give the final word to Robert Heilbroner, an economist and historian of economic thought who died in 2005:

> Suppose we . . . knew with a high degree of certainty that humankind could not survive a thousand years unless we gave up our wasteful diet of meat, abandoned all pleasure driving, cut back on every use of energy that was not essential to the maintenance of the bare minimum. Would we care enough for posterity to pay the price of its survival?[43]

What if we knew that global warming and ecological destruction would cause the collapse of human societies and the deaths of billions of people over the course of this century unless we did all those things? Would we care enough to pay the price by altering our lives? Would we?

4

Living Beyond Our Means

or,

Embracing Simplicity Whether We Want To or Not

> *We have lost sight of how large the human enterprise has become relative to the earth's resources.*
> —LESTER BROWN[1]

> *Humanity is already in unsustainable territory. . . . The collapse will arrive very suddenly, much to everyone's surprise.*
> —DONELLA MEADOWS, JORGEN RANDERS, AND DENNIS MEADOWS[2]

Can nine billion people be my neighbor? Good question, and one we had best answer in a hurry. When Jesus told the story of the Good Samaritan, when he reiterated the Hebrew scripture's mandate that we must love our neighbor as ourselves, the global population was approximately 300,000,000, only a small portion of which lived in what is now the Middle East.

That's significantly less than the population in today's United States. Lots more to go around in those days—space, frontiers, room to expand, as the Roman Empire knew so well, land to give to chosen peoples, land to be conquered and put under cultivation, the earth covered in forest, seas teeming with fish and other sea life, wildlife in abundance that we cannot even imagine anymore. If one place was wrecked, people could move on to another. The concept of sharing loaves and fishes, with abundance for all, more than enough to go around, along with justice for the poor—as in Luke's

Gospel or the prophets of the Hebrew scripture—might have been possible if humans had chosen to live this way, if oppression had not already been the problem that it still is. No profit-making corporations running the global economy, no stock portfolios and pressure on quarterly earnings reports, no World Trade Organization. The potential for Jubilee looks different in a world so sparsely populated than it does to us now, with most land under production of one kind or another, resources claimed, owned, "developed," already exploited or even permanently depleted, on a planet growing more crowded with every passing day. The monarchies and empires of Europe that destroyed much of that continent's natural resource base were not even on the horizon yet, though in subsequent centuries a way of human settlement that laid waste to the land was already entrenching itself, inspired in part by a religiously motivated mission to dominate and subdue nature in the service of "man." The United States had yet to manifest its destiny—a destiny to conquer the frontiers of this continent, to conquer nature itself for the benefit of our nation's expansion, no matter what "godless heathens," or wild animals, or grasslands, forests, rivers, and mountains might be in the way.

In the Great Plains, more than sixty-five million American bison roamed the vast grasslands before the Europeans arrived, supplying food, clothing, and materials for shelter for native tribes that lived and thrived for thousands of years before we found them in the way of US destiny. Along with the bison, many other animals were over-hunted; forests were chopped down; rivers and streams were dammed, "redirected," and depleted; land rich in minerals needed for industrialization was laid waste, ravaged for our growth and development; and rich ecosystems were destroyed forever. The original beauty of this land is left now to the imagination, the stuff of dreams or movies.

And so it has continued, right up to the latest exurban development beyond suburban sprawl, the latest housing tracts constructed across deserts and mountains, the latest wetlands drained for shopping malls and big box stores.

If you think the last three chapters were full of bad news, hang on, because the story gets a lot worse. We are just now getting to the really big problem, the most dire threat to our future on this planet, a problem that would exist whether or not we were super-heating the atmosphere, though global warming is one of its results: ecological overshoot.

What is ecological overshoot? We need to know, because this is a hurdle that cannot be jumped, a limit that cannot be surpassed. This is the one that will come crashing down on us even if global warming trends are reversed and the world begins to cool down. So, even if at this point we find the ecological challenges described in earlier chapters frighteningly daunting, this is the one that really means we have to change how we live—not temporarily, but forever.

In the important and highly disturbing book *Limits to Growth*, the authors define some terms with which we need to become very familiar, to make part of our daily lives as we examine how to address our multiple ecological crises. They should become the substance of our ongoing faith reflection, the content of weekend sermons and religion classes, part of the conversation at the family dinner table and among our neighbors, the substance of the calls to action we need to make, and soon. These terms must become part of the framework of our religiosities, our spiritualities and theologies, the framework of meaning that we give to our daily lives, the values by which we live in every aspect of our lives—because of what is at stake here.

One of the terms that has become popular in the "green" lexicon these days is *ecological footprint:* "the total burden humankind places on the earth. It includes the impact of agriculture, mining, fish catch, forest harvest, pollution emissions, land development, and biodiversity reduction."[3] *Ecological overshoot* is what happens when that footprint exceeds the capacity of the earth to recover, renew, and replenish what that footprint has cost it. "To overshoot means to go too far, to be beyond limits accidently—without intention."[4] We didn't mean to do it; we didn't mean to consume so far beyond the limits of the planet that we are now drawing down its very "capital," but saying that doesn't mean it has not happened. And when we overshoot, we have to turn around and correct the mistake.

You see, this isn't just about reaching the limits. This is about going way beyond them. And because we have built a whole global economy around this way of doing business, the correction isn't going to be easy.

In the Introduction I mentioned a reflection by former World Bank Deputy Director Sven Burmeister that changed the way I view my world. I have used the following quotation over and over again when addressing various audiences. It is always followed by silence in the room. Keep in mind that Burmeister wrote this in 1991. Sixteen years have passed from that writing to this one, a lot of time wasted.

> Our current handling of the environment and its resources might lead to our ultimate destruction. In fact, if we continue on our present course, the question is not whether destruction will happen, but when. Acid rain, deforestation, ozone depletion, and global warming are clear signals that we are misusing and exhausting the resources of the planet. . . . All resources are finite in the end. . . . The important question is how we conceive of our relationship with nature. Are we here to exploit the earth and use up its capital? Or are we here to find an equilibrium with our fellow creatures, or to live as stewards off the income that the earth can yield without destroying its capital? . . . The ultimate constraint on resource use is the carrying capacity of the globe:

per capita resource use should not exceed the level the globe can sustain for all the world's people. Today's per capita resource use in industrial countries is not sustainable for all inhabitants of the earth. . . . The planet is capable of carrying only 500 million people indefinitely at the level of income and technology in the United States today. If resources were used more prudently as in Europe and Japan, the planet might carry one billion people indefinitely. Demographers estimate that, if present trends continue, the world's population . . . will stabilize sometime in the twenty-first century at nine to twelve billion human beings[5] (emphasis added).

You see? Not sustainable. *Limits*, that bad word. And we have already passed them. Ecological overshoot was reached sometime during the 1980s. It would take "1.4 earths" to support our current level of consumption. Another way of looking at it is by the year. On October 9, 2006, we reached overshoot; for the rest of the year what we took from the earth was no longer its "interest" but its "capital." And that date comes sooner every year.

As Lester Brown, president of the Earth Policy Institute in Washington DC, wrote in *Plan B 2.0*: "The bottom line is that the world is in what ecologists call an 'overshoot-and-collapse' mode. Demand has exceeded the sustainable yield of natural systems at the local level countless times in the past. Now, for the first time, it is doing so at the global level."[6]

And despite the science-fiction dreams of colonizing other planets one day, we are products of *this* planet, and we have, unlike in the days of Jesus Christ or Columbus, nowhere else to go. We are going to be competing for or sharing, depending on the choices we make, a rapidly depleting amount of "earth product" with a greater and greater number of other human beings, not to mention the plants and the animals, the birds of the air and the creatures of the sea, whose numbers in many cases are in rapid decline as ours rise (the two being connected, of course).

Spending down life

We are spending down the life sources of the planet; we are rapidly moving toward severe shortages of fresh water, arable land, forests, fish, along with fossil fuels—all the things we need to live—and we are doing this on an increasingly crowded planet.

Can nine billion people be my neighbor? And if this remains a central mandate of our faith traditions, to love our neighbor as ourselves, what will this mean in a world where scarcity is an overarching framework of the human presence on this planet?

For a long time, many of us wanted to believe that justice was a matter of "lifting all boats" without having to sink ours. Now we know this is not possible. To raise everyone to the US standard of living—to our luxury yacht, so to speak, on this ocean of life—would require five planet earths.

It is those of us in the United States and the wealthy of the G-8 countries (the United States, Canada, the United Kingdom, France, Japan, Germany, Italy, and Russia) that are really spending down the capital of the earth. We are the ones who, more than any other societies, have put the planet into overshoot. And it is only by drastically reducing the consumption of those of us at the top end of the global economy that our beloved earth can be restored to life-sustaining equilibrium.

So you see, we have a problem. And we in this affluent US culture especially have a problem—how are we going to share this planet with nine billion people in a way that makes it possible for all to live with dignity; to not be poor; to protect the rights of all species along the whole chain of life upon which we depend, absolutely, for our own existence, to be respected and preserved for future generations? Do future generations matter in our moral calculations?

The problem with arriving at the limits of carrying capacity, and going beyond them, is that what we are using up now will no longer be available for those generations. When we drain the High Plains aquifers that lie under eight western states, the water is gone. It's gone. That's it. Time to pack up and leave. Why? Because it takes so long for the aquifer to replenish itself naturally that groundwater from this source is considered to be a nonrenewable resource. It's not as if you can just turn it off for a few hours and, presto, it comes back on again.

This is what happens when we take water out for our use at a higher rate than the aquifer can replenish, a classic case of overshoot. We then add to the problem by paving over more and more of the wetlands that once soaked in the rains, allowing the water to drain down to the aquifers. Meanwhile, our greenhouse gas emissions have warmed the atmosphere, which increases the rate of evaporation, which in turn affects rainwater, rivers, streams, wetlands, glaciers, and snow melt. Hence, there is even less available water. Simply put, given current trends the US West will begin to run out of water—in our lifetime.

Not only the West. Also the Midwest, also New England, also parts of the Pacific Northwest, some areas with the fastest growing populations. Any sane person would say this kind of development has to stop.

Right now we are so far beyond the carrying capacity of the dry western states, it is breathtakingly reckless that development continues at all, much less at this accelerated rate, more population moving in, more homes going up, more tourist industry being developed—because *we know we are doing it.* (Remember the Roman Catholic definition of mortal sin? One requirement is knowledge that what you are doing is grievously wrong.)

David Brooks, in a column in the *New York Times*, describes driving out to the White Tank Mountains outside Phoenix and from there looking out "over a barren desert floor ... nothing but scrub, tire tracks and desert washes."[7] Yup, Brooks looks out on that desert, and all he sees is barrenness. It wants—guess what?—developing! He cheerily reports that this expanse of desert has indeed been bought by developers, and he proclaims heartily that by 2025 one million people will live in this "empty space," empty presumably because there are not yet any developments on it, no housing tracts, schools, churches, or shopping malls.

Not a humble project, to be sure. Brooks notes that 100 billion square feet of new housing will be constructed. And to emphasize his joy in this new wave of exurban development, he also notes that "half of the buildings in which Americans will live, play and work in the year 2030 don't even exist yet. We are in the middle of a $25 trillion building boom that is changing the face of the country, and *most of it is happening in desert places like this one*" (emphasis added).[8]

Are we out of our minds? In the desert? Where will the water come from? And what of that $25 trillion boom of pavement and roads and buildings and water and loss of trees and wetlands across this already overdeveloped country? What of the ecosystems, the migration patterns of species, the fossil fuels that will be required to run all this development?

Brooks wrote this column in the beginning of Arizona's seventh year of drought. I am writing this in its eighth.

Meanwhile, in Colorado, groundwater from bedrock aquifers of the Denver Basin is being depleted at a steady rate. "Aquifers that sustain suburban Denver, Colo., are dwindling at rates of 30 feet per year due to exponential population growth over the past few decades. ... Ever since Denver residents drilled the first Arapahoe well in 1883, withdrawal has exceeded recharge." At the rate that water is currently being extracted, natural recharge "is not possible."[9] What are we doing about it? Building more developments to support one of the fastest population growth rates in the country.

> The carrying capacity is a limit. Any population that grows past its carrying capacity, overshooting the limit, will not long sustain itself. And while any population is above the carrying capacity, it will deteriorate the support capacity of the system it depends upon. If regeneration of the environment is possible, the deterioration will be temporary. If regeneration is not possible, or if it takes place only over centuries, the deterioration will be effectively permanent.[10]

A very big problem.

As we passed into the twenty-first century, the United Nations commissioned a study to address the growing concerns of member nations about the state of "ecosystem services" around the world. The crisis of resource diminishment was being felt in many countries, and the study was intended as a systematic assessment of the situation. Just how bad are things?

Part of the Millennium Ecosystem Assessment series, the study focused on "the linkages between ecosystems and human well-being." The work was carried out from 2001 to 2005 and resulted in a multi-volume report, a condensed version of which was published as *Ecosystems and Human Well-Being, Our Human Planet: Summary for Decision Makers.*[11]

The findings do not comfort. Thirteen hundred scientists from ninety-five countries found that 60 percent of the earth's ecosystems are already in trouble, that much of this damage has been done in just the past fifty years or so. "As summarized in one leading British newspaper, *The Independent*, Planet Earth stands on the cusp of disaster and people should no longer take it for granted that their children and grandchildren will survive in the environmentally degraded world of the 21st century."[12]

Yikes! That is *this* century, the very one we are in, the very one that our children and youth are inhabiting.

The article quotes Walt Reid, leader of the core of the two thousand authors involved in writing the report: "The bottom line of this assessment is that we are spending Earth's natural capital, putting such strain on the natural functions of Earth that the ability of the planet's ecosystems to sustain future generations can no longer be taken for granted."[13]

The report indicates that fifteen of the twenty-four ecosystems required for life have been seriously degraded or overused. And while we degrade these systems, we are adding two to three billion more human beings. The report states:

> The problem posed by the growing demand for ecosystem services is compounded by increasingly serious degradation in the capability of ecosystems to provide these services. World fisheries are now declining due to overfishing, for instance, and a significant amount of agricultural land has been degraded in the past half-century by erosion, salinization, compaction, nutrient depletion, pollution, and urbanization. Other human-induced impacts on ecosystems include alteration of the nitrogen, phosphorous, sulfur, and carbon cycles, causing acid rain, algal blooms, and fish kills in rivers and coastal waters, along with contributions to climate change. In many parts of the world, this degradation of ecosystem services is exacerbated by the associated loss of the knowledge and understanding held by local communities—knowledge that sometimes could help ensure the sustainable use of ecosystems.
>
> This combination of ever-growing demands being placed on increasingly degraded ecosystems seriously diminishes the prospects for sustainable development.[14]

That term *sustainable development* sounds very tame, and I think we should get rid of it. Because what we are talking about here is not how to develop sustainably, but how to stop developing in some ways altogether, while developing wholly differently in others. However we state it, the message here is clear: we cannot go on like this any longer.

Without major and immediate changes, this world will be dealing very soon with widespread famine; acute water shortages; greater impacts from natural disasters; more epidemics of diseases like malaria, influenza, West Nile virus, and dengue fever; overwhelming amounts of raw sewage and other wastes (some cities have already maxed out their landfill space and are shipping out their waste); collapsing fisheries; depleted soils from overused or badly used and abused agricultural land; sick oceans and dying coral reefs; and the list goes on.

I know we have difficulty with overwhelming numbers of facts, but I think we need to have a clear picture of what is going on already on this earth. Therefore, I want to run through some of the conclusions summarized in *Ecosystems and Human Well-Being, Our Human Planet: Summary for Decision Makers.*

Being better off is killing us

According to the report, human well-being has improved greatly in the past couple of generations. We live longer and we are healthier doing so. However,

> in part these gains in well-being have been made possible by exploiting certain ecosystem services (the provisioning services, such as timber, grazing, and crop production), sometimes to the detriment of the ecosystem and its underlying capacity to continue to provide these and other services. Some of the gains have been made possible by the unsustainable use of other resources. For example, the increases in food production have been partly enabled by drawing on the finite supply of fossil fuels, an ecosystem service laid down millions of years ago.[15]

Using fossil fuels (for farm machinery and tractors, for chemical fertilizers and pesticides, and for transport of crops, to name a few uses) to increase agricultural production to feed more and more people has become unsustainable. This miracle of food production is now undermining our ability to feed the global population in the next generation.

We are also undermining biodiversity by producing mono-crops over huge areas of arable land:

Variations among genes, populations, and species and the variety of structure, function, and composition of ecosystems are necessary to maintain an acceptable and resilient level of ecosystem services in the long term.

For ecosystem functions such as productivity and nutrient recycling, the level, constancy of the service over time, and resilience to shocks all decline over the long term if biodiversity declines. (16–17)

Resilience is one of the most important dynamics of a healthy ecosystem. When we break that down through widespread mono-cropping, deforestation, introduction of GMOs, large-scale use of pesticides and fertilizers, and so on, we undermine that resilience and the whole system becomes vulnerable to shocks, shocks like drought and wildfires, insect infestations, wind and rain storms that cause widespread erosion of depleted soils. Or we reap the results of damming and dredging and controlling, like those of the Mississippi River that made the delta and the City of New Orleans more vulnerable to floods and then to a shock like Hurricane Katrina.

Genetic variability is the raw material on which plant breeding for increased production and greater resilience depends. In general practice, agriculture undermines biodiversity and the regulating and supporting ecosystem services it provides in two ways: through transforming ecosystems by converting them to cultivated lands and through unintended negative impacts of increased levels of agricultural inputs, such as fertilizers, biocides, irrigation, and mechanical tillage. (17)

Among plants and vertebrates, the great majority of species are declining in distribution, abundance, or both, while a small number are expanding. . . . The observed rates of species extinction in modern times are 100 to 1,000 times higher than the average rates for comparable groups estimated from the fossil record. . . .

The current rate of biodiversity loss, in aggregate and at a global scale, gives no indication of slowing. . . . The momentum of the underlying drivers of biodiversity loss, and the consequences of this loss, will extend many millennia into the future. (18)

Among the findings to which the Millennium Ecosystem Assessment scientists gave a high level of certainty are these: 23 percent of animal species are threatened with extinction, 12 percent of bird species, and 25 percent of conifer species. At a medium level of certainty, they believe that 32 percent of amphibia for which they have "reasonable" information are also threatened—all of this evidence of the assault on biodiversity because of our heavy human footprint.

The Millennium Ecosystem Assessment report points out that the human population growth rate will begin to decline, but will still increase by two to three billion by mid-century. More and more of this population will be moving to cities. "The world's urban population increased from about 200 million to 2.9 billion over the past century, and the number of cities with populations in excess of 1 million increased from 17 to 388" (19). These massive urban populations will, of course, have massive demands for food, water, energy, transportation, housing, and consumer goods.

New York City's population, by the way, is expected to increase by another one million between 2007 and 2012. Where, oh where, will it put all those people—and their cars?

This burgeoning urban population will also produce massive amounts of waste, which has to go somewhere. And all of this waste will create an additional pressure called *eutrophication*, or *oversupply of nutrients*. *Ecosystems and Human Well-Being* says

> [this] is an increasingly widespread cause of undesirable ecosystem change, particularly in rivers, lakes, and coastal systems. Nutrient additions on the land, including synthetic fertilizers, animal manures, the enhancement of N-fixation by planted legumes, and the deposition of airborne pollutants, have resulted in approximately a doubling of the natural inputs for reactive nitrogen in terrestrial ecosystems and an almost fivefold increase in phosphorous accumulation. The reduction of biodiversity at the species and landscape levels has permitted nutrients to leak from the soil into rivers, the oceans, and the atmosphere. Emissions to the atmosphere are a significant driver of regional air pollution and the buildup of the greenhouse gas nitrous oxide (and to a small extent, methane). (19)

It's all connected. We put land under cultivation with big machines for mono-cropping—corn or wheat or soybeans. To increase production, we use fertilizers and pesticides (made with fossil fuels). These inputs make it possible to keep producing on the same land, which depletes the soil. Many crops are now being raised on fully depleted soil, growing solely out of chemically induced production. Nearby, cows graze on wide expanses of pasture land, again, a once diverse ecosystem broken down for meat and dairy. Animal manure and chemical runoff are washed into rivers and streams, altering those ecosystems as well. This type of agricultural production produces greenhouse gases, carbon dioxide from the fossil fuels used, nitrous oxide, and methane. This adds to global warming, which leads to climate change that affects these habitats and ecosystems further, making them even more vulnerable, and on and on in a cycle that is becoming increasingly deleterious to the well-being of the planet.

Meanwhile, fossil-fueled transport brings all these needed goods to grocery stores for that burgeoning urban population, who take the stuff home, cook it, eat it, throw a lot of it away (like all that packaging and wrapping that the food came in), and then deposit a whole lot of human raw sewage down sewer systems into, hopefully, some sort of fossil-fueled filtration plant. This massive urban consumption drives the continued cultivation of land for mono-cropping and cow and hog production, and there we have the full circle.

Now add global warming to the picture: "climate change over the next century is projected to affect, directly and indirectly, all aspects of ecosystem service provision" (20).

Something within this circle is going to crack. It has to.

Meanwhile:

Habitat loss is the fastest-growing threat to species and populations on land and will continue to be the dominant factor for the next few decades. Fishing is the dominant factor reducing populations and fragmenting the habitats of marine species and is predicted to lead to local extinctions, especially among large, long-lived, slow-growing species and endemic species.

Habitat fragmentation (the reduction of natural cover into smaller and more disconnected patches)—compounds the effects of habitat loss. (20)

Some species get caught in those little fragments and are no longer able to migrate; their paths are cut off by development, more and more pavement, highways and parking lots, shopping malls and high-tech corridors; they just die off.

The Millennium Ecosystem Assessment report speculates that half of all fresh-water wetlands have already been lost since 1900 (not including rivers, lakes, and reservoirs), a result of "development (dams, dikes, levees, diversions, and on and on), land conversion at the catchment, overharvesting and exploitation, introduction of exotic species, eutrophication and pollution, and global climate change." The report estimates that "by 1985, 56%-65% of available wetland had been drained for intensive agriculture in Europe and North America" (30).

Why does this matter? Wetlands are among the most important sources of ecosystem resilience, health of soils, buffers for storms, removal of waste and pollution, and biodiversity. We continue to lose them at our peril.

"The construction of dams and other structures along rivers has resulted in fragmentation of almost 40% of the large river systems of the world. . . . Several of the world's largest rivers no longer run all the way to the sea for all or part of the year (such as the Nile, the Yellow, and the Colorado)" (31).

This wreaks ecological havoc all along the way, especially along the river estuaries and at the river deltas. Overuse and contamination of groundwater is endemic around the world, in which between 1.5 and 3 billion people depend on groundwater for drinking supplies.

"Forests have effectively disappeared in 25 countries, and more than 90% of the former forests have been lost in another 29 countries" (31). Each year, says the report, we lose an estimated 9.4 million hectares more. Okay, you get the idea. We have attempted to meet the growing needs and demands of the global population by doing more and more of the very things that are now undermining our ability to continue to meet the growing needs and demands of the global population.

Here is another one of those simple facts that puts the picture into focus: "The number of buildings that will be built in the 21st century is on the order of the number of buildings built in the entirety of human history."[16] Wow! Just think about the amount of energy that will be needed to support all those buildings. Where will it come from? Coal under the mountaintops of Appalachia? The tar sands in Alberta, Canada? Natural gas and oil shale in the Rocky Mountains? Solar? Wind? And what of the land turned over and paved over for all those buildings? What rate of habitat loss are we talking about here? Where will all the water come from to pump into those buildings?

Multiple collapses

Now, what the Millennium Ecosystem Assessment report predicts is not so much sudden global collapse from the weight of all these indicators, but rather multiple local collapses all around the planet. Some of these collapses are already occurring—the decimation of ocean fish species, for example, or the loss of coral reefs; desertification in large areas of Africa and Asia; dead zones in off-shore waters in dozens of locations, including the Gulf of Mexico and the ocean off Oregon's coast; and the beginning of the "sixth great extinction," a rate of species extinction that has happened only a few times in evolutionary history.

Lester Brown writes:

We are now in the early stages of the sixth great extinction . . . this one is of human origin. For the first time in the earth's long history, one species has evolved, if that is the right word, to where it can eradicate much of life. . . . As various life forms disappear, they diminish the services provided by nature, such as pollination, seed dispersal, insect control, and nutrient cycling. The loss of species is weakening the web of life, and if it continues it could tear huge gaps in its fabric, leading to irreversible changes in the earth's ecosystem.[17]

Meanwhile, as water and arable land are increasingly overused and depleted,

> demand for food is expected to grow 70%-85% by 2050, resulting in a
> 10 to 20 percent decline in forest and grasslands. Rising demand for
> fish will likely result in major and long-lasting collapse of regional
> marine fisheries. Hunger will remain a major problem, most wide-
> spread in South Asia and Sub-Saharan Africa. South Asia will reach an
> "environmental breaking point as deforestation spreads, industrial ag-
> riculture grows, water use goes up and sewage discharges increase."[18]

Water is one of those limits we will not be able to get around. On a global
level the crisis of overshoot in regard to human water usage has already
arrived. A 2006 report from the International Water Management Institute
in Sri Lanka indicates that demand for water could double over the next
fifty years. The report notes that the amount of land irrigated for food production tripled from 1950 to 2005, supporting the so-called Green Revolution that fed the fast-growing populations of Asia. The report also says,
basically, that we can't do that anymore. In places like China and India, Central Asia and the Middle East, we have already run into the limits of available
water, yet these areas have some of the fastest population growth rates in the
world.[19]

The first paragraphs of this report are worth a moment of sober reflection:

> Imagine a channel of water a meter deep, a kilometre wide, and 7 mil-
> lion kilometres long—long enough to encircle the globe 180 times.
> That's the prodigious amount of water it takes each year to produce
> 3,000 calories of food a day for each of the world's 6.1 billion people.
>   Broken down into smaller quantities, a calorie of food takes a liter
> of water to produce. A kilo of grain takes 500–4,000 liters, a kilo of
> industrially produced meat 10,000 liters. Surprising numbers, indeed.
> Add 2–3 billion people by 2050 and accommodate their changing di-
> ets from cereals to more meat, and that will add another 5 million
> kilometres to the channel of water needed to feed the world's people.
>   Where will that water come from? Will it reach the poor and hun-
> gry? Will it produce enough food? Will it continue to sustain the envi-
> ronment?[20]

The authors then issue this troubling conclusion:

> The Assessment . . . finds a multitude of water, food and environmen-
> tal issues that add up to a crisis. Water is a constraint to acquiring food

for hundreds of millions of people. Important aquatic and terrestrial ecosystems are damaged or threatened. The competition for scarce water resources is intense. And in many basins there is not enough water to meet all the demands—or even for rivers to reach the sea. These local problems could grow in number and severity, or shrink, depending on whether and how they are addressed.[21]

The study points out that the water scarcity crisis that looms before us is exacerbated by urbanization, waste, contamination, and climate change that is reducing glaciers and seasonal snow melt and increasing evaporation of surface water.

A quarter of the world's population lives in areas of water scarcity (including the US Southwest). In many of these areas, the report indicates, water sources are already over-committed (like the Colorado or the Rio Grande in the United States and Mexico), not only for meeting the demands of humans, but also to have enough flow to keep the ecosystems along the way from coming apart. Water scarcity exists where water is naturally scarce; it also exists in places where development has overshot the available supply, or where massive irrigation (in desert areas like southern California) has supported a way of agricultural production that cannot be sustained.

In poor countries, like those of Sub-Saharan Africa, the funds, the infrastructure, and the natural resources do not exist for the kind of agricultural development we take for granted in the United States and Europe. They can't do massive irrigation projects there. At the same time, global warming and environmental degradation of many of these dry lands are increasing the rate of desertification. In short, parts of our world are becoming uninhabitable—places that have hundreds of millions of inhabitants.

Add all this together and you see why one of the concerns of UN agencies and NGOs around the world is the increasing population of environmental refugees—millions of people who will not be able to live where they are. Think about how some countries and their populations already are responding to the migration/immigration increase: shutting down borders, creating legal blocks to immigration, clamping down on undocumented people with arrests and deportations, and so forth. This becomes an integral part of our moral dilemma.

According to the Millennium Ecosystem Assessment report, "Increasing consumption per person, multiplied by a growing human population, are the root causes of the increasing demand for ecosystem services."[22] And those ecosystems are now stretched to the point of breakdown. This is another way of saying that we are living beyond our means.

On second look, it is not quite so simple, because we have to add to this picture, again if we are coming from the perspective of faith and values, the glaring fact of injustice. It is not that everyone is feeling the looming crisis right now, or that all of us have an equal burden of scarcity. Not everyone's consumption is increasing, and not everyone is faced with the imminent threat of water running out or of not being able to get enough to eat. In fact, our inordinate wealth here in the West shields us from experiencing the enormous scarcity that already exists.

While we address growing concerns about the health risks of obesity and diabetes in rich countries, hunger and even starvation are afflicting a greater proportion of the world's population. According to *Limits to Growth:*

> Current modes of growth perpetuate poverty and increase the gap between the rich and the poor. In 1998 more than 45 percent of the globe's people had to live on incomes averaging $2 a day or less. That is more poor people than there were in 1990, even after a decade that saw astonishing income gains for many. The fourteenfold increase in world industrial output since 1930 has made some people very wealthy, but it has not ended poverty. There is no reason to expect that another fourteenfold increase (if it were possible within the earthly limits) would end poverty, unless the global system were restructured to direct growth to those who most need it.[23]

Alas, that is not the direction in which we are headed. That is not the way the rules have been rigged. They are meant to reward the wealthy with more wealth; investors, after all, deserve a hefty return on their investments. The global maket as currently constructed is not, in fact, interested in lifting all "boats," but rather in making bigger "yachts" for those who already have them (or bigger houses for those who have houses, or bigger dividends for those who own stock, and on and on).

But even if we switched the direction of the global economy, restructured it to raise the standard of living of the poor, unless we also drastically reduce the consumption of the wealthy, we would still need to grab hold of another few planets to exploit as we have this one in order to make that possible.

Here are some other disturbing facts in this regard. Population growth is happening at a far faster rate in poor countries than rich. In fact, growth rates among the rich have already flattened. According to Thomas Homer-Dixon, director of the Trudeau Centre for Peace and Conflict Studies at the University of Toronto, global population will grow by 700 million in each of the first two decades of this century:

> Almost all of this increase will occur in poor countries, and half will come from just nine nations: India, Pakistan, Nigeria, Congo, Bangladesh, Uganda, the United States, Ethiopia, and China. What this boils down to—and what we should pay good attention to—is that

by 2050 the population in rich countries will be almost exactly what it is today—about 1.2 billion—while that of poor countries will have surged from about 5.3 to 7.8 billion.[24]

And to add some perspective to our recent geopolitical troubles, Saudi Arabia's population will double by 2050, at the same time that many fear the monarchy will be encountering rapidly depleting oil fields, its main source of national income. In Afghanistan, the population is expected to triple.

Now there's a recipe for upheaval.

What to do with all those poor people

Are all these people my neighbors? Do I really have to love them as myself? Does the total accumulation of our possessions begin to feel a bit heavy in such a world? Do we think we can go on like this without something having to give?

According to Homer-Dixon, "In 1950, there were about two poor people for every rich person on Earth; today there are four; and in 2025, when the world's population will be about 8 billion, there will be nearly six poor people for every rich person."[25]

Perhaps this brings some of the grievances around the world toward the United States and Western Europe into sharper relief, the tensions we have seen deepening through our lifetimes. Do people really hate us "because we are good," as Senator John McCain said after the terror strikes of 9/11? Might such glaring injustice in the face of such glaring human misery have anything at all to do with this? Is it really our democracy and our freedom that people who hate us find so threatening, or could it be, perhaps, the pressures of widening injustice in a world of growing scarcity?

If we look at the situation from the point of view of, say, equity or justice, we are faced with a starkly serious set of moral questions. We did not intend to create such a world. It has happened, I suspect, much to our surprise, and so quickly—in the span of a lifetime, really—that we can forgive ourselves a bit for reeling, for having a hard time grasping it all. But while we were absorbed in our lives, creating a better life for ourselves and our children, working hard in a challenging world, this is the reality that unfolded. And it did not unfold evenly or equitably.

Our faith tells us that the poor cannot be made to bear the burden of the changes required, of the choices *we* made, whether or not we ever intended the outcome. As Meadows, Randers, and Meadows point out: "Generally speaking, the ecological footprint of a rich person is much greater than the ecological footprint of a poor person." And they give this example: "One German . . . has a footprint 10 times that of a Mozambiquean, while one Russian draws as many resources from the planet as one German—without even getting a decent standard of living out of it."[26] And the footprint of a person in the United States is greater than that of the German.

The UN Environment Programme says: "The continued poverty of the majority of the planet's inhabitants and excessive consumption by the minority are the two major causes of environmental degradation. The present course is unsustainable and postponing action is no longer an option."[27] And then we went ahead and postponed action.

Part of the problem, of course, is that there is no national dialogue about any of this, no concerted ongoing action plan or strategic thinking, no call from our churches or other cultural leaders to address these issues—you know, like that traditional Ash Wednesday reading when we are called to repentance, something on the order of *Call an assembly! Gather the people! We have sinned, we need to repent. The covenant is broken. Creation, that incredible gift of God, has been violated. Rend your hearts, not your garments, because our world is very broken and there is work to do! We are called to conversion and there is no time to waste.*

It seems to me that we are living in times that need precisely this kind of radical call to action and a protracted struggle within our faith communities to live in a way commensurate with the challenges and the exigencies of faith within *this* world. We assume so much about our way of life that we forget that it all has moral content, especially now. When plans come up for the next subdivision, when the latest family farmer sells his farm to be subdivided for development, when we buy a house there, we don't think about how this is part of a pattern that defines the enormity of the human enterprise on the planet, or that we are part of a process that is destroying the earth's ability to sustain life. We think, okay, just this one more time, or just for me, or what can my little piece of property do to hurt anybody.

But I want to give us some perspective on how maladapted our responses are to the multiple ecological crises before us. This is not by way of judgment but a self-reflection. We have to begin to see that our behavior and our automatic reactions have been bred into us by a consumer culture from birth; they now feel like part of our DNA.

In the winter of 2005–6, the country faced possible natural-gas shortages as tight supplies encountered rising demand, causing prices to rise and, along with them, fears about the costs of heating our homes and businesses through the winter. Economists worried that this would tamp down consumer demand and have ripple effects throughout the economy.

Then, in January 2006, we experienced unusually warm weather, record-breaking warm weather, in fact. That month the US average temperature was thirty-nine degrees, the highest ever recorded for January, 8.5 degrees warmer than average.[28] There was great relief, needless to say.

This could have been one of those "teachable moments," an opportunity to raise consciousness about our use of fossil fuels, about the need to reduce consumption through conservation and efficiency because of coming short-ages, about the impact of natural-gas production on the environment, about the need to develop new cleaner technologies.

But what did US Americans do with the money we didn't need to spend on heating our homes? You know the answer—we went shopping. Business columnists and economist were buoyantly cheerful and relieved. Rather than focus the country on the meaning of the crisis and the multiple forces at work, and then the need to mobilize around the urgency, we went shopping, we emitted more carbon, we spent more of the earth's capital.

> The global challenge can be simply stated: To reach sustainability, hu-manity must increase the consumption levels of the world's poor, while at the same time reducing humanity's total ecological footprint. There must be technological advance, and personal change, and longer plan-ning horizons. There must be greater respect, caring, and sharing across political boundaries. This will take decades to achieve even under the best of circumstances. No modern political party has garnered broad support for such a program, certainly not among the rich and powerful, who could make room for growth among the poor by reducing their own footprints. Meanwhile, the global footprint gets larger by the day.[29]

What would Jesus say about this—to those of us with the heavy footprint? Is this not the stuff truly worthy of our faith, which is, after all, about the meaning of life, a challenge worthy of being placed at the centerpiece of what it means to be a person of faith in this generation and a human being on this planet at this time in its evolutionary history?

The setting of religion must enlarge

It is time to reread the Gospel of Luke in a vastly enlarged setting, be-yond a local world of tribes and ethnic groups in a desert region grappling with the Roman Empire and the moral and political compromises of reli-gious and tribal leaders. It is time to wrestle with those pesky Beatitudes and Woes, with Jesus's concern for the poor and the marginal, with his denun-ciations of the wealthy and the hypocritical, of the political and religious leaders, with his call to love of enemies, and with the recognition of him in the breaking of the bread. It is time to consider our world of ecological overshoot, environmental degradation, and a vast and growing chasm be-tween rich and poor.

In recent generations our monotheistic religious traditions in the West have not exactly encouraged us to develop a sensitivity to our integral place *within* creation. The human project has been seen as somehow separate from nature, or worse, nature has been viewed as at the service of the human

project, or, in religious terms, at the service of the project of human redemption. Now nature is reminding us of how much we are a part of it, a
species connected organically with all other species. Their fate is our fate.
What we do to them, we ultimately do to ourselves.

Our traditional religious stories do not include our planet's ecological
crisis, having never encountered it. We can probe scripture all we want,
along with the writings of doctors of the church and religious philosophers
of past centuries, and most church documents and pronouncements, but we
won't find the narrative that shows us how to deal with this crisis. So we will
either remain stuck in a religiosity that cannot help us in this, or we will find
the courage to recognize that and come up with something adequate for the
times, something large enough and relevant enough to speak to it.

What we know now is that we are a species among species, that we are in
fact a species way out of line with the balance of nature, and the earth must
put us back in line in order to restore that balance, either with our cooperation or without it.

It is time that we enlarge our own view beyond the setting in which the
gospel story was first situated, that we begin to search for a framework of
meaning, values, and faith that arise from *this* reality, this real world of today, this crowded planet whose very fabric of life is in danger.

Among the truths we ignore at our peril is that we are the result of a long
process of evolution and that all that happened in that evolution is what
made us possible. Most life forms can do just fine without us, but we cannot
do without them. We are the dependent ones; we are the ones cutting off
our own noses to spite our faces. At some point, that sixth great extinction
will take out from under us what we need to live.

We have thrown the earth way out of balance, and it is struggling might-
ily to hang in there with us. There are two ways the earth can restore that
balance—through our conscious cooperation with it, or by doing it for us. If
we choose the latter, the processes of nature will do it the way it has been
done many times before in the earth's evolution, through various modes of
mass die-offs. If we choose the former, then we must choose to live in a way
that the earth can support. And if we want to do this justly, then we must
allow the poor to *increase* their ecological footprint—allowing them to no
longer be poor—while we *reduce* ours, a lot.

The authors of *Limits to Growth* put it this way: "Down is the direction
that throughputs will eventually have to go after the overshoot, by human
choice or by natural limits."[30]

"*The human world is beyond its limits*, and we have to 'grapple' seriously
with the question of what to do. . . . Now, at the turn of the millennium, it is
inexcusable to deny the awful reality of overshoot and ignore the consequences."[31]

Sven Burmeister gave us a golden rule for how to approach this challenge: "per capita resource use should not exceed the level the globe can sustain for all the world's people";[32] that is, our per capita consumption must shrink to a level that the globe can sustain for all people. But more, far more, per capita consumption in wealthy countries must shrink enough so that the per capita consumption of the poor can rise while keeping consumption overall at a level the globe can sustain.

Moral challenges just don't get any starker than this, or more personally threatening. We have expended a lot of energy in this generation trying to ward off this day of reckoning, or hoping it wasn't true, not yet anyway, or mitigating its impacts on our lives. But the day was bound to come, and we are the generation in which it has arrived. We are the ones who have to begin making the really big decisions about the fate of life on this earth.

As Lester Brown writes: "If we cannot stabilize climate, there is not an ecosystem on earth that we can save. Everything will change. As the number of species with which we share the planet diminishes, so too does the prospect for our civilization." The fate of the planet, he says, depends upon whether or not we are able to stabilize both climate and population.[33]

I can't find much in the Hebrew or Christian scriptures to help me here, or in formal Western institutional religions, most of which are also in a bit of a defensive mode regarding the truth of our planetary condition. It affects some orthodoxies and theologies we are loathe to let go, and it affects a lot of comfort and privilege to which some of these institutions, their leaders, and their congregations have become accustomed. We are dealing with realities, with social and economic dynamics, and with a new understanding of the place of the human in planetary history that are not addressed by our Western religious traditions, so they can feel very threatening. Yet, these realities will shape everything from this point on for the human being, affecting everything we think and do, how we live, how we think about the content and meaning of our faith, how we see our presence in this world and its meaning, how we identify ourselves within creation, and how we see our role within the fabric of life, being the only species we know of that can make a conscious choice about what to do.

Keep in mind that the story of overshoot and collapse does not have catastrophe as its inevitable conclusion. None of the writers I have quoted in this chapter believes that all is lost. In fact, their work is intended as wake-up calls to what we can do to save life on this planet, if we begin to act now. Disaster and untold human suffering are where we are going if nothing changes. But if the answer to the question of who is my neighbor does mean all nine billion people with needs for survival and dignity, and if we believe that a central tenet of our faith is to love our neighbor as ourselves, then we have some pretty big life changes to make. Our willingness to make those changes will indicate whether or not we believe that this original charge of our Judeo-Christian faith is still relevant.

We have degraded the natural systems of this earth. None is left undamaged. We have made the planet mortally sick, and soon perhaps incurable. What are we going to do about it? And how do our faith and values inform our answers?

But before we open that reflection, which is part of the destination of this book, let's look at another aspect of our crises, another one that faces this Western society with crucial choices—the rising political violence in a world of scarcity. It is inevitable, and we are going to have to figure out what to do about it.

5

A World of Trouble

or,

It's Going to Get a Bit Tense Out There

*As land and water become scarce, we can expect
competition for these vital resources to intensify
within societies . . . The shrinkage of life-support-
ing resources per person that comes with population
growth is threatening to drop the living standards
of millions of people below the survival level. This
could lead to unmanageable social tensions that will
translate into broad-based conflicts.*
—LESTER BROWN[1]

*Just as shrinking global oil supplies are becoming
ever more concentrated in some of the planet's most
dangerous and politically unstable regions, more
countries desperately need cheap energy to maintain their consumption-driven growth—a situation
that raises the likelihood of wars over oil in places
like the Persian Gulf. And just as gaps between
rich and poor people are widening fast within and
among our societies, new technology has put
staggeringly destructive power in the hands of
people who could be enraged at those gaps.*
—THOMAS HOMER-DIXON[2]

*The upshot of all this is that we are entering a
historical period of potentially great instability,
turbulence and hardship.*
—JAMES HOWARD KUNSTLER[3]

The problem with needing to rid the planet of some eight billion people in order to ensure our way of life within the carrying capacity of the planet is that they are not likely to go away quietly or willingly.

The day I sat down to begin writing this chapter, I came upon this story in the *New York Times:* A group described as "young protestors" attacked an oil pipeline hub in the Niger Delta. The result was a 30 percent cut in Nigerian oil production.[4] This occurred in mid-May 2007 during a period in which gasoline prices in the United States were already on the rise. Nigeria is this country's fifth largest supplier of oil.

At the time of the attack, another group of Nigerians had already been occupying a Chevron oil field for more than a week, cutting supplies to an Italian oil company by 100,000 barrels a day. Three pipelines had been blown up.

None of this was exactly new. Attacks on Nigeria's oil-production infrastructure have been going on for years; it is a target for groups vying for a share of the local wealth, or seeking to assert local power for their ethnic group, or protesting the corruption of the national government.

Also "not new" was what the local violence in Nigeria did to the price of gasoline in the United States. The price of a barrel of oil shot up by 71 cents in a matter of days, and it kept on rising through the month. Over the next couple of weeks the price of gasoline at the pump rose in response, shattering US records on a nearly daily basis.

By the end of May 2007, the price averaged $3.25 per gallon across the United States, in some areas approaching $4. Oil companies were raking in huge profits (ExxonMobil, in particular, was shattering all previous US corporate records).

The violence in Nigeria was only one factor involved in the spiking prices. Also involved were tight domestic refining capacity, which meant turning to more expensive imports to meet demand; the Iraq war, which was going very badly; and fears of a US attack on Iran, another country with huge oil reserves, fears that were rattling nerves across Europe, Russia, and Asia.

This is the world we live in now. Among its defining characteristics— ever-rising energy prices; oil-driven violence; a brittle, overstretched production and supply system; and the potential for sudden shocks from a host of potential disruptions, both natural and political. And that's *before* peak oil.

We are not immune to the forces of history or of nature, though we have tried to live as though we are. No world power lasts forever, and most empires and superpowers tend to overextend and overshoot, simply because it takes increasing amounts of energy and other resources, including a larger and larger military, to maintain and defend such states. Unmatched power attracts other dangerous characteristics, as well—hubris and an air of entitlement from within, and envy and resentment from without.

The vulnerability we face in the United States now has been encountered by great powers many times before. By overusing resources, especially energy and land resources, for the expansion of empire, or economic growth, one day the superpower runs up against the inherent limits of its power base—finitude. Yes, it's true. Against conventional economic wisdom and hubristic blinders, we must insist—the world is actually finite.

Our industrial expansion after World War II relied on cheap and abundant oil, creating the most mobile society in human history, converting farmland to suburban and exurban sprawl, building a vast transportation network for the production and consumption of goods, and then, by the growth logic of capitalism, spreading that system across the globe, helped along with communications networks of increasing complexity and speed that make it possible to get business done in real time 24/7.

Oil remains the fundamental energy base of our economy, the fuel that drives economic growth, which itself is now dependent upon a vast system of globalized capitalism that has seeped into just about very nook and cranny of our world.

As Thomas Homer-Dixon points out:

Without oil, our societies, as they're currently set up, couldn't function. It provides nearly 40 percent of the world's commercial energy supply—that is, energy bought and sold in the marketplace. It's essential for farming, much manufacturing, and countless petrochemicals. And, as we're reminded every time we put gasoline in our cars, it provides nearly all our transportation fuel. Oil powers virtually all movement of people, materials, food stuffs, and manufactured goods—inside our countries and around the world.[5]

As this essential resource grows scarce and its remaining reserves are increasingly concentrated in troubled regions of our world (some of which have stored up rather intense animosity toward the United States and the West), and when we consider in addition the competition for oil reserves from incipient economic giants such as China and India, well, what we have here is a perfect recipe for international tensions of all sorts. And I hate to say it, but because of the way we have organized our economic life in this country, and our wealth, we are among those most likely to fall through the cracks when the weight of demand begins to collapse the energy base of the global economy. Just imagine, for example, living in the exurbs when the oil begins to run out, or trying to find affordable produce in the grocery store. Imagine your energy and food bills. Imagine the cost of getting to work, should you still have a job.

Cheap and abundant oil helped the United States create one of the most dynamic societies in history, but we are quickly approaching its limits, which means that society is about to begin losing some of that dynamism. We simply do not have the technology or energy sources to replace oil in the near future. And it is not possible to put enough land under cultivation for various biofuels to fill our gas tanks; any attempt to do so will compromise our ability to raise enough food to feed the people of this planet. Solar, wind, and geothermal steam do not put fuel in the gas tank. Liquified coal is a fossil fuel that produces dirty CO_2 and acid rain. That direction would be dangerous indeed. Hydrogen power is decades away from practical use. Nuclear energy will not fill a gas tank, even if enough uranium could be found to churn out more of this dangerous power indefinitely. Some of these sources might power rechargeable, battery-operated electric cars, but not on the scale of the mobility we count on or to power ships across oceans and trucks across continents. Nor are we anywhere near being prepared to turn in hundreds of millions of gasoline-powered cars to be replaced by hundreds of millions of electric cars that do not yet exist. Nor have we even considered the amount of electric power—and where it would come from (coal?)—to plug them all in at night.

I might just throw in here that the United States is also woefully, and I mean *woefully*, lacking in mass transit infrastructure (like the efficient, fast, and clean national rail systems they have in much of Western Europe and Japan) to make it possible for us to get out of our cars (you can't demand that people drive less if there are no alternative sources of transportation).

The new foreign policy: It's all about access

Meanwhile, our economy's insatiable thirst for oil (for mobility, transportation, and most global production) and natural gas (for much of our heating and cooling) has become a leading driver of US foreign policies, which are increasingly oriented toward finding and securing access to energy sources in far-distant places at ever-mounting costs to our public finances and our family budgets—not to mention the human costs of staffing military bases around the world (more than 700 in some 130 countries, not counting those in the United States) and the violence this presence tends to exacerbate.[6]

I found this little factoid in Lester Brown's book, *Plan B 2.0*, just to give an example of how insane this has become. He cites a study by Rand Corporation analysts looking at US military expenditures devoted to protecting access to Middle Eastern oil: "Before the most recent Iraq war [such expenditures fell] between $30 billion and $60 billion a year, while the oil imported from the region was worth only $20 billion."[7] That was *before* the war; imagine the ratio now.

Makes sense, doesn't it? Now imagine if we were instead spending that money on reshaping the economy and our "way of life" away from oil.

The energy used for these ventures only hastens the day when we will arrive at peak oil in a society pretty much unprepared for the consequences. Homer-Dixon writes:

> We've already found and tapped the biggest and most accessible oil and gas fields, and we've already exploited the best hydropower sites. . . . Now, as we're drilling deeper and going farther abroad in our search for oil and gas, and as we're turning to alternatives like tar sands and solar, wind, and nuclear power, we're finding that we are steadily spending increasing amounts of energy to get energy.[8]

Like building coal-fired power plants to provide energy for the new ethanol plant that transforms into fuel corn that was produced with huge energy inputs and that replaced crops grown for food which now has to be shipped from farther and farther away to get to your grocery store—all this to find something to replace the gasoline in your car and reduce our dependence on foreign oil. Got that?

Locked into this energy-intensive model, our economy is becoming less "resilient," more "brittle," harder to change, whether because of a consumer mind-set, a tax and investment regimen, or production models that cannot keep up with a rapidly changing world. Just one example, despite the mounting oil crunch and rising gasoline prices, Detroit auto makers still build their business strategies around gas-guzzling vehicles, like enormous SUVs— a strategy that certainly worked for a while. Many of us got addicted to these powerful behemoths. Auto companies guessed correctly about the US American self-image of power and comfort, that in-your-face attitude on the road.

When environmentalists began to challenge car companies and SUV owners in the face of rising evidence of human-caused global warming, auto makers and some politicians tried to convince us that patriotism was involved in our vehicle choices, and that democracy and freedom mean being able to buy whatever vehicle your heart desires.

As prices rose and consumers began turning to more fuel-efficient cars, US auto companies changed not their vehicles (which would have meant investing in new assembly lines and products) but their sales pitches. The federal government took part by offering tax credits on SUV purchases.

As the US auto industry went into financial crisis, Toyota and Honda sales rose steadily. In 2007, Toyota, maker of the hybrid Prius and other fuel-efficient cars, temporarily surpassed the "big three" US auto giants in worldwide car sales. Was anyone really surprised?

Societies that can't adjust quickly to reality, especially in a world going through rapid and profound upheaval, that can't make the shift toward a world of scarcity in accordance with our ecological crises of overshoot and climate change, are headed for decline, or worse, collapse, especially as sudden shocks emerge that can push unprepared societies over the edge—and, friends, shocks are inevitable, as inevitable as 9/11 and Hurricane Katrina. Certainly no one can accuse us of having been prepared for the destruction of a major US city. The portents here are not good.

In most of the countries that still have significant oil reserves (for example, Saudi Arabia, Iraq, Kuwait, Iran, Venezuela, Nigeria, Angola, Sudan, Chad, Russia) and nations with natural-gas reserves (Russia, Central Asia, and Iran), high prices mean greater opportunities to take advantage of countries without these resources, using oil and gas—whether for profit or political leverage or out of sheer desperation—as a base of power, or to apply pressure internationally, or as a weapon in conflicts that are sometimes global in effect but often intensely national or local. What it means is that more and more nations, societies, or small disgruntled groups are able to match our power by striking at our vulnerable spots; they are able to level, or, if not exactly level, certainly bring a new "balance," or imbalance, to power relationships, affecting old alliances, national self-interest, and international security.

Nigeria has oil, and the world's remaining reserves of conventional crude oil and natural gas are concentrated in a few very troubled regions of our world. Because of our dependence on oil, what happens in Nigeria (or Angola or Sudan or Venezuela) now affects us enormously. Because of our dependence on oil and gas, we are headed for more difficult relations with a country like Russia, with whom we will have less negotiating clout on issues that range from climate change to human rights to political reform to trade agreements to military treaties.

Because the "genius" of capitalism in our time is its absolute global reach and fast-paced movement of goods and services, and because it has been fueled by the availability of cheap oil, this energy crisis, combined with our global ecological crisis, is going to show us by direct experience just how interdependent our world has become—or just how dependent we in this country really are. It is not a good time to be making enemies.

Blowback and the balance of power

Beneath many of our current international tensions—blowback from our invasion and occupation of Iraq, corruption in Nigeria's government leading to local insurgencies, our belligerent relationship with Iran, internal crises in Sudan and Chad, our soured relationships with Russia and Venezuela, and a host of other examples—political mines are ready to explode, the fallout from which will affect every single thing that we consume, what we pay for it, and how we move about from place to place, whether to work, to school, to the store, to our kids' soccer games, or to our family vacations.

The United States is but one of many nations that will be competing, with increasing desperation, for dwindling oil and gas reserves. China, with plenty of money to spend, is investing. Where? In Sudan, Nigeria, Venezuela, Zimbabwe, Angola, Chad, Brazil. China needs oil to fuel its breathtaking economic growth rate, 11.1 percent in 2007. It has the money to cut deals and back them up, to return the favor of oil contracts with money for roads and ports. In May 2007, for example, China contracted with Nigeria to put a communications satellite in place for them, maintain it, and then train Nigerian technicians to take it over.

A lot of that money comes from US consumer debt. To fund our huge trade imbalance, the Chinese government has bought up a lot of US currency, loaning that money back to us so that we will continue to purchase China's cheap imported goods. By 2006 China held more than $321 billion worth of US Treasuries (by the end of that year, nearly 45 percent of US debt was foreign owned), leaving us less leverage to pressure the Chinese government on things like human rights, international labor standards, or mandatory carbon reductions.

Might be interesting to point out here that China is expected to become the world's largest economy by 2015.

Russia, meanwhile, sits on enormous oil and natural-gas reserves and is using them in a bid to revive its superpower status in the world. Russian President Vladimir Putin became more openly hostile to the United States during the Bush administration, challenging its swagger in international affairs, especially in Iraq and Iran, where Russia has strategic interests at odds with those of the US government, especially over energy.

Hostility between countries could have serious consequences. Western Europe found this out the hard way. In 2006 a dispute broke out between Russia and the former Soviet republic of Ukraine when Russia's energy giant, Gazprom, raised the price of natural gas that it pumps into the country. Ukraine protested vigorously, and its government began siphoning off some of the gas. So Gazprom turned off the pipeline. The problem was that Russia's supply of gas to Western Europe comes through the same pipeline. Europe went nuts, and Russia promised never to do it again, but the message sent was plenty clear.

Central Asia has been a central focus of the politics of natural gas because it holds large reserves and potentially vital pipeline routes. In an attempt to counter Russia's influence in the region, the Bush administration began negotiations with two former Soviet republics, Turkmenistan and Kazakhstan in Central Asia, over the route for a proposed natural-gas pipeline from Central Asia to Europe. Russia, of course, wanted the pipeline to pass through the Gazprom grid, purchasing the gas from the Central Asian governments then reselling it to Europe at a handsome profit. This was classic power diplomacy competing for vital energy resources.

The Bush administration views Russian control of such a vast flow of natural gas as a strategic threat. Vice President Dick Cheney, with his usual diplomatic aplomb, didn't help things any when he accused Russia of using its energy supplies as "tools of intimidation or blackmail."[9]

In the end, the United States lost this battle. The deal was brokered in May 2007, and the pipeline will go through Russia.

I'm guessing that, a decade ago, none of us would have imagined that two countries whose names we have difficulty remembering or spelling correctly would have such an impact on global politics, on the fate of Europe, and on our lives.

Meanwhile, in Iran, another story was unfolding in 2007. While the Bush administration sat on the sidelines refusing to talk with Iranian leaders until they shut down their nuclear-enrichment program, other countries began stepping into the breach. I'll bet you can guess which ones. Right. Russia and China.

Iran sits on the world's second-largest proven reserves of conventional crude oil and enormous natural-gas reserves, second only to Russia. The government has been desperate to get the investments it needs to bring these reserves into production. China has money to invest, while Russia has the expertise. As one foreign-policy expert, Flynt Leverett, director of the Project on the Geopolitics and Geoeconomics of Energy Security at the New America Foundation, put it, "By refusing to consider a 'grand bargain' with Iran . . . the Bush administration is courting failure in its nuclear diplomacy and paving the way for Russia and China to win the larger strategic contest."[10]

In terms of the global balance of power, Leverett pointed out something that should give us all pause when we think about how the United States will proceed in this increasingly energy-challenged era: "Together, Russia and Iran control almost half of the world's proven reserves of natural gas. If they coordinate their production and marketing decisions, these two countries could be twice as dominant in international gas markets as Saudi Arabia is in the global oil market."[11]

What comes to mind is that line from the Gospel of Luke where Jesus says, "Make friends for yourselves by means of dishonest wealth" (Lk 16:9). Maybe we should have been a bit less arrogant, a little more humble, a little less superior, a bit more caring and compassionate about the rest of the world. Maybe instead of swagger and domination, we should have made more friends. Just a thought.

As all these power dynamics shift, the global economy will be shifting as well. For the past few decades we have seen the rapid globalization of the capitalist system, with more and more corporations moving off shore in search of cheaper labor and resources. In a world of energy scarcity, we may soon discover what a bad long-term strategy this was because we have lost a good percentage of our domestic production capacity. Much of it has been dismantled and moved to faraway places. It is no longer "ours." This means that we are now at the mercy of a globalized production infrastructure for the vast majority of what we consume, not just our energy and food, but also the clothes we wear and the technology we use, like our computers, iPods, and TVs. As energy becomes more scarce, we may begin to see the consequences of having destroyed our local farmlands for suburbs and dismantled our factories in search of cheaper labor overseas.

Homer-Dixon writes:

> Our societies are like the marble that wants to roll back down to the bottom of the bowl, and compared with ancient Rome we're holding that marble much farther up the bowl's side. Colossal flows of high-quality energy make this possible. If we can't sustain these flows, our societies will fall back toward equilibrium—which means, essentially, that their complexity will unravel. And that unraveling, should it occur, would make Rome's decline pale by comparison.[12]

This is quite a world we have made. Some of us might see these words as a wake-up call, an alarm to rouse us from our complacency, to rethink what we are doing here. Perhaps we ought to begin trying to figure out how to make sure that marble flows as gently down the side of the bowl as possible as the energy flow to our way of life begins to decline in a world where we have made many enemies and where some of those holding the energy card are not exactly shining lights in regard to things like respect for human rights, or the rights of women and minorities, or protection of the environment, or tolerance, or economic justice.

Oil = corruption and repression

Okay, let's go back to where we started this chapter, Nigeria. What does all this mean in one impoverished oil-producing nation? And why is it that most nations holding oil reserves are also among those with the largest gaps between rich and poor, or with the most repressive and corrupt governments? What does oil mean to Nigeria?

Well, it means 99 percent of its export revenues and 85 percent of government revenues, according to the World Bank.[13] Oil also means fabulous wealth—for somebody. Where does all that money go? In 2005 the World Bank reported that 80 percent of the country's oil revenues went to 1 percent of the population, while 133 million people, 70 percent of the population, lived on less than $1 per day.[14] Remember that this country is on the list of those with the fastest population growth rates; its population is expected to double by 2050.

The people of Nigeria have almost no other source of export or government revenue, creating a perfect situation for increasingly turbulent internal violence and the potential for social collapse (a failed state), with repercussions throughout the world.

Where will 266 million people go if that happens?

This, too, is what our thirst for oil brings about in our world.

The history of Western colonial domination of Africa is now reaping its
whirlwind. Western powers, either by direct political domination through
empire, or economic domination in more recent decades, have laid waste to
parts of the continent, stolen its natural wealth, and left lasting grievances in
their wake, now being played out among rival ethnic factions or political
insurgencies. We have bled many parts of Africa (and Latin America) dry,
sucking out their abundant natural resources for the benefit of our profit
margins, our economic growth, and our consumer ways.

The price we pay now for the Western world's neglect of things like equity, justice, human rights, local and regional ecosystems, national sover-
eignty, and self-determination will be paid at the pump, the grocery store,
and the shopping mall—and in a mounting defense budget. It is no coinci-
dence that the United States is creating a military presence in Northern
Africa right now. Because of the volatile mix of large oil reserves and political instability, the Pentagon has developed what it calls another "front" in its
"war on terrorism." The Trans-Sahara Counter-Terrorism Initiative, started
in 2005, is working with several African governments to provide military
training and equipment to meet the "threat" of militant Islamic groups—
which many Africans say are a minimal presence at most. But oil is very
present.

Some Africa experts fear the US program will only make things worse,
providing cover for repressive governments while enraging local insurgent
or political opposition groups. Jeremy Keenan, an expert on Saharan Africa
at the University of East Anglia in Britain, says that there is no proof of a
terrorist threat to the United States in the Sahara and that only a "growing
dependence" on African oil can explain the US presence.[15] Keenan worries
that the program is more likely to *attract* terrorism than to counter it, something we might have learned from our experience in Iraq.

Meanwhile, as political turbulence intensified in the wake of reputedly
fraudulent elections in Nigeria, the United States had to ponder what would
happen to the 1.2 million barrels of oil per day that it imports from that
country, about 10 percent of the total consumed here.

Keep in mind that the supply of oil is about as tight as it can get in the
context of the daily functioning of the global marketplace. Each day we humans pretty much consume every drop of oil that is produced and put into
the market. There is little "wiggle room" in this system. What happens in
Nigeria, our fifth largest supplier of oil, truly matters.

In the same way, most of our consumer goods imported from overseas are shipped on demand in real time. Companies don't stock inventory anymore (it is not efficient in the global marketplace); instead, orders are filled as they come in, thanks to computers and satellites, and shipped out, often on the same day. Given this taut system of production, delivery, and consumption, it would not take much to cause serious disruptions to the global economy.

As Homer-Dixon writes: "Today our global, social, technological, and ecological systems are so tightly linked together, and they now operate at such velocity, that the duration of any future breakdown or collapse is likely to be dramatically compressed."[16]

In other words, things will break down faster than we are likely to be able to cope.

The United States spreads its military tentacles

Empires or superpowers seldom have the tendency to say, gosh, we're in overshoot; we must shrink the empire, reduce consumption, and cooperate with the international community to bring our lifestyle back into balance with the earth's ecosystems. Would that it were true. Sadly, the United States is doing what so many other great powers have done in the past—spreading its military weight around the world to try to keep control of the chaos and protect our "vital interests." This poses special moral and ethical challenges for us.

But the part of this story on which I want to focus here is the toll that the military takes on an already damaged and depleted earth. What we decide about how we use the military in this world of trouble will also shape the prospects for the future of human beings and the life systems of the planet. This is because, of all the weighty ecological footprints in this world, none is heavier or more destructive than that of the military, in both human and ecological terms.

The US military is an enormous, wasteful, oil-consuming machine. It is also the world's biggest purchaser of fuel:

> According to the DESC [US Defense Energy Support Center], the Defense Department consumed 132.7 million barrels of oil in 2005! . . . Over the past three years the DESC has bought over 419 million barrels of oil for the DoD at a cost of $21.2 billion. Refiners produce 19.5 gallons of gasoline from every one barrel of oil. So, the 419 million barrels consumed by the DoD over the past three years is equal to about 8.2 billion gallons of gasoline.[17]

In 2006, the Army calculated that it was using about 40 million gallons of fuel every three weeks in Iraq.[18]

Since oil is crucial to our military, you can be sure that it has been looking at the peak-oil scenario and that its estimates of remaining reserves deserve to be taken seriously, given what is at stake for it. The Army concluded a strategic report on oil production that managed to find its way into the public domain in 2006, entitled *Energy Trends and Their Implications for US Army Installations.* The study was conducted by the US Army Engineer Research and Development Center (ERDC). It reinforces the information in our previous chapter regarding peak oil and natural gas.

According to the study, domestic natural-gas and oil reserves are nearing depletion (at current consumption rates, 8.4 years for gas and 3.4 years for oil), while at the global level

> world oil production is at or near its peak and current world demand exceeds the supply. . . . The proved reserve lifetime for world oil is about 41 years, most of this at a declining availability. Our current throw-away nuclear cycle will consume the world reserve of low-cost uranium in about 20 years. Unless we dramatically change our consumption practices, the earth's finite resources of petroleum and natural gas will become depleted in this century. . . . We must act now to develop the technology and infrastructure necessary to transition to other energy sources and energy efficient technologies.[19]

No kidding. Imagine the panic that must keep military leaders awake nights as they ponder this predicament. If this is the situation, then how in the world will the United States be able to project military power around the world by, oh, say, 2020?

"Time is essential to enact these changes. The process should begin now," the report states.[20] Corn ethanol for F-16 jet engines? I don't think so.

To keep the worst from happening—suddenly being unable to fill all those jet fighters and aircraft carriers with fuel—the military is beginning to look at alternative fuel sources, and it is of course looking back here at home to see what we might have available. And what do we have in abundance? Right: coal. Liquified coal. And if this is where the military turns, it will be very bad news for our planet.

Yet, the move has all the appearance of inevitability, unless we can find the political will to ratchet down radically the US military project in every way. If a planetary presence of this size turns to coal for fuel, we will be dealing with a scale of ecological destruction unmatched thus far. And if it is done under the mandate of national security, we mere citizens may be allowed little say in the matter, just as we were allowed little say in the decision to secure the oil assets of Iraq.

On May 14, 2006, the *New York Times* reported that the military is already testing a synthetic fuel, one that will initially be a mixture of traditional crude-oil-based jet fuel with natural gas, and then ultimately with liquified coal, "which is plentiful and cheaper."[21]

Michael Aimone, Air Force deputy chief of staff for logistics, told the *New York Times:* "The United States is essentially the Saudi Arabia of coal. It can be mined relatively inexpensively. We really believe that one of the things we can do to help our country's energy needs is to use the abundance of coal reserves."[22]

Inexpensive? Just what value is he putting on those 470 Appalachian mountaintops already blown to bits?

"Energy is a national security issue," Aimone claims, and God knows how much of the planet will be sacrificed in the name of national security, until there is no security to be had anywhere on this earth.

"Once peak oil occurs, then the historic patterns of world oil demand and price cycles will cease."[23] Eloquently understated. Just let that sentence sink in for a moment. Think about what is being said here. The implications are enormous.

Michael T. Klare writes:

> The end of abundance is not the same thing as outright scarcity. Some commodities, like oil, may become truly scarce in later decades of the 21st century, but they will not disappear altogether. Those with the means will still be able to purchase gasoline and air conditioning and other soon-to-be luxury items. But the *end of abundance* will create a new international environment—a new gestalt, if you will—in which expectations are lowered and struggles over what remains become fiercer and more violent.[24]

Those struggles will involve expenditures of all sorts of capital—military, political, economic, human, and environmental. If we choose to use the weight of the US military to try to be the last society on earth with "the means," we should be prepared for a very violent path, because those with the means will face the fear, the rage, and the resentment of most of the globe's suffering population.

Now ponder putting oneself in this position—just for a moment—from the standpoint, say, of the Beatitudes and Woes.

Whether or not we are comfortable hearing this, the deployment of the US military around the world to fight wars, to carry out clandestine "counter-terrorism" operations, to run secret prisons, to detain and "disappear" suspected terrorists, and more, is directly related to defending the extravagant (by planetary standards), inequitable, and wasteful production and consumption patterns of this global economy, in other words, the lifestyles of the affluent. It is related directly to the presumption of this society that how we are living is how we are entitled to live—forever. That is what is being protected by the projection of US power in a world reaching the end of the fossil-fuel era.

So, as we ponder our ecological future and the moral and ethical demands of a world of scarcity, these issues of power and the temptation to use military force and violence to defend our way of life are inescapable subjects of our reflection. We will have to take a stand, and soon, because we are running out of time for an effective change of course.

Water and food, you know, what we need to live

Unfortunately, energy shortages are not our only problem. As population grows, land and water shortages will also grow more acute, affecting populations in some of the poorest countries of the world. Energy shortages will contribute enormously to this problem, because it takes so much energy to support the model of agricultural production that dominates right now. Homer-Dixon made this point in a 2007 interview with Terrence McNally of the progressive online news publication Alternet. McNally comments that we have created economic and agricultural systems "as if energy would never run out":

> HOMER-DIXON: We've quadrupled the human population in the last century, from 1.5 billion to 6.3 billion, in part because we've had a lot of cheap energy. In particular, that cheap energy has allowed us to increase the amount of energy in our food production systems by 80 fold.
>
> McNALLY: So it takes 80 times more energy to feed four times more people.
>
> HOMER-DIXON: Exactly. We've created a food system, a water system, and cities that are fundamentally dependent upon a resource that is not indefinitely available.[25]

Once again, you see the problem. It's a bit like spending more than $60 billion a year in military expenditures to defend $20 billion worth of oil supply. Mega-agriculture, the Green Revolution, made it possible to feed more people, and so even more people came into the world. Obviously, no one planned that this massive scale of food production would cause exponential increases in population growth and unsustainable overuse of arable land and energy to the point where the whole system could collapse on itself, leading to famine, massive refugee populations, and a death toll one resists contemplating. No one planned this.

But there it is.

The amount of land cleared for agriculture reached a peak over the past couple of decades and is now decreasing. Development in the form of cities, suburbs, parking lots, and other habitat destruction has taken a good portion of it, while other farmland has been depleted through overuse and is now suffering steady erosion from water and wind, as well as increased salinity.

> The world's existing topsoils were generated over thousands and millions of years at a rate averaging an inch per 500 years. The amount of soil available to farmers is now decreasing at an alarming rate, due mostly to wind and water erosion. In the US Great Plains, roughly half the quantity in place at the beginning of the last century is now gone. In Australia, after two centuries of European land-use, more than 70 percent of land has become seriously degraded. Erosion is largely a function of tillage, which fractures and loosens soil; thus, as the introduction of fuel-fed tractors has increased the ease of tillage, the rate of soil loss has increased dramatically.[26]

The guy who wrote this is Richard Heinberg, an expert on peak oil and a research fellow at the Post Carbon Institute in California. His article contained some other pretty depressing information, for example, that 85 percent of fresh water in this country goes into agriculture. To maintain this, we are "drawing down ancient aquifers at far above their recharge rates." To get to that deeper water, we build more powerful pumps, which uses more energy. And he reiterates a point made by Worldwatch Institute: "By 2020 . . . virtually every country will face shortages of fresh water."[27]

Aidan will turn twenty-two that year, and Maya twenty-seven. Francesca and Elliot will still be in high school

They have a rough road ahead of them.

All of this will add to our world of trouble. If you think the world will battle over oil and natural gas, just wait until you see what water shortages can do. This is already a factor in the Middle East, and tensions are rising among states of our own Southwest over how water, especially the Colorado River, will be allocated. In recent years there has been tension between Mexico and the United States over shares of the Rio Grande and the water that flows through the All American Canal, California's Imperial Valley's only water source. In 2006 plans by the local US district water utility to repair the canal and stanch its many leaks drew protests from Mexican farmers who used the seepage from the canal to irrigate their crops. While farmers worried about their crops, environmental groups feared that the repairs could cause local wells to dry up.

José Antonio Rodríguez, chief advisor to Mexico's National Water Commission, told Reuters: "There are more than 100 countries in the world that share watersheds and most of them don't have treaties to cover disputes."[28]

Just imagine the chaos in places like Bangladesh and India, Israel, Palestine and other Arab neighbors in the Middle East, or among the nine African countries along the depleted Nile River, or the dozen nations along the Danube in Europe, or the several Latin American countries along the Amazon.

But while we may not hear much about this, the story apparently not being newsworthy, *somebody* has been thinking about this a lot—the world's militaries. Some of them have started to look at water sources as national security assets, that is, an issue for which one might go to war if necessary. "Are we heading for an era of 'hydrological warfare' in which rivers, lakes and aquifers become national security assets to be fought over, or controlled through proxy armies and client states? Or can water act as a force for peace and cooperation?"[29] Good question. Which approach is the United States likely to choose, given recent history?

Most estimates say that by 2025 more than two billion people will live in areas where there will not be enough water to meet all their needs. Meanwhile, here in this country, we have used water as if there were no tomorrow, which may be the case, and no limits, as if the skies would just keep opening up and giving us what we need. We trust that our ingenuity will get it piped or pumped from wherever it is to wherever we want it.

Dominate and subdue this earth. Bring it into submission for our wants and desires. We have squandered vast amounts of this resource without which we, and our planet, are dead. Around the world, rivers are running dry, lakes are being drained, and aquifers are being depleted. At the same time, more surface water is evaporating because of global warming.

There are few things that will make people more desperate than the need for water. We need it for everything, from sustaining our life to agriculture to running factories. It will take a tremendous level of international cooperation to ensure that more than nine billion people have the water they need for survival. But we aren't the only living creatures in need of water, and nothing will destroy local ecosystems more quickly than the rivers and wetlands running dry. So there is a lot of life out there that needs water.

In the Middle East, where water is perhaps the single most crucial geopolitical issue, "more than 90 percent of usable water crosses international borders. Forget oil: The most precious resource in the region flows in the River Jordan, or resides in the aquifers that link Israel and the occupied Palestinian territories."[30]

Who gets to pump that water out of the ground? And who ensures that it is not done, as it is now, beyond the recharge capacity?

In 2006 Britain's Defense Secretary John Reid noted that global warming was enhancing the potential for "violent collision" between water scarcity and population growth, and that political conflict was one likely result, including increased terrorism. Reid said that military planners were already studying the possible impacts on the country's armed forces and that they must begin preparing for "humanitarian disaster relief, peacekeeping and warfare to deal with the dramatic social and political consequences of climate change."[31]

Well, at least someone is thinking ahead.

The US military has been looking into this as well, concerned that abrupt climate change resulting in water and food shortages could cause conflict across borders, including among nuclear powers (India and Pakistan, for example), and result in hundreds of millions of refugees.

Think of Bangladesh, for example. Lots of people do, worried about the 140 million people who will be vulnerable to rising sea levels and storm surges in the Bay of Bengal. Areas closest to the coast could become inundated, and these folks would have nowhere to go.

"If 60 million people could not survive in Bangladesh," said Paul Rogers, a professor of Peace Studies at Bradford University in England, "yet they are kept there, you would have A) gigantic human suffering and B) progressive very deep radicalization—very, very angry people—and that is not in anybody's security interest."[32]

No, of course not. It's not in anybody's interest in terms of human decency either.

By spring 2007 the US Congress was beginning to get tuned in to these potential threats, perhaps the change in the majority having something to do with it. A bipartisan proposal to require the CIA to undertake a National Intelligence Estimate (NIE) to study the potential impacts of climate change won wide support, despite opposition from some Republican climate-change nay-sayers. The legislation was the first time that climate change was considered a matter of national defense in US public policy, language that makes me feel extremely uncomfortable. The agency was tasked to assess those parts of the world most vulnerable to major political and humanitarian disruptions as a result of climate change. The bill also required the Pentagon to carry out war games that would focus on US security in the event of a catastrophic weather event.

Meanwhile, the UN Security Council held its first-ever discussion of global climate change. The Bush administration and some other members opposed even having the conversation, saying the Security Council was not the appropriate forum for the subject matter, but the discussion went on anyway.

Why is it important to know about these initiatives? For this reason: military and intelligence analysts are already planning for a world that no one is really telling us about. While every day many of our political leaders fan the fears of Islamic terrorism, we are staring right in the face of another crisis that is likely to engulf our world—shortages of the basics of life. This crisis is not being talked about in any of our major cultural institutions (heard a sermon about it yet?). But the US military is making preparations. We are seeing the horrible human and ecological costs of wars, invasions, and occupations to secure energy access and supplies. We have considered the grim prospects for a world in which billions of people, broken nation-states, and small groups of angry people with very destructive capabilities carry out a life-and-death struggle for what they need to live.

Given this situation, wouldn't it be a good idea to start having some serious conversations about how we are going to proceed? Because if we are going to start looking at food, water, and energy shortages, combined with ecological catastrophes, from a national security vantage point, I want to be sure that the people involved in that reflection and analysis are not nationalists, are not motivated by power or profit. I want them to define *security* in the broadest context of dignified life and equitable sharing in a world of scarcity among a growing human population within the context of our life-sustaining biosphere—which means the entire earth community—within the carrying capacity of the planet, ensuring its rich and essential biodiversity for the next generations. I want to be sure that people bring to these discussions profound ethical and moral values, and that will only happen if we make it happen. But first, we need the information about our world that is being kept from us.

Finally, inescapably, 9/11

On the morning of September 11, 2001, I was listening to National Public Radio's *Morning Edition* as I drove into the parking lot of the building in Washington DC where my office was located. About 8:55 they broke in to a story on education to announce that there had been an explosion at one of the World Trade Center towers.

Eight years before this 2001 news bulletin shattered our world, US Americans had shared the shock of the bombing that took place in the World Trade Center underground parking lot. And there were other attacks on US targets over the years—Beirut, the embassies in Africa, the *USS Cole*—each one an announcement of something new taking place in our world. We were not prepared for one of the fastest growing dynamics reshaping our world in the Persian Gulf region, the Middle East, parts of Asia and northern Africa, and dense urban neighborhoods of Europe: the rise of a version of fundamentalist Islam that was spreading like wildfire. There was plenty of fuel to fan the flames—historic grievances, disenfranchisement, marginalization, disrespect, oppression, and US support for governments that clamped down on these movements with ruthless repression, not to mention the generations of grievances among Palestinians who never got the state they were promised.

Just as I was about to turn off the car, the news broke that there had been an explosion at the second tower. Life had changed forever.

Within half an hour, another breaking story reported that a plane had flown into the Pentagon and the building was in flames. This was followed by chaos and confusion. The impression in the moment was unforgettable—the sense that the nation, that Washington DC, was under attack. How bad was it going to be? We didn't know. No one knew.

Then came the reports that a plane had disappeared over Pennsylvania. This fourth hijacked plane was the other flight headed for Washington DC, for either the White House or Congress. The passengers on flight 93 successfully battled to bring that plane down far short of its target.

Just one week after the 9/11 attacks there was more. In early October, a lethal strain of anthrax mixed into a white powder had poured out of envelopes delivered to various media outlets and the offices of two US senators. This was shocking enough, but immediately fears were raised about possible contamination all along the postal route of these envelopes. Eventually, five people died.

Terror had indeed become a part of our lives.

Several years later, with the war in Iraq still raging and the story of the destruction of New Orleans now part of this unfolding drama of our altered world, I ask myself if it is possible that nothing fundamental changed in this society after all these events. Have we integrated them into our lives somehow and just moved on? Every one of them was an announcement about our world screaming for some attention. Every one of them was a mirror reflecting back to us something about ourselves. Every one of them was an alarm going off, a chance for us to wake up, to begin to do something differently. Did we just turn off the alarm and go back to sleep—over and over again?

If even these events haven't changed us (in fact, it became an odd mark of defiance and patriotic bravado *not* to change our lives), what will? What will it take? A war gone out of control with a death toll in the thousands for Americans, tens of thousands of lost limbs and eyes and battered brains and wounded psyches, hundreds of thousands of Iraqis dead, injured, millions displaced? Will that do it? How about a nuclear weapon set off in a major US city, as some intelligence experts fear? Would that do it? And if it did, what kind of human beings would we be then? How would we react? What kind of world would we make in response?

What kind of world did we make after 9/11? After Katrina? How did this country respond to those two unprecedented events?

In a world of scarcity, like the one unfolding in this generation, we are going to have decide what is most important to us. That is not going to be easy. It will ask a great deal of us, but there is no avoiding the challenge. It is right here.

We are living in a world of trouble. It will be a volatile, turbulent, violent world for a long time to come as we pass through this difficult stage, this transition from our industrial and post-industrial world to, well, something else. In Chapter 1, we reflected on our need to recover after disasters, with their huge toll in human lives—earthquakes, hurricanes, and floods. We will need this resilience as never before in our human evolution, because this violence among the human community, reflective of and also in part a product of the violence we have done to the earth, is going to be with us for a while. Verses from our gospel tradition will shriek at us from the pages, and we will be asking ourselves how it will be possible to live them—"love your enemies," "turn the other cheek," "if anyone wants to sue you and take your coat, give your cloak as well," "leave your gift there before the altar and go; first be reconciled to your brother or sister," "woe to you who are rich."

What role will our fading superpower play in this turbulent world? While we will feel challenged and vulnerable on all sides, we will still have enormous power to fan the flames of violence—inevitably so if we still believe we are entitled to grab and hold whatever we need to try to keep our way of life going for as long as we can.

Each one of us will have to wrestle with this question: do we believe we have such a right? Much is riding on our answer.

6

The End of the American Dream

or,

When Dream Turns into Nightmare

> *There are two things we can say with certainty: never in history have the differences of income and opportunity among us been so great, and these differences are prima facie evidence of a moral failure of almost incomprehensible magnitude.*
> —THOMAS HOMER-DIXON[1]

> *The human species is, in a word, an environmental abnormality. It is possible that intelligence in the wrong kind of species was foreordained to be a fatal combination for the biosphere.*
> —E. O. WILSON[2]

Perhaps as one example, the American Dream . . .

When I was a kid growing up in Wauwatosa, Wisconsin, I lived with my big Catholic family on a dead-end street with a field near the end of the block and a clear path down to the Menomonee River. This was the "sticks," the end of the line, a heavily wooded suburb sitting on the west side of the City of Milwaukee. Beyond us just down the road a mile or so the pavement turned to dirt, and on to the countryside.

In those days the sky was so clear we could see the Milky Way at night. In mid-August and mid-autumn my mother would bring us all outside to watch the annual meteor showers right there from the backyard. On warm summer nights the evening air was aglow with fireflies. Some weekends, when my mother stayed up nearly all night long cleaning the house, she managed to catch glimpses of the northern lights from the front porch.

Through the years, the chase to the suburbs moved on all around us. First came the decision to build the freeway, I-94, a straight shot west from Milwaukee to Madison and on to Minnesota. Then came the first suburban shopping mall just a mile down the road. Then we lost our precious dead-end as the city cut the north-south road through for traffic flow to the interstate. Roads beyond Wauwatosa were paved over and small towns connected by highways.

The sprawl eventually engulfed us and continued on west beyond the suburbs all the way to Waukesha, some fifteen miles away. It trampled the local farms and thousands upon thousands of acres of woods until now it crawls up the hills of the glacier-carved Kettle Moraine area right up to the border of the state parks.

Meanwhile, south of the city was the farm belonging to Henry and Violet Mahr, just about the oldest friends my parents had. When we were kids, we would visit the farm from time to time—the barns and the cows and the cornfields. Despite the "yuck" factor for us city kids, we drank unpasteurized milk there fresh from the cows and ate corn plopped into hot water right after picking.

Then I-94 was cut right through their property, making its way down to Chicago. By 1963 the old North Shore Line, an inter-urban rail company that connected the towns between Milwaukee and Chicago, was gone, the tracks ripped up. Southeastern Wisconsin made way for automobiles, and the suburbs kept growing.

You can't see the Milky Way from our family home anymore; in fact, most nights you can barely see all the stars of the Little Dipper. The best viewing for the meteor showers is at least fifty miles away. A few fireflies sparkle here and there on warm summer evenings, nothing like those nights when we were kids, when they glowed by the hundreds and we went out with our jars to capture them (they were always dead in the morning, an early childhood lesson in how nature will not submit to us, even to our love for it).

The family house was built in the 1930s, and my folks bought it in 1947, bringing the first two babies, and soon after the third. I came along in 1949, and then three more after me. Onto our beautiful lannon stone home, my folks built a large addition for the growing family. There was a big backyard, no fences up or down the block, so we kids had the run of the neighborhood. Neighbors talked to each other just about every day in the yards and across the alley. We had a wiffle ball "field" in the alley with tar marks as bases. Next door were two elderly women, sisters, both widowed. We all watched out for them, and then for the one that was left alone for many years after her sister died. Sometimes she would walk over to our house and sit in the kitchen and grouse with my father about the stock market. Always there was a homemade strawberry schaum torte for our birthdays and pea soup in the winter.

My folks paid $18,000 for that house (about $167,000 in today's dollars), and they paid that off in five years, burned the mortgage, one of the great rituals of middle-class life back in the 1950s. The addition cost another $5,000 ($38,000), a big family room and a bedroom above for three growing boys. That was a pretty nice life in those days.

My father was in the music business, had his own big band and was a music contractor. He was much loved in the city, a local star. He met my mother when he hired her out of high school to sing with the band. She did that for more than a decade, until too many babies made the night gigs too difficult. My father has his name, Steve Swedish, carved on the Wall of Fame in the city's Performing Arts Center.

He also never finished high school. Sixth child of a Croatian immigrant family, he grew up in dreadful urban poverty after his father died in a typhoid epidemic in 1910, leaving his Ma with nine kids. His older brothers went to work as teenagers, and the oldest paid for the music lessons. Despite joining the upper middle class economically, my father was always more comfortable with his cruder, less educated, working-class roots. He was not sophisticated, but he was talented, and he knew exactly how to play to the City of Milwaukee.

My father was frugal and successful; though never *rich*, especially with seven kids to support, he made a comfortable, if crowded, life for his family. He paid for each of his kids to get through college. My first semester at the University of Wisconsin–Milwaukee cost him $175 for fifteen credit hours ($1,082 in today's dollars). My last semester at the University of Colorado cost just under $900 (about $4,100 today) for out-of-state tuition.

This was the quintessential twentieth-century American Dream, the promise of a hardworking generation passing on a better life to its children, the myth of the self-made man made incarnate there in Milwaukee. My family rode the wave of the post–World War II middle-class explosion, built on the industrialization boom that was birthed in the war factories that had so successfully helped defeat the empires of Germany and Japan.

What a time to grow up in America. For the first time, nice homes, pretty cars, and good education were not just the privilege of the wealthy. A guy like my father could create a music business from nothing and build a solid upper-middle-class dream in the new suburbs for his wife and large family, while my uncles bought homes and cars from the union wages they made in the factories or the railroad.

Who wouldn't want to believe this would never end? Who in the world would want to see the dark side of something so wonderful?

The problem was, this was a brief and unique time in US history, indeed in the industrial, capitalist development of the West. But when it is the social framework that contains your whole life experience, when you know nothing else, as with my baby boomer generation, you make assumptions about the world. Unfortunately, that is what we have done—made assumptions—that this way of life, and this linear progression in affluence within the span of a generation or two, is not only the norm but the model for quality of life, the standard, what I need to feel good about myself, what I need to believe I have either attained or can aspire to in order to give my life meaning. Rather than examine the reality base of this mythology, we prescind from it.

Now this world view, this generational experience, is in our way as we try to address the most profound crises ever faced by humans. It is our blind spot, our stumbling block, the root of our denial. We keep picking the splinters out of our eyes (replacing light bulbs, looking for alternative fuels for our cars, purchasing hybrids if can afford them, recycling) so that we can see a clear path to our future comfort and well-being, but we've got a beam in there so big we cannot see what's happening all around us.

My mother turned ninety the year I wrote this, and she was still living in that house where she raised all her kids. It remained for her a symbol of something very important. She, too, had known poverty, in this case as huge and tragic loss since her family was clobbered by the Depression of the 1930s. A German family with deep roots in Milwaukee over three or four generations, her father and grandfather and other ancestors were upstanding business people well regarded in the community.

After the crash of 1929, my grandparents and their four daughters saw their lives quickly unravel. First they lost the summer cabin on a lake island, then the bank took the car, then they were evicted from their home. It was the first eviction; there would be others when they could not make rent, each move representing a descent into worse urban poverty. My mother worked in a candy factory after high school to bring home a couple of bucks for her mother to buy food, and on weekends they pulled a wagon to the site where the county handed out free cheese, flour, butter, and other staples.

When my father bought the house, it meant dignity. It meant she would never know such degrading poverty again. One has to understand where that early twentieth-century generation came from, the one that went through the Depression and World War II, many of them from recently arrived immigrant families pulling themselves up by their own will and hard work, to appreciate the deep roots of this cultural orientation that continues to form our national mythology, to appreciate why my mother has such spiritual and emotional need to die in her home.

From those psychological roots, and from this still point of our lives that is that house, my siblings and I have had an amazing vantage point from which to view the rise of that generation and the expectations that grew out of it, what affluence meant to them from *their* experience, the meaning of the beautiful house with a big backyard. From there we witnessed the beginnings of the suburban sprawl that soon surrounded us, the sprawl that began to swallow up that dream and sap it of its original meaning, the connections with those origins long gone. From that vantage point we viewed the transition through the lifetime of the baby boomers, who had been given so much of material things and well-being from a generation whose motivations we ignored or forgot, until we saw those lifestyles as birthright, normal expectation of a fully mature adult life. We saw our generation transition from an economy that produced things to one that consumes things, from an economy that had a place for people like my uncles and their aspirations within a middle class to one that no longer has much space for them at all.

Meanwhile, few people are so stationary anymore; life became frenetically mobile in my generation, social ties were cut as people moved around the country chasing the Dream, a higher salary, a new position in the company, retiring to a warmer clime, or selling from here to there all across the country and then beyond our borders. Symbols of "making it" now had to do with each move meaning a bigger, more valuable house and a higher standard of living, not relationships or community. Enormous pressure was put on nuclear families to take care of relational and emotional needs, and in many cases they were simply not up to it. Extended family was now really extended; children lost cross-generational intimacy with grandparents, aunts, uncles, cousins.

My mother and her children lost all of that as her family chased the Dream, moving to Southern California back in the 1950s, when the population explosion took off around L.A.

For us, that old family home in Wauwatosa maintained a sense of roots, of family, even after we too were long scattered. But it also provided us this scenic overview of a societal journey that is now leading our nation toward the edge of a cliff. We didn't just go with the changes; we also stayed in one place and watched them happen all around and beyond us.

My father was frugal, that is, he saved. Because he saved, he never carried significant debt. Because he saved, we didn't have a lot of *things*. Instead, we shared the one TV and two cars, never had a room of our own, went to school and friends' houses on city buses, and spent a lot of time in "unstructured play," meaning creative and spontaneous. Because my father saved, my mother has the resources to stay in her house with quality home care until the day she dies. This freedom from financial worry in one's elder years is now becoming a privilege for a shrinking minority of well-off people in this country. For the rest of us, we can hardly imagine so secure an old age.

An unaffordable middle class

This was certainly a privileged life within a society always marked by vast injustice (for example, how "white" that suburban world was—and still is), but it was a life shared more widely throughout the society than we can ever imagine now. Through this one lifetime that is mine, our society morphed from one built upon a growing middle class saving for a secure future and passing on the inheritance of its hard work to its children, to a society of consumers and the most indebted nation in the world, a society with a rapidly shrinking middle class holding a negative savings rate, a nation consumed by things that we buy and discard, mostly on credit, in the firm belief that this is the only way to create jobs and have a decent life. We have watched people chase the Dream as it became more and more illusory, an exclusive possession of the privileged, while most people struggled to keep up, fell behind, or were left out altogether.

Now for the past couple decades or more, we have been chasing an ever-more expensive and frenzied American Dream with credit cards and refinanced mortgages, working more hours, taking fewer vacations, spending less time doing the simple things we enjoy. More and more of our monthly expenses are paid out as interest on our debts, money straight from our pockets to banks and other lenders.

Meanwhile, so many of the gains won by the workers of that generation—from the forty-hour work week to decent pay to health benefits to pensions, gains won for the most part by organized labor—are disappearing right along with the Dream they helped enable.

Something important happened while we were out shopping and refinancing our mortgages to take out cash for still more consumption, those bigger houses, or trips to shopping malls, or an SUV or two. What happened is this: the era of the American Dream came to a crashing end. Shh! Don't tell anyone. They don't want you to know. Because if you ever jump off this Sisyphusean treadmill, if you decide to pay your bills, get out of debt, get rid of the credit cards, turn in the SUV, take public transit to work and school, and scale down to a simpler lifestyle, you will be betraying an economic system and the ideology upon which the wealth of corporations and their stockholders absolutely depends. Most of all, you will be dangerously exposing the great fallacy of this economic system—that it cannot, and does not intend to, support a large middle class that can assume a socially secure way of life or make a place for everyone on the upward climb up the economic ladder. It cannot afford it, and it knows it cannot afford it. It cannot keep its wealth, much less increase it and concentrate it, and afford to do that. That's why it has collapsed the life support of the middle-class worker.

The economic transition witnessed by my generation—from an economy that built the middle class to one that can no longer afford one—is part of the story of what happened in this one lifetime that is mine, this generation of post–WWII baby boomers. If you think about it, the change has been breathtakingly swift, the era of the mythical stable suburban middle class strikingly brief. Yet, we have constructed a whole cultural value system around it.

One of the most interesting characteristics of this new economic era is how economic growth has detached itself from production, from the wages of workers, from the ability of the poor to participate in the system. It is detached from *real things*. Wealth flows to fewer and fewer people, and the number of workers needed to support growth, or wealth generation, is shrinking. The economy *grows*, wealth *grows*, yet workers' wages slump, benefits for workers are lost, and production moves off shore. When companies say they can no longer afford health insurance for workers or begin reneging on promised pensions, they are saying the same thing—we cannot afford a large economically secure middle class and still increase profits.

It is also within this one generation that the global population grew from 2.5 billion to the 6.5 billion that it is as I write this in June 2007. In that lifetime, the US population doubled from 150,520,000 to 301,100,00—so no wonder we are feeling a bit crowded. That's our share of the global population explosion, with another hundred million expected by 2025, surpassing 500,000,000 by 2045. That's how many people Aidan and Francesca and Elliot will be living with when they are forty-seven, forty-three, and forty-one.

If we consider these economic trends in the context of all we have learned in the previous chapters, do we really believe that this linear Dream of increasing affluence for generation after generation has any basis in reality?

The suburban working/middle class created by high-wage factory work is disappearing. It is being replaced by upper-middle-class professionals as the costs of houses, health insurance, and school tuition ascend beyond the reach of most wage earners. Those still working at places like GM, or on construction sites, are finding themselves *descending* the economic ladder, taking losses in pay and benefits that once belonged to their parents' generation. The largest job-growth sector is the service sector, and to be sure, data-base entry or managing a McDonalds franchise or being a bank teller will no longer buy you a nice house in a pleasant suburb, and most new jobs will not guarantee you health insurance, much less a pension—pensions are turning out to be ephemeral, an odd phenomenon of a few decades of the twentieth century. They have been replaced in some companies, if you're lucky, with 401(k) investments, funds put into the stock market, a shift of burden from the corporation to the individual, and, by the way, good luck.

I lived for a long time in a little section of Takoma Park, Maryland, made up mostly of small brick capes and tiny square colonials built in the 1940s. When I moved there, the neighborhood was quite mixed—retired government workers living on their pensions, middle-aged workers raising their kids, and people like me—folks working in the non-profit sector without exactly great salaries. Neighborhood parks dotted the town; it was progressive, family friendly, had good public schools, and a large number of rent-controlled apartments. In the space of five to ten years, these little houses shot up in value from an average $150,000–$160,000 to today's $400,000–$600,000 and higher. Many apartment buildings, whose owners always chafed against the profit-making limits of rent control, are converting to condominiums. One-bedroom apartments are starting at $160,000–$180,000.

Good schools and sweet parks are no longer affordable for that disappearing class of workers and retired, much less we activist types. Takoma Park is dramatic, but a version of this is going on all across the country. Why does this happen? Well, though *we* may not be able to afford to live there anymore, *somebody* can, somebody with a lot of money. And the change in class structure of home ownership will change the dynamics of the neighborhood very quickly.

Let's look at it on a global scale. If we cannot absorb 300,000,000–500,000,000 people in what is currently the world's richest country into a "growth economy," what about the rest of the world? It would be problematic to try to integrate the 2.5 billion people on earth in 1950 into this economy (remember that Burmeister put the limit for living at the level of the United States at half a billion); in a world of 6.5 billion, the belief that we can continue to grow wealth like this, especially for a shrinking minority of rich people, is leading very rapidly to disaster. As we learned in Chapter 4, the earth is being crushed in the attempt, and the deepening inequities are leading to more resentment and political instability. After another two to three billion people join us, if we continue the trajectory of this global economy, ecosystems all around the world will begin to collapse and social violence will be a hallmark of our times.

If we approach this from the perspective of faith and values, or even just basic human decency, we begin to realize that the attempt to hang on to such privilege in a world of growing scarcity and multiple ecological crises is quickly becoming morally repugnant—before the 1.1 billion people who live on less than $1 per day, before the 2.7 billion people living on $2 per day, before the two to three billion soon to join us, and before our children and their children's children on to the "seventh generation."[3]

The capitalist system, the global economy as it currently functions, cannot provide a decent life for the vast majority of human beings on the planet. And it cannot continue on the course it is on right now without destroying the planet. The sooner we admit this, the sooner we can get about the business of finding another way to live on the earth.

I can wish that it was not my generation, but unfortunately we are the one saddled with this responsibility—to tell the generation coming up behind us that this way of life is over, not because we are making a virtuous choice, but because it has become impossible. We are the generation that must tell them that most of them will not be able to achieve the middle-class and upper-middle-class status that so many of us once assumed by birthright, much less aspire to have more. We are saddled with the responsibility of telling our young people that they will have to learn to live without all that the affluent of our parents' generation assumed was the meaning of "making it" in the United States of America.

Now I wonder how we will do that, face them with this truth, if we are not willing to accept responsibility for the situation we have created, to be honest with them about it, and begin doing the things we need to do to ensure a habitable world for them.

We cannot possibly do this to our children—hold on to our "way of life" while telling them they cannot have it, and oh, by the way, we are leaving you a depleted world in the meantime. Like it or not, as the generation of "the boom," we need to become the bridge generation, the one that begins the transition, and with our young, do all we can to ease that marble down the side of the bowl.

The very economy of the world has changed in any case. We are not going to become a world of nine billion consumers living a middle-class dream (remember, we would need to find another five or six earthlike planets to do so). What is really happening is that this global economy has less and less room for all of us now. Income gaps are widening, and wealth is concentrating. We feel the pain of the transition without understanding what is happening to us and how permanent it is.

The economic reality is not separate from all the other dynamics of our world—of ecological overshoot and global climate change, and the potential for greater conflict over increasingly scarce basic resources. To think we can have a growth economy in a world of scarcity and ecological stress is wishful thinking.

We must become downwardly mobile. The American Dream is not sustainable. For a long time it has been unjust and inequitable—now it has moved beyond the means of the earth to support it.

Road kill

Some writers have compared our consumer way of life to drug addiction. We are addicts to the power of money to buy things. But the fix wears off

pretty quickly after we buy the "thing," so we go back out to get the next
high, and then the next.

We are certainly an insecure people; we appear to need outside measures
to feel okay about ourselves, measures established by others, not from within.
We at times seem to be an amazingly gullible people, pulled by fads and ads
and the power of the media that guide our behavior, our consumer choices,
our lifestyles.

But we should not underestimate the power of corporations to manipulate us through the mass media. They are the "pushers" of the drug to which
we are addicted, creating needs and discontents that can only be eased by
what they are selling, whether the "affordable" home financed with interest-only, subprime mortgages, the latest credit-card offer in the mail, the
ads that flash at us through our computer screens, what shrieks at us from
the TV while watching the Super Bowl. These guys understand the US
American consumer more than I like to admit, and they are master manipu-
lators.

In my age of innocence, I remember my surprise, when working to complete my degree in psychology back in the 1970s, that many of the recruiters
who came to our department were from corporations—what did corporations need with psychologists?

Television, always intended as a means to sell products, is a mesmerizing
and socially cohering media. It works in more ways than we may care to
admit. Think, for example, of the cultural unifying factor of the *American
Idol* phenomenon spawned by the Fox TV network—we watch the show
and then we watch news stories about us watching the show, and then there
is a whole national conversation about it among bloggers and IM-ers, and
then you feel left out if you're not in on it, and then you find yourself actually spending many hours of your precious life on this earth taking part in
this national fad. And what is the show, after all, but reaffirmation of, well,
the American Dream? Living vicariously through TV game shows and con-
tests has always given Americans a boost of adrenaline.

Along with shows like *American Idol* (that name alone is so revealing of us,
isn't it?), another example of the mesmerizing and distorting power of television is the way it gives us the news, tells us what is important. I will give
just one example. I turned on MSNBC one day in June 2007 to catch up
on the day's events. The first story was a very powerful, moving, and deeply
disturbing account of one military unit in Iraq that had suffered several
casualties from snipers and explosive devices. The account was accompanied by grim photos. The soldiers' stories were laced with shock, grief,
courage, anger, and a lot of doubt about what they were doing there. Immediately following this story, with no break at all, came a story about the
travails of Paris Hilton facing a jail term for violating parole on a drunk-
driving charge. The newscasters, taking an almost imperceptible pause and

an exchange of glances (left me wondering if they knew how appalling this was), switched in a moment from a very somber tone to lighthearted and cheery.

What are we to make of such a society? And why should we be surprised that we have such a hard time understanding what is truly important, even worth a moment of our time?

In searching for more examples of what is wrong with us and why, I was amazed all over again by the constant flow of manipulative messages and images that fill our days. Newspapers have become vast advertising journals, the ads getting more print space now than the news, because it is the only way the papers can stay in business. On the front page of a special real-estate advertising section of the *New York Times* on September 5, 2006, there was an enhanced photograph of a very appealing corner of an isolated home tucked in a beautiful natural setting. What we saw was the edge of a deck at sunset overlooking a lovely waterfront landscape, warm lights coming from the elegant room adjacent to the deck. The ad had just these words: "Show us how you want to live. We'll help you get there." Inside the section were photos and information for real estate that only the wealthy can access. But the message is one this society has bought into for a very long time—tell us how you want to live, and it shall be done to you.

Here is another, an advertising cover for *Time Magazine* that showed up uninvited at an old address. The ad is for the investment firm Smith Barney. On the cover, it reads: "I am working wealth." Inside is this message:

> Working wealth—earn your first dollar by your labors. Get up early, work late. Get up the next day and do it again. Keep doing it, even after the dollars start adding up. Smile at the challenges. Curse at idleness. Be true to your dream. Don't stop until you achieve it. Then dream another dream. And work to achieve that. Pass on your values. Not just your assets. Give your family a better life, too. Leave no statues. Leave signs of significance. Working wealth wears no uniform and meets in no club. But you know who you are. We at Smith Barney would like to say one thing to you. Welcome.

I get tired, anxious, and stressed just reading it. Actually, I can hardly find a better definition of a life of alienation that can kill the spirit, along with alienation from everything we need now to save ourselves.

Sometimes what the advertising world offers us is more direct, cruder, but right to the point. During the 2005 Major League Baseball post-season telecasts, one commercial really struck me. It was an ad for a Chevy pickup truck, tearing over the earth. It included the words: "Lead, follow, or be road kill."

Yikes!

A yawning gap

To give us a sense of how much the economic realities of our world have changed, the context for the argument I am making about the demise of the American Dream, I gathered up some of the facts that present a rather grim statistical picture of our situation, that show just how exclusive the club of the economically secure and wealthy has become.

Here are some of those facts:

We have known for a long time that the distribution of global wealth is inequitable, but it is becoming dramatically worse. The gap between rich and poor is vast—now it is widening as never before. A report from the World Institute for Development Economics Research of the United Nations University shows that by 2000, "the top 1 percent of the world's population—some 37 million adults with a net worth of at least $515,000—accounted for about 40 percent of the world's total net worth. . . . *The bottom half of the population owned merely 1.1 percent of the globe's wealth.* The net worth of the typical person—whose wealth was above that of half the world's population and below that of the other half—was under $2,200." This article notes that rich countries, most especially our own U.S. of A., have "experienced . . . a spectacular buildup of assets" (emphasis added).[4] Those assets include stocks, government bonds, land and other property, and they are concentrating into fewer and fewer hands.

The United States accounts for 4.7 percent of the global population but holds 32.6 percent of global wealth. Nearly four out of every ten persons among the richest 1 percent is a US American.

Do we still think people around the world resent us for our freedoms?

While a billion of the world's children suffer from severe lack of nutrition, water, health care, decent housing, and education, in 2006 the world had

> 793 billionaires with a combined wealth of $2.6 trillion—equivalent to 20 percent of the United States' annual gross domestic product (GDP). Between 2003 and 2006, the number of billionaires increased 66 percent, and their total net worth rose 86 percent. If they'd liquidated this wealth in 2006, they could have hired the poorest half of the world's workers—the 1.4 billion workers who earn a few dollars a day—for almost two years. Indeed, an average billionaire could have hired nearly 2 million of these workers. Never before have so few had the ability to command the labor of so many.[5]

But they don't, despite having the ability. They just keep on accumulating more wealth. What they command is the ability to control the global economy to their benefit; what they command are resources that could help change the fortunes of this suffering world.

Meanwhile, the disparities within the United States are as great as those without. In fact, the United States is second in the world in wealth disparities—only Switzerland outdoes us. In 2007 income disparities were near the records set in 1928, just before the stock market crash and the Great Depression. Data reported in the *New York Times* in March 2007 showed that income gains in the United States in 2005 went mostly to the richest one percent of us—an average gain of $139,000, resulting in an average income of $1.1 million. Over the past three decades, the share of the wealth for the top 1 percent doubled. "The new data also shows that the top 300,000 Americans collectively enjoyed almost as much income as the bottom 150 million Americans. Per person, the top group received 440 times as much as the average person in the bottom half earned, nearly doubling the gap from 1980."[6]

Now, this was happening in a time of modest economic growth and record gains in the US stock market. And it points out one of the least attractive trends of this era of global capitalism—economic growth is disconnecting from the production of goods. It is instead increasingly connected to investments, and wealth is going disproportionately to the investors. More than ever before, wealth is generated by growth in the stock market and corporate profits. In other words, if you are rich, you are getting richer. If you have money to invest, you are likely becoming better off. If you have a large diversified stock portfolio, you have a shot at a comfortable life. If you are working for wages, your share of wealth is declining steadily.

The article also points out that

> the top 10 percent of Americans collected 48.5 percent of all reported income in 2005 . . . an increase of more than 2 percentage points over the previous year and up from roughly 33 percent in the late 1970s. The peak for this group was 49.3 percent in 1928.
>
> The top 1 percent received 21.8 percent of all reported income in 2005 . . . more than double their share of income in 1980.[7]

Numbers to boggle the mind—"The top tenth of a percent reported an average income of $5.6 million, up $908,000, while the top one-hundredth of a percent had an average income of $25.7 million, up nearly $4.4 million in one year."[8]

Meanwhile, a study conducted by McClatchy Newspapers revealed a stunning increase in poverty in the United States. Results reported in February 2007 showed that the number of us living in "extreme poverty" is at a thirty-two-year high: "Nearly 16 million Americans are living in deep or severe poverty. . . . The number of severely poor Americans grew by 26 percent from 2000–2005."[9]

What is the definition of severe poverty? A family trying to exist on $9,903 per year, or an individual on $5,080.

Try it sometime.

So now let's look at corporate wealth. Here the numbers can stop normal brain function. Skyrocketing pay packages for top corporate officers have been raising eyebrows in recent years, and they should—they should raise more than that. From 1990 to 2004, while the average worker's pay "remained almost flat at $27,000," the "average chief executive pay has risen from $2.82 million to $11.8 million, representing a ratio of more than 400 to one."[10]

Societies with wealth this skewed don't usually do well. And, by the way, while we know that a family cannot be raised in this country on an income of $9,900, millions of others are trying to do it on that current average worker's pay of $27,000. Yeah, try doing that, too. Millions of us are, and having a very hard time getting by. Actually, some 35 percent of us had an income of $25,000 or less in 2005. Another 36 percent were getting by on incomes of $50,000 or less, which means different things depending on where you live—an okay life in Iowa, but barely making it in New York City. The median income in 2005 was $46,326 ($31,000 in 1990 dollars). Meanwhile, just 7 percent of us had incomes above $100,000.[11]

We've come a long way from the middle-class dream we grew up on, at least the one we used to envision, the one in which my uncle, my father's oldest brother, could work all his life for the railroad company, in his later years as a train conductor, make a decent wage, buy a house, retire, and live in that house on his railroad pension and Social Security until his ripe old age. He even had a little inheritance to share with his nieces and nephews when he died.

In our time, just a couple of decades later, the "middle" has become quite economically stretched, stressed, and insecure. It is having trouble making mortgage payments, meeting college tuitions, paying for doctors, and even keeping food on the table. According to the Urban Institute, in 2002, four million "nonelderly low-income *families* said they had used a food pantry at least once in the past 12 months" (emphasis added).[12] Nearly half of those seeking help from food pantries were *working parents* with children. For a growing portion of the population in this country, the American Dream is fading indeed. In fact, we have crossed the threshold. A study conducted by a group of NGOs released in May 2007 indicated that US men in their thirties are now making less than their father's generation.[13]

Living on credit

So if all of this is true, how is it, then, that we continue to be one of the world's leading consumer nations? How are we able to buy all this stuff? Well, that's that other part about being the world's biggest debtor nation. Simply put, we have been doing it on credit. We have been paying for our increased consumption with a whole lot of personal debt.

To help us keep doing that, the Federal Reserve has been keeping interest rates low, reducing our incentive to save and increasing our incentive to borrow. This keeps us buying things; this keeps the economy churning. And it kept us buying houses, as mortgage interests rates tumbled during the 1990s. This made houses more affordable since the cost of borrowing was cheaper. This caused speculation in the housing market, and prices in many markets soared. To keep us buying, mortgage lenders started sweetening the package, offering three- and five- and seven-year adjustable rate mortgages, and eventually even interest-only mortgages. More people were borrowing to buy homes they actually could not afford. Then, with the value of homes rising, millions of people refinanced at lower rates, taking money out not to save or to pay off debt but to spend, to consume, and we really went on a spending spree. Between 2000 and 2006, mortgage debt rose from $4.8 trillion to $9.5 trillion. It felt like having money, but what we were actually spending was *debt.*

Meanwhile, our credit cards were in overdrive as well. Despite interest rates that hovered between 13 and 20 percent, we made lavish use of them. Over the past decade, credit-card debt as a portion of GDP rose to 18 percent. Millions of people are making only their minimum monthly payments, which means their interest debt just keeps rising. By 2006, the personal savings rate of Americans had dropped to zero.

So what the Fed was calling economic growth was actually debt expansion. Debt spending by consumers has kept the economy afloat, and a terrible reckoning may be in the offing. Corporations and the Fed wanted you to keep spending to keep the economy "growing," but since we couldn't afford it, they lowered the cost of borrowing. If this appears insidious, that's because it is. If it appears unsustainable, well, yes, to say the least.

Why in the world would they do this? It's simple—because the US consumer keeps the global economic engine running; it is the single most important factor in economic growth. If we stop consuming things, the global economy collapses. That's why, after catastrophic events like 9/11 or Hurricane Katrina, or to honor sacred feast days like Christmas, we are urged to go shopping. People made fun of George Bush when he told people to go to Disney World or back to shopping malls a week after the 9/11 attacks, but he knew what was at stake—heaven forbid that a moment like that actually brings us back to sanity, to the most basic values of life and community and meaning and faith—because the engine just might break down—and we have not exactly prepared for another way of doing business. Wealth is at stake, and lots of jobs, and the ability for people to keep supplying the engine. So use those credit cards, buy stuff, make your minimum payments, pay that interest to the banks—keep the engine running with your consumption and your personal debt.

This way of doing business is not going on in isolation from the rest of the world. It is deeply entwined with the economies of the developed and developing worlds. China, as one glaring example, is growing its economy on the basis of the production of cheap exports and is counting on us to buy them. Wal-Mart is a major customer for the Chinese export market, one of the reasons it can underprice its competitors. This is China's economic life-line, what fuels its breathtaking growth. With the income, China is industrializing, creating factory jobs to make things for the export market, creating in the meantime the Chinese consumer, whose demands will just keep rising, building those 562 coal-fired power plants, cutting deals for oil with Sudan, Angola, and Venezuela. For this reason, it is in China's interest that we keep buying its stuff. To make sure we keep doing that, they are lending the money they make on our purchases back to us to keep us shopping.

China is now one of our biggest creditors, financing our government's extravagant defense spending and tax cuts for the rich, along with our consumer debt. The Chinese have been doing this in part by buying US Treasury bonds. This helps prop up the value of US currency vis-à-vis their own, which helps keep their exports cheap so that we keep buying them. "Asian central banks in particular have been buying large quantities of dollars and dollar-denominated securities. Chinese purchases of US bonds in 2005, for example, are estimated to have risen as high as 2 percent of our G.D.P., a very significant portion of America's foreign borrowing."[14]

The Chinese are lending us back our own money and propping up our currency so that we will keep buying their stuff.

It is not only the Chinese who have been engaging in the accumulation of dollars and dollar-denominated securities. The Japanese have been nearly as active, as have other Asian economies. Middle Eastern oil producers have also been running large trade surpluses, thanks to high oil prices, and investing at least some of the proceeds in the United States.

As a result, there has been an immense rise in foreign ownership of American securities of all kinds, but especially government bonds. *Foreign ownership of the US federal debt passed the halfway mark in June 2004.*

About a third of corporate bonds are now in foreign hands, as is more than 13 percent of the US stock market. One analyst has half-seriously calculated that at the current rate of foreign accumulation, the last US Treasury held by an American will be purchased by the People's Bank of China on Feb. 9, 2012.[15] (emphasis added)

Now I have no intention here of appealing to a nationalist or protection-ist sentiment. We are long past that in any case—there is no such thing as a purely national economy anymore. What I am doing is describing this new world in which we live, some of the sea changes in the global economy that have made our situation here in the United States a lot more precarious than my parent's generation was even in times of war and economic depres-sion, in part because economic decisions that affect our lives are now part of a global system over which national governments have less and less power.

How bad is it?

So if we are borrowing money like crazy to keep the economy afloat, just how indebted are we? On the day I wrote this, June 8, 2007, the national debt stood at $8,843,871,008,172.46.[16] It is increasing by an average of $1.34 billion *per day*, amounting to more than $29,000 per person. By March 2008, with this average, the debt will have risen by more than $400 billion. It grew by $3 trillion in the first six and one-half years of the presidency of George Bush.

That nearly $9 trillion national debt is only part of the story. If you in-clude all US debt—government, household, business, financial, and foreign—the total US debt in 2005 was $40.1 trillion! In 2004 the $40 trillion debt amounted to 437 percent of national income.

This is not good news. While carrying some debt is not necessarily a bad thing—and can be a very good thing for a home buyer, for example, or a government if it is investing in things like schools, technology, or infra-structure—debt of this size can cripple the generations that follow the ones who created it. Debt is real. It carries obligations, among them, debt-service payments—interest plus a portion of the principal. In 2003, debt-service payments on the US debt totaled $4.09 trillion.

Now this is bad, but there's an additional worry, one that may be clearer by the time you read this. The Federal Reserve has been keeping interest rates low to keep us spending—refinancing mortgages, buying cars, bor-rowing from savings, and so on. But interest rates are going to rise, and when that happens so will the interest payments on our national debt. This will be trillions and trillions of dollars paid out to our creditors and there-fore not available for our very real growing needs—like emergency response systems for disasters, like replacing our aging infrastructure, roads, bridges, sewers, like investing in alternative fuel technologies and building mass transit systems, like universal health insurance or social programs for the poor—pick your favorite need and add it to the list.

The federal deficit, which is part of the national debt, skyrocketed during the Bush administration, a combination of defense spending, imperial war, and tax cuts for the rich. Each year of deficit spending adds to the debt. Because the White House did this, and because Congress has let this go on for so long, the country is facing increasingly horrible choices. Financing the deficit will mean real and painful loss of income for many families. The pain will be even worse for them if tax cuts for the rich remain in place, because it means they will have a greater share of the tax burden as well.

Thanks to George Bush, and most especially thanks to his war, the interest bill that must be paid out with your tax dollars rose to $220 billion in 2006, an increase of $36 billion from 2005. The Congressional Budget Office predicts the bill will rise to $270 billion in 2008. And a good chunk of this money will end up with foreign creditors—$77 billion in 2005.

In order to be able to continue borrowing to meet debt obligations, Congress raised the debt ceiling four times in the first six years of the Bush administration, to a staggering $8.96 trillion in 2006! But you see how we are already approaching that sum. Meanwhile, as our debt and interest burden grew, the United States crossed a threshold in 2006—the government is now paying out more to foreign creditors than it receives in investments.

So add this to all the other ways our world has changed in this generation; in economic terms we now live in a very different world.

But we're not happy!

Okay, this is hard stuff, feels like piling on, which is exactly what's happening. Life is piling on, and it's no wonder we would rather fold the blinders in a little closer. But before we give way to despair, I want to say this about the American Dream—it is good for us that it is over. That Dream, romantically rendered as poor hardworking people coming to the Promised Land to pursue happiness, and then passing it on to the next generation and the next, morphed into a way of life that is killing the spirit and destroying the earth. Right now our culture manifests all the symptoms of a stressed-out, discontented society struggling with basic values and meaning, running on a treadmill that we do not know how to stop and off which we are too afraid to leap. Vague feelings of emptiness are a national plague. This is also nothing new. We have been reading about the spiritual impoverishment of consumerism for a long time.

Here are just a few examples:

1989, the book *Poverty of Affluence: A Psychological Portrait of the American Way of Life* by Paul Wachtel:

> It is ironic that the very kind of thinking which produces all our riches also renders them unable to satisfy us. Our restless desire for more and more has been a major dynamic for economic growth, but it has made the achievement of that growth largely a hollow victory. Our sense of contentment and satisfaction is not a simple result of any absolute value of what we acquire or achieve. It depends upon our frame of reference, on how what we attain compares to what we expected. If we get farther than we expected we tend to feel good. If we expected to go farther than we have then even a rather high level of success can be experienced as disappointing. In America we keep upping the ante. Our expectations keep accommodating to what we have attained. "Enough" is always just over the horizon, and like the horizon it recedes as we approach it. . . .
>
> Our entire economic system is based on human desire's being inexhaustible, on there being a potential market for almost anything we produce. Without always recognizing what we are doing or how we do it, we have established a pattern in which we continually create discontent, and we attribute the restless yearning to the spontaneous expression of human nature.[17]

1995, the essay "Are We Happy Yet?" by Alan Thein Durning:

> Psychological evidence shows that the relationship between consumption and personal happiness is weak. Worse, two primary sources of human fulfillment—social relations and leisure—appear to have withered or stagnated in the rush to riches. Thus many in the consumer society have a sense that their world of plenty is somehow hollow—that, hoodwinked by a consumerist culture, they have been fruitlessly attempting to satisfy with material things what are essentially social, psychological, and spiritual needs.[18]

2006, the book *The Upside of Down: Catastrophe, Creativity, and the Renewal of Civilization* by Thomas Homer-Dixon:

> In essence, then, the logic underpinning our economies works like this: if we're discontented with what we have, we buy stuff; if we buy enough stuff, the economy grows; if the economy grows enough, technologically displaced workers can find new jobs; and if they find new jobs, there will be enough demand to keep the economy humming and to

prevent wrenching political conflict. Modern capitalism's stability—
and increasingly the global economy's stability—requires the cultivation of material discontent, endlessly rising personal consumption,
and the steady economic growth this consumption generates. Without economic growth, rich and poor people in our societies would
soon confront each other in a fierce zero-sum conflict, and over time
the widening gap between these two groups would tear our societies
apart.

Our economic role in this culture of consumerism is to be little
more than walking appetites that serve the function of maintaining
our economy's throughput. Our psychological state is comparable to
that of drug addicts needing a fix: buying things doesn't really make
us happy, except perhaps for a moment after the purchase. But we do
it over and over anyway. . . .

Consumerism helps anesthetize us against the dread produced by
empty lives—lives that modern capitalism and consumerism have
themselves helped empty of meaning.[19]

Sounds like madness, doesn't it? We could find many volumes on this; these
are just the ones I had at hand.

Sometimes our mental illness, or soul sickness, makes it into the press,
too. In June 2006, the *Washington Post* reported that US Americans are becoming more socially isolated, many complaining that they have few friends,
if any, who really know them, in whom they can confide. "A quarter of Americans say they have no one with whom they can discuss personal troubles," a
number that doubled from 1985. The article notes that social ties are connected to psychological and social health.[20]

As we grow lonelier and more stressed, we have been aiding and abetting
a pharmaceutical industry that seems to come up with a pill for every troubling emotion. We are depressed, anxious, hypertense, overweight or un-
derweight, and there are pills for each of these ailments. Our children are
heavily medicated. According to Greg Critser, who wrote the books *Fat
Land* and *Generation RX*, spending on drugs to treat adolescent behavior
problems "rose by 77 percent between 2000 and 2003, 'with 65 percent of
all children on such drugs taking at least one antidepressant.'"[21]

So, to ease our loneliness and depression, our loss of meaning and intimacy, we are buying stuff and we are popping pills. Fake relief from an emptiness bred by the culture of economic growth.

It goes on. A study released in 2005 predicted that nine out of ten men
and seven out of ten women in this country will become overweight.[22] So
while we are buying things and popping pills, we are also eating ourselves to
early deaths.

Our young people are suffering terrible stress and anxiety due to unrealistic expectations from parents and society. Pressures are enormous for kids to succeed, or at least not to fail. Some psychologists are now saying that a culture that views children's self-esteem as extremely fragile and vulnerable has reached extremes of overprotection that has left kids unable to deal with the real world or to have the self-confidence to go out into it. Anxiety disorders have become a plague among adolescents, perhaps the clearest indication of a cultural pathology, yet another "canary in the mine" telling us something is very wrong with the society.

Tens of millions of us are in therapy. Are we really this incapable of living whole and self-fulfilling lives? Are we really this helpless to solve our problems?

Or are these problems symptoms of the great upheavals of our world, completely appropriate responses to a planet in grave trouble and a society under great stress and discontent? Are all these feelings of anxiety and depression, rather than being symptoms of illness, actually healthy responses to a sick society? Should we be listening to them instead of anesthetizing them?

I want to cite just one more article here that may shed some light. Studies show that money can't buy you happiness—you know that old cliché.

> A wealth of data in recent decades has shown that once personal wealth exceeds about $12,000 a year, more money produces virtually no increase in life satisfaction. . . . Dramatically changing one's wealth does create happiness, but it will last only until people get used to their newfound status, which can be a matter of months or a couple of years at most.[23]

The journalist who wrote this article, Shankar Vedantam, quotes from an article in the journal *Science*:

> The belief that high income is associated with good mood is widespread but mostly illusory. People with above-average income . . . are barely happier than others in moment-to-moment experience, tend to be more tense, and do not spend more time in particularly enjoyable activities.[24]

Studies show that people actually care more about things like family, intimate relationships, and long walks in the park, not only things that money can't buy but that our stressed-out lives keep us from having time to enjoy. And while money might pay for the prescription pills, it can't heal the wounded spaces of our relationships, whether family or friends. Our stresses compound these troubles while leaving little of the time that healing requires.

So also of our earth.

So perhaps rather than fearing the end of the American Dream-turned-nightmare for our planet, for the poor of our world, for the spirits of our people, we should embrace it.

So often in my life I have been warned not to use the word *sacrifice*, not to scare people too much, and not to tell people that they have to be downwardly mobile—because it will just turn off my audience. In this book we are learning that we will have to sacrifice, that there is plenty of reason to be scared out of our wits, and that, in order to save the planet and the human prospect, we must become downwardly mobile in a hurry.

Because our affluence, our mind-numbing consumerism, and our technology can provide powerful shields from reality, can put off the fear, can keep the changes at bay longer than most of the world, putting the distractions of our consumer lifestyle aside may be pretty wrenching at first—that first full view of the world as it really is. I know what it meant for me the first time I laid eyes on a so-called third-world country back in 1983, my first trip to Central America. I remember as if it were yesterday. I never quite got over it. I realized then that I was looking at the vast majority of the world, that Wauwatosa, Wisconsin, my norm, was norm for only a handful of people on this planet.

So who are we really?

What does all this say about who we are? Some of the diagnoses are not exactly complimentary. A marvelous paper written by Robert A. McDermott, a philosophy professor and former president of the California Institute of Integral Studies, describes the culture of the United States as one "which has much more power than wisdom." He continues:

> There is overwhelming evidence that . . . the United States . . . is greatly lacking in wisdom, out of balance and approaching self-destruction concerning the ecosystem, gender, generations, health, education and its sense of justice. . . .
>
> The "American way of life," which appears mostly to do with goods and services, continues to increase its domination throughout the world. Wherever it is imitated American economic energy brings with it American short-sightedness, rapaciousness, neglect of healthy daily rhythms and an alienation from the inner life. Both at home and in its influence abroad, American culture shows itself to be at an adolescent

stage of development: it looks ahead with idealism, passion and confidence, but with inadequate insight nor foresight.[25]

Harsh. Difficult to hear. But don't we detect that ring of truth somewhere in the midst of all the noise of the culture?

This is what we have to change now, for the sake of our people, for the sake of all the world's people, for the sake of the earth. "It is essential that the dark side of the American story be candidly acknowledged," McDermott writes, "and if humanity—and, more urgently, the Earth—is to survive, that it be accepted and overcome."[26]

It is not that we are a bad people, it's that we have a hard time believing that a society so rich and bountiful (supposedly) could have such morally compromised foundations. We forget that we would never have risen on this continent without destroying the populations here before us and enslaving millions upon millions of Africans. We forget sometimes how long it took for people of color to be recognized as full human beings or for women to be acknowledged as having equal rights. We forget the exploitation that led to the necessity of child labor laws or that labor activists were murdered in the struggle for the forty-hour work week.

We forget that much of our wealth has been taken from other lands across the globe, and that the labor that assembles our consumer items is largely exploited and poorly paid. We don't see that this one more wetland destroyed for the new housing development where I want to live is part of a relationship of destruction that lies beneath our suburban and exurban sprawl and that our insistence on getting into our own individual car every day is causing polar ice sheets to melt and weather to go crazy.

We don't want to acknowledge how much violence it takes on our behalf to support this way of life.

We are in a hard place now. It is over. This way of life is, must be, over. It will take great spiritual strength to get through this transition to another way of life. But we should be assured that giving up the aspirations of a society of consumption and materialism promises not to leave us less happy. The studies tell us this will not be so. But it will take some courage.

So as we move to the next step on this journey, I want to take up the challenge of Robert McDermott and go down to the depths beneath the society to examine the values that support it. I want to pose the crucial question of what of our values and belief systems we need now to shed, to let go, as we try to find our path toward ecological hope, as well as what we can salvage of our cultural values, or recover, to help us move in a new direction. Let's be courageous about this. There are some powerful assumptions and religiosities that no longer serve us. That's okay. God will not strike us with lightning if we are prepared to embrace new revelations about this earth story and who we are within it. Indeed, one could argue rather forcefully that it is the Creator God herself that is urging us to this task; more, that we are in our questioning and our anxiety and our discontent expressions of that very creative dynamic urging us toward the next leap in our evolution.

7

Alienation from Nature

or,

Letting an Old Story Go

> *Hurrah, boys! We've got them! We'll finish*
> *them off, then go home to our station.*
> —LT. COL. GEORGE ARMSTRONG CUSTER

> *Our combat operations in Iraq have ended.*
> *In the battle of Iraq, the United States and*
> *our allies have prevailed.*
> —PRESIDENT GEORGE W. BUSH, MAY 1, 2003

Some lessons are hard to learn. If you have walked with me this far, and I hope you have, one thing seems clear from the reality of the world presented here—something has gone very wrong with us, and our world reflects it. A torn fabric of life, a biosphere in great distress, an atmosphere ready to cough us up and out of its system, a degraded planet, a completely unsustainable, destructive way of life that we seem convinced we are helpless to do anything about, a set of crises so grave that it will wipe away most of what we think are daily concerns—and still we go on.

See the little hand waving out on the vast sea as we drown in an ocean of the mess we have made? Help!

Are we the wrong species for the planet? Did evolution put consciousness in the wrong brain?

I love that Custer quote. I came upon it at the site of the Battle of the Little Bighorn on my cross-country road trip in 2005. I had a profound day there, wandering the open fields and rolling countryside of the battlefield under a blistering hot sun, a meditation on hubris, on the mentality of the conqueror, subduing lands and peoples in the name of a manifest destiny, on the arrogant violence that has so often been the underpinning of our expansions and our grandiosity, grabbing what we want when we want it, invading other lands, as if we really do have some birthright. Just who was it that decided we had that destiny after all? God?

It was a much larger battle than I had imagined. Thousands of Sioux and Cheyenne Indians had left their reservations in 1875 in defiance of the US government. On June 25, 1876, a grand alliance of Teton Sioux, Northern Cheyenne, and Arapahoe Indians under the leadership of Sitting Bull were encamped along the Rosebud River. Meanwhile, Lt. Col. George Armstrong Custer and the Seventh Cavalry were on a mission to force the Sioux and Cheyenne back to the reservations.

The Indians vastly outnumbered the soldiers, but Custer did not know this. Stumbling on a scouting party and fearing that the village would get wind of the army's approach, Custer, despite orders to wait, decided to launch an attack. It would be easy, he thought, a walk in the park. His hubris caused him to make a grave strategic error that day, and it cost him his life and the lives of more than two hundred of his soldiers.

When the reinforcements arrived the next day, there were bloated bodies of US Army soldiers scattered across the fields.

I also found this quote from a Cheyenne warrior named Two Moons: "We circled all around them, swirling like water around a storm." Sounds like the streets of Baghdad, or the world we live in now.

We think we see it coming. We think we see the whole picture, as Custer did that day. We have a plan. But then comes reality, what we don't see or don't want to see, swirling around us like water around a storm—like New Orleans.

I wonder what Custer thought in his last moments. I wonder if he had a moment of regret about his overblown self-confidence, a moment of "uh oh!"

The US Army, of course, paid the Indians back in spades. Their victory was short lived. Massacre sites dot the countryside all across the northern Great Plains and elsewhere across this land.

Who are we? And what values are *actually* reflected in our history and way of life? We may be shocked at times to realize how different our behaviors are from the values we espouse. But the only reason we are shocked is because we have not learned this history very well, or have believed that in our case it was okay because we are so special, or have put up blinders because we simply don't want to know what our way of life has cost other human beings, much less the planet.

It has happened often in my life that I have been attacked or criticized for bringing up actual historical events—like the US covert training of death squads in Latin America, or the massacre of women and children at Wounded

Knee, or the connection between the ravaging of the Appalachian Mountains and our air conditioning. It's as if stating these realities is an offense against the national psyche, an attack of some sort, an agenda of the left.

The market, too, is reflection of our values. So is the gaping chasm between rich and poor. I'm not making up or inventing the information stuffed into these chapters; it is what it is, and we need to stop being afraid of looking at it for fear of what that look will tell us about ourselves, and what it will ask of us.

Some religious institutions and ministers have tried to make this easier for us by focusing our moral lives on our private personal behavior, even though our Western scriptures are focused decidedly somewhere else. It's easier to worry about sex and marriage than it is about how we spend our money, what we buy, what corporations are doing, what habitat once thrived in the new development where I bought my house, how my electric power is produced, the reality in oil-rich countries—who really pays for how we live. Yet I can't find any Beatitudes or Woes regarding private morality in the Gospels, nor a vision of the final judgment focused on marriage, same-sex relationships, or reproductive rights.

And it is becoming glaringly clear that many of the problems that are breaking apart our families and intimate relationships, that are causing fractures in our communities, that are making us depressed and anxious, are organically connected to the ecological and economic stresses of our society. But it's hard to preach the Gospel of Luke or Matthew 25, much less apply them to the crises of climate change and ecological overshoot, when your congregation is likely to get mad at you.

We have a lot to talk about here, and we can hardly cover all the questions and ramifications that these realities present to us within the scope of this book. That's why I think of this as only the beginning of a conversation, one that needs to start happening in church halls, around dining room tables, among families and neighborhoods, in community settings all across the country.

In this chapter I want to look in the mirror of our world, how it reflects us at this moment, in particular in this US culture. I want to reflect on what seems wrong with us, where the problem seems to be, and how this begins to suggest the different way of living required of us now. This is not a conversation about what to do, but a reflection on values, on the spirit, on the soul of this nation.

Later, we will make an attempt at articulating a spirituality of ecological hope—not in any finished way because this dialogue is very much in process, an act of creation going on with urgency in many places, and it may be years before we have the words, the language, for the new framework of meaning for this next phase in the human/earth journey.

Living wrongly

We are living wrongly on the planet. This has become horribly obvious. This we know. How we are living is altering the planet itself in a way that is breaking down the balance in which this magnificent era of evolution occurred—a phase brimming with rich, diverse life out of which came the human.

Part of the problem is just getting used to the idea that we could be this *big*, or that all of our little individual activities could add up to something on a planetary scale. It is unsettling, to say the least. Gerald Barney, director of President Carter's *Global 2000 Report*, spent many years developing computer-simulation models for sustainable national planning for the Millennium Institute, assisting more than twenty countries. He is founder and director now of Our Task, Inc., a project aimed at empowering young people to act as advocates for the earth they would like to inherit. In an interview for this book conducted in May 2007, he reflected: "I think it has genuinely come as a surprise for people to discover that we have collectively managed to do damage to the entire planet. We never dreamed that we'd have power to influence anything so big. So that's a big change, and it is rocking and challenging our sense of identity at the moment."

Ironically, despite our surprise at the bigness of our human footprint on the planet, the US culture has always tried to do things "big." With our sense of manifest destiny and grandiosity about the mission of the United States, we have tried to shape a world in our image. No matter how much it backfires, we just keep doing it, because once we *did* conquer frontiers and make native peoples and nature submit to us. We helped win two world wars in the last century and outlasted the Soviet Union in the forty-year-long Cold War. We invaded or intervened throughout Latin America and made it into our "sphere of influence," with largely unchallenged access to its vast natural wealth, propping up dictators when needed. And we became very rich in the process.

While many others, of course, became quite poor in the process.

Why not invade and occupy lands for oil when this is the next thing we need to do to keep the destiny manifesting itself? I cringe every time I hear a politician or pundit talk about "our" oil—ours by birthright again, ours by the sheer gloriousness of the project that is America.

But underneath this American project there is a grave misunderstanding: we mistook mere physical power and a lot of good luck for entitlement. We mistook wealth for proof of success and righteousness. We mistook the might of arms for might of a powerful God who takes sides in our wars. We mistook our ability to fell trees, turn over vast swaths of land for mono-crops, drop atomic bombs on Japan, beat the Soviet Union to the moon, and blow off mountaintops for electricity as testament to our ingenuity and superiority. We thought the world as endless as our aspirations; we thought the world big enough for our grandiose self-identity.

We considered ourselves masters of the universe, assigned this role by a God with whom we could identify, who commanded his chosen to occupy the promised land no matter who happened to be there already, a God who would crush his enemies, even blessing those who would dash the heads of the enemy's babies against stones (Ps 137:9), as we did in the Great Plains wars, or in Vietnam, and as our Latin American military allies did as recently as the 1970s and 1980s. I suppose it's not a stretch to believe this God would also "disappear" people into detention centers, torture and abuse them, for fear they might be terrorists and therefore opposed to his will and our destiny.

I know we squirm at these violent Bible passages now, but our actions show that as a political culture we have lived by them more often than we like to believe, however narrowly and self-servingly they have been interpreted or divorced from the cultures in which they were first articulated. Economic and military might have been the guarantors of the US superpower role in the world; they have been the guarantors of our way of life. Not only many pastors, but even politicians these days, have constructed a religious narrative to justify this and often use the Bible as an ideological weapon, stripping it of its essential insights and meaning, its *stories* of human beings grappling with their relationship with a God whom, just like us, they only dimly understood and too often confused with their own wants, needs, fears, and ambitions.

One reason we are willing to go to such lengths to extol the glories of America is because it is, after all, such an alluring and amazing, indeed, a stunning way of life. We believe it to be so wonderful that we assume everyone aspires to it, and those who don't are somehow suspect. We forget what it has cost—the richness of the planet, the resources belonging to other peoples, the oppression of others that has made this life affordable for us.

Because we have not experienced, seen, felt very often the cost to others, the cost to the earth, of this way of life, we think it has come relatively pain free, simply by our hard work, ingenuity, and entrepreneurial spirit—and we have certainly had plenty of all those things. But each improvement in our standard of living comes at a cost somewhere through the fabric of life—whether the labor of impoverished miners in Kentucky or Bolivia, an ecosystem here and there, a habitat disturbed or destroyed, a few more particles of pollutants in the air, a few more pounds of greenhouse gases. We have sincerely believed that we created such an advanced and enlightened way of life that we are called by some historical destiny to pass it on to others around the world, until now we find that it was created in large part by exploiting human beings and the planet to the point where we are exhausting both.

Our incremental contributions seem so small, so isolated in the moment—you know, just a levee here and there along the banks of the Mississippi to channel the flood waters, a little dredging here and there to get the barges through, a few canals in the delta to facilitate shipping around the refineries, a few levees to hold back the Gulf and the lakes so that communities can develop in the areas below sea level. We don't see the storm that's coming.

Or maybe just this one more house in the new exurban development, with parks and big yards, good schools, sitting atop a wetland that was once part of a functioning ecosystem. We don't see how this one more development adds to the others that have destroyed local farming, that are bringing about the extinction of meadow birds, obstructing animal-migration patterns, increasing local flood dangers, adding to greenhouse gas pollution from our longer commutes.

We don't see what our thirst for fine wood for our floors and our furniture or our using and discarding of millions upon millions of throw-away chopsticks and brown paper bags are doing to the pine forests of Latin America and Asia. We don't pay attention to what the plastic water bottles mean for greenhouse-gas emissions and our monumental piles of garbage, or what it means that the water that fills them comes from aquifers in Maine, or fresh springs in Iceland, the Fiji Islands, or the Adirondack Mountains.

We don't pay attention because we don't want to, because it is so hard, because we're too tired, too stressed, because my little gesture doesn't make any difference when everyone else is doing it, because it is just too easy, while filtering water from the tap, cleaning out reusable bottles, or fighting for the right to clean fresh water for everyone takes too much time in our over-stressed lives.

Once the earth as a whole could withstand these many assaults, even heal and renew some of the wounds, but no longer. The assaults are now reaching a global scale and the earth is not able to hold the balance.

Now these things are adding up; they are adding up to a planetary crisis.

"The reality is we're up against a situation where it must change," said Gerald Barney in our interview, "or it's going to destroy us."

We started out our journey looking at the Katrina metaphor, at how our attempt to tame and control the Mississippi River led to the disaster in New Orleans, thousands of our sisters and brothers standing on rooftops begging for help, or sweltering, abandoned, in the Superdome as we watched on national television. Despite political promises, some 180,000 people ended up displaced permanently. Oh well.

A whole world engineered and developed, used as resource for humans, used as resource for wealth generation, leading to a world of New Orleans—environmental disasters, toxic waste, unsustainable and inappropriate development, massive flooding, collapse of infrastructure we thought could control weather or hold it at bay, poor disaster response, neglect of the needs of the poor, and racism. We saw it all in the wake of the hurricane.

The Katrina metaphor reveals attitudes deeply embedded in the US psyche. It reveals religious, cultural, and national *values*. We have one self-image, New Orleans reveals another, as do the levees in California, the toxic streams and polluted lakes across this land, exurban sprawl, and a baking atmosphere with steadily rising temperatures that still can't get us to change how we live. We think we can do anything, manipulate any reality, make anything work. We keep thinking we can get on top of all this, fix it, but it keeps spiraling out of our control—which is the point—it is not in our control.

The US Army Corps of Engineers is a perfect example. As I was writing this book, I read about its plan for the Gulf Coast—to build islands and new sea walls and a pipeline to bring Mississippi sediment to the delta, billions of public dollars worth of flood and surge "protection," efforts to reengineer the natural systems that were destroyed by the previous engineering. Yes, indeed, like the dams and levees of yesterday, we can beat this river into submission, we can get it to behave properly. The problem is that we simply have not engineered it enough yet.

On the other hand, unless we are willing to relocate an enormous human population along the Louisiana coastline, we may have no other choice, that is, if New Orleans is not to one day soon be washed out into the sea. But, given the record, I wouldn't bet on New Orleans.

The problem with social justice

All that we have covered in this book reflects a construct, a way of being, that is doing grave harm to the planet, breaking apart our world like the levees that cracked and collapsed around the Lower Ninth Ward. It describes a relationship with nature, our sense of place and identity, and often a religiosity that undergirds that relationship. Our lives are out of balance with the natural world that holds us and all life, and our being out of balance is putting everything out of balance. That balance cannot be restored with a little recycling here and there, or replacing our light bulbs (though, please, do those things!). In fact, it cannot be restored. Too much damage has already been done. The earth can heal, if we get out of the way, if we learn to live within the limits of our creation, but the balance will be new, and one of the questions is what of life as we know it will remain in that new balance.

Even in my social justice world, the context of most of my life's work and vocation, we see indications of the same problem. We were going to fix things, build just societies, and humans were at the center of this project. "Social justice" provided a powerful framework, a highly rational way to see the world and the suffering of human beings within it, a framework from which to struggle for human dignity and freedom. It seemed to get to the heart of the matter. Those with power built unjust structures, structures of wealth, structures controlled by elites who control the global economy, structures of military power that guaranteed the world order. We worked hard under the assumption that if we could make the structures just, like fixing the levees, then the world would become just.

In many freedom struggles of the last century, the ideological core was centered on a belief that the project of history was the liberation of the human from oppression, and that this process was inevitable, historically determined. Societies would be built around the "new man." The human being was the master manipulator, the one that could bring this about or force the change through struggle (la lucha), including armed struggle. Capitalism, which had created such gross disparities in the world, would be transformed or overturned, to be replaced by popular democracies and socialist economies. State-run economies sought to change the rules of the game to provide more economic resources for workers, impoverished urban dwellers, and peasant farmers.

I grossly oversimplify here, but to make a point. The capitalist world was not alone, or even singular, in the ecological destruction it caused by the way it viewed the role of the natural world—as the environmentally ravaged countries of Eastern Europe and China show us only too well. It is not only the problem of the economic model at work, but of the relationship between the human and what we have so mistakenly referred to as "natural resources." By putting "man" at the center and natural resources at the service of our economic development, we have ravaged the earth to the point where one of the prerequisites for justice is under grave threat—before there can be justice, there must be life.

Meanwhile, for all this work to change structures, those structures remain deeply entrenched. They reflect still the power of global and national elites making rules largely to their benefit, including the power of the human over nature. They reflect a view of nature as "resources" for human gain or enrichment. Control of them goes increasingly to those with money to invest. They are expressions of power relations and of the values and world views that guide those relations. Institutions like the World Trade Organization, the International Monetary Fund, the World Bank, or the US Federal Reserve make up the rules that govern and enforce those relations. They are hierarchical in nature, undemocratic, and jealous of their powerful roles in world or national governance. In rare moments when advocacy or conscience come into play, they can become venues for figuring out how to bring economically improved lives for the poor, an AIDS program in Africa, for example, or micro-loans for subsistence farmers, or keeping interest rates low so more people can afford to buy homes. These programs offer *assistance* or better terms on credit, but not a change in how business is conducted, or the power dynamics that shape the global economy. Mostly, the struggle is around issues of access to resources and how those resources will be distributed, the question for social justice activists being whether or not the distribution of those resources is just.

But even if we could get these institutions to change the rules of the game to the benefit of the poor of our world, if this work does not have in its sights a way to bring human consumption and waste down to levels that fall within the balance of life, this model will also fail to end the suffering of humans and all our other fellow species.

We need 1.4 "earths" to support our current levels of consumption and waste. We can make that just and equitable by dividing up the share of that consumption and waste more equitably—but we would still require 1.4 planets.

Meanwhile, micro-loans won't mean a whole lot to villagers and farmers in Africa whose lakes are receding and whose land is becoming desertified and uninhabitable because of global climate change, caused for the most part by industrial and post-industrial societies whose elites control the institutions handing out those loans.

Structures are an expression of our values, and the most fundamental thing in any civilization or society or culture is what values shape the structures, the way of life, the values by which we live, in our case, what we buy, what we value, what we consume, and then all of the things that are at the service of that and this entitled way of life to which we believe we have a right. Values are not what we proclaim, but how we live, what we spend our life doing.

Social justice expresses something essential, the requirement of human-to-human justice, justice within the human community, but we have tended to see this as something apart from all the rest of nature, to see nature as a "resource" at the service of this moral and ethical requirement and separate from it. The human drama is at the center, the primary moral imperative above and beyond the needs of the natural world, as if these realities are somehow detached, or that one is subsidiary to the other. Too often this logic has turned out to be very destructive indeed.

Theologian Rosemary Radford Ruether, who has played a leading role in the articulation of ecofeminist theology in this country, describes two critiques of "development" models that have shaped the policies and orientations of both government organizations and NGOs as they address the economic and ecological challenges of our generation. One comes from a vantage point of the so-called Third World, seeing poverty in the world as a result of "misdevelopment" and exploitation by rich nations. "Western colonizing countries had stripped the colonized countries of their wealth which now underlies Western capitalism."[1] The remedy from this point of view is not foreign "assistance," but the end of this type of exploitation. Many liberation struggles of the latter half of the twentieth century were motivated by this desire to throw off the yoke of the colonizers.

Another critique came from environmentalists from the so-called first-world who looked at realities of carrying capacity and resource depletion and said the urgency was to stop development altogether, to try to stabilize the economic system and population where they are, an approach that would protect the affluent for the most part and lock in place the glaring inequities in the world. Needless to say, folks in poor countries had reason to be suspicious of the motives of many "green" activists in the West. It was a case of bad communication and sometimes a glaring lack of solidarity with the poor majorities on our planet. Easier to support funds for population control programs in Africa, for example, than to become downwardly mobile so that the poor can have what they need for dignified lives.

Ecology and social justice movements appeared to be in conflict, writes Ruether:

> The liberation viewpoint stressed pulling control over the natural resources of poor countries out from under Western power so that the developmental process could continue under autonomous, socialist political systems. The First World ecological viewpoint often sounded, whether consciously or not, as though it were delivering bad news to the hopes of poor countries. Stabilizing the world as it is seemed to suggest stabilizing its unjust relationships. . . . Social justice and the ecological balance of humanity with the environment were in conflict. If one chose ecology, it was necessary to give up the dream of more equal distribution of goods.[2]

In Latin America, source of so much inspiration in my own life over three decades, liberation theologians articulated a solidarity with the poor rooted in their experience of oppression and their discovery of God at work among them in the project of liberation from oppression. They often aligned themselves with socialist political movements working for liberation from the colonial powers and the dictatorships that were at their service.

Brazilian ecofeminist theologian Ivone Gebara wrote of this movement: "Liberation theology asks the question: 'How to speak of God in the face of hunger, injustice, misery, dictatorship, the destruction of entire peoples?' It offers a more collective understanding of God and stresses the social nature of sin. God becomes the God of life and of justice who has a preferential love for the poor."[3] This insight sparked a four-decades-long reorientation of many pastoral workers, theologians, and "first-world" faith-based activists to a solidarity movement with the poor of Latin America that did courageous work in defense of human rights and economic justice, even to facing threats to life and limb in the process. Many local faith communities through-out the Americas were invigorated by this struggle, finding in it an imme-diacy of their gospel faith like none they had experienced before in their lives.

But, these many decades later, and with misery, social violence, and pro-found injustice still realities for much of the continent's peoples, Gebara suggests that liberation theology also had a problem:

> God has always been used by both the left and the right to justify par-ticular political programs. . . .
>
> There is a growing suspicion that the age-old conviction that "re-demption through suffering" might not be true. There is growing dis-satisfaction with liberation theology. The promise of a new society founded upon justice and equality just hasn't happened. We are tired of the struggle, which is often violent and which promises our libera-tion at the end. All we have seen is destruction and death, never vic-tory. So we are suspicious of this approach, tired of yet another docu-ment. Analysis on the political and economic situation of our people is very important, but it is not everything!
>
> Instead, we look at the air, the water, the earth. We look at all the garbage surrounding us, and we sense deep within ourselves that our planet is not just a place—it is our own body. Ecofeminism proposes a new relationship with the earth and with the entire cosmos.[4]

How do we bring that relationship about? It is perhaps not quite in the way we have thought for so long about our social justice work.

> We must first change our image of men and women within the cos-mos. And when we change that image, our image of God changes. Any image of God is nothing more than the image of the experience of the understanding we have of ourselves. We must re-situate the human within—not above—the cosmos. This is diametrically opposed to a Christian anthropology that insists humanity is "Lord of Creation" ordered by the Creator to "increase and dominate the earth." In the current anthropology, the human's right to dominate, control, possess has been legitimized by the Creator and thus becomes part of human nature, pre-established—and therefore impossible to change.[5]

Not just a problem of right-wing theologies, but of any theology that puts the human outside, over and above creation.

One of the breakthroughs in consciousness that is happening in our world today is precisely that more and more of us are breaking with the much-criticized anthropocentrism of this religious world view to something more holistic, more in keeping with what we are coming to know about our planet and our universe.

Gebara writes:

> I am convinced that this way of thinking is shifting. Today we are beginning to experience who we are in a different way, more holistically. Why? Because we are beginning to suffer because our water is dirty, our rivers and oceans are dirty, because our food isn't any good anymore. We feel great pain at the destruction. We sense at a gut level that we too are "dirty," somehow "polluted" as well. Our intuition tells us what many so-called primitive peoples have always held: that we are all in all.
>
> The scientists are also showing us how our very "power over" is tragic because it is not only causing our own destruction as human beings, but it is destroying life itself! We humans cannot live if we destroy the rest of our body.
>
> And so we are beginning to discover our interconnectedness. We humans are not "Lords of Creation." Instead, we are the Earth's thought, the Earth's reflection of itself; one type of consciousness present on the planet.
>
> Therefore, when we behold the sick body of the poor, and see the injustice they suffer, we see it as our own body. There is no other. The other is myself. We are part of one immense, pulsating body that has been evolving for billions of years—and is still evolving.[6]

I have quoted Gebara at length for this reason: I think her reflection offers us a new spiritual and theological framework for the work of justice. In the face of such a testimony, and appreciating the limits that the social justice model is now facing as we address the ecological crises of our times, I would suggest, as have many others, that we separate the word *social* from justice. Our notion of justice needs to expand, needs to encompass a deep sense of restoring right relationships with all the earth. As Gebara writes, we do not have some natural right beyond all other species to live out of balance with nature, to use and exploit this planet for our own desires or material gain. Besides, if we truly care about justice and the poor, we have to become passionate about what is happening to this planet before we destroy any hope that the poor can live decent and dignified lives by destroying what they need to live.

Again, this is not a new insight so much as the unfolding or evolving of a profound awareness growing as a seed, or a ferment, inside our religious traditions for some time now. In the early 1960s the great monk and mystic Thomas Merton, writing in another era when humanity faced possible extinction, in this case through thermonuclear war, wrote in a little book entitled *Life and Holiness*:

> The task of the Christian is . . . not simply to concern himself with social justice, with political order and fair trade practices. It goes much deeper than that. It is a question of the very structure of society and of man's cultural heritage. The task of each Christian today is to help defend and restore basic human values without which grace and spirituality will have little practical meaning in the life of mankind.[7]

No question that the male pronouns speak of the time in which he wrote this book, but the meaning suggested here is clear and powerful—the social justice model is not enough: a wholesale shift in "the very structures of society" and in the "cultural heritage" of the human is required of us now. That heritage allowed us to justify creation of a weapon that could destroy life on the planet. That same heritage has brought us to our ecological crisis, our cultural and spiritual tipping point. I don't know exactly how Merton would address this challenge of our times, but I think I can make a good guess. At the very least, the work of *justice* evokes a far bigger task now than the *social* justice that Merton critiqued more than four decades ago.

As for structures, we simply need new ones. Clearly, an ecological vision would be reflected by utterly different sorts of structures than the ones shaping global or national environmental, economic, development, or fiscal policies now. The old models cannot produce ecologically whole, healing, regenerative results. New structures must be created that more closely resemble the way this creation actually works, the balance of nature, the democracy of living creatures, the interweaving of life forms that make possible the diversity of ecosystems that nourish and replenish the planet's biosphere.

And, however uncomforting the thought, creating this new "culture of life" (I want to steal that phrase for this much worthier project) will require nothing less than re-creating how we live in just about every aspect of our lives.

Is our religion up to it?

Part of our difficulty is that we have a very powerful religiosity here in the West that undergirds our approach to nature, and there is just no way to avoid this difficulty if we are to address the need for a new way of life. The major religions that grew out of biblical monotheistic traditions contain stories of creation and of God's relationship with humans that have opened spaces for a variety of interpretations, including those justifying the assault on nature. In Genesis we read that, following a wondrous process of creation of day and night, earth and sky, land and waters, and all living creatures, God creates the human and says, "Be fruitful, multiply, fill the Earth and conquer it. Be masters of the fish of the sea, the birds of heaven and all living animals on the earth" (Gn 1:28–29).[8] The human is given dominion over nature, created by an act of God from outside nature—a hierarchy of creatures, with humans at the top, closest to the divine.

However, the intent here is certainly not that nature, God's work of creation, be ruined and destroyed at the hands of the human. This is hardly justification for blowing up 470 Appalachian mountaintops. On the contrary, creation is gift and is to be honored and respected as such.

In the second creation story Adam and Eve are expelled from the Garden of Eden, an idyllic natural world, because they ate fruit from the tree of knowledge, which also happened to be delicious, against the command of God. In this version the human is made to suffer because of the sins of desire and disobedience, and the punishment is hard work, painful birth labor, and death. This is a pretty bleak view of the human condition, alienated from God and nature by guilt and shame.

The first creation story paints a very different picture from the second, a creation process that takes place over time through a series of commands, the penultimate creation being the human, the one made in God's image. All of it is pronounced "good." In the second, the human is created right out of the earth, "fashioned" out of "dust from the soil" (Gn 2:6). But this time, things are not so good. In this story, some fundamental flaw in the human gets us thrown out of the garden.

In each of these two stories we can find source of alienation, but also connection, a reason for human superiority as well as human failing, of closeness to the divine and separation because of that failing. In many ways they express down through time an ambivalence that appears deep in the human psyche about our own human condition, an alienation we have internalized whose origins may always be a bit mystifying—because it does not exist in nature. There is no inside and outside of nature or the cosmos, no alienation except that which we create in our psychological and spiritual lives.

What we know now of the *real* creation story, that dazzling, brilliant, breathtaking narrative that has come to us in our generation through the new physics and new cosmologies, the Hubble Space Telescope, and paleontological and archeological work all around the world, not only shatters the story of alienation from nature and the cosmos, but adds stunning breadth, depth, and scope to the original biblical narratives.

By now, the story is familiar—some fourteen billion years ago there was a Big Bang, a "flaring forth." An unimaginably dense microdot containing all that is within our universe, including space and time, blew up, and eventually our solar system came to be, an ordinary star around which there settled into orbit a small planet brimming with all the ingredients, given the right conditions, for life to begin oozing from its surface. And so it was. Hundreds of millions of years later, Homo sapiens emerged from this ferment. Everything that came before made us possible, and all that is now will make the next phase in this evolutionary journey possible, and then the next, and the next—until one day the earth begins to die and the sun explodes a few billion years from now.

After that, the cosmos will go on—more explosions, more stars created, more galaxies, potentially more life somewhere else.

In this story, as in the first creation story, there is no original guilt, no original exile from nature and the body. There is here no sudden onset of sin that separated us from God and immortality. Death is not a punishment; it is what makes life possible; it is part of the constant unfolding of the earth story, of the evolution of the cosmos as it expresses itself on this one small planet, as far as we know unique in all the observable universe (I wonder what is going on in the part of the universe that we cannot observe, which is most of it).

Stars have been birthed and then have disappeared forever, whole galaxies have come and gone. That this happens to us as well is quite unremarkable in the context of the cosmos, and certainly not something that implies moral failure. It is part of the essence of evolution, what propels it on, whether toward a certain direction or fate, no one knows, though the topic gives way to lots of passionate discussion and debate among scientists, philosophers, and theologians.

Now this creation story can certainly shake up our sense of things, our identity, our sense of place or location. It can be a bit dizzying—and very, very frightening. What could be more disconcerting than to find the human displaced from the lead role in the story of creation?

Some writers have compared this unsettling advance in evolutionary consciousness to the Copernican revolution, when science proved that the earth and sun were not the center of the universe. There was an outcry among church leaders and philosophers, yet a faith rooted in Western scriptures survived that upheaval, and I suspect it will survive this one.

But it seems obvious to me that these discoveries will reshape our experience of that tradition, closing some doors (like the God who takes vengeance against his enemies) and opening others (as in the "new creation" account in Isaiah 65—"they will do no hurt, no harm on all my holy mountain" (v. 25), say, for example, in Appalachia).

The tradition that speaks of alienation (to search for this thread, of course, one can look at Gnostic traditions, the early meeting of Christianity and Greek philosophers, right up to Newtonian physics, the Age of Enlightenment, the Puritans, and Western economics, especially capitalism) is collapsing under the weight of the damage we have done because of that alienation until nature itself is being altered in ways deleterious to human beings and other species.

The other more organic and dynamic tradition sings the praises of nature, the work and life-giving presence of God herself:

> Let earth praise YHWH;
> sea-monsters and all the deeps,
> fire and hail, snow and mist,
> gales that obey God's decree,
> mountains and hills,
> orchards and forests,
> wild animals and farm animals,
> snakes and birds . . .
> all rulers in the world,
> young men and girls,
> old people, and children too! (Ps 148:7–12)

This is an earth not alienated but giving voice to praise for the Creator from deep within its very reality.

Now not all religious institutions are prepared to embrace this creation story, for its implications will affect these structures as well. That there is resistance is no surprise. The ground is quaking underneath all human constructs, whether or not we believe them to be divinely inspired. What the new creation story is showing us is that hierarchy and centralized authority, dynamics of power and domination, grand temples and strict orthodoxies, are all poor models for how creation actually works, for how we experience the sacred within *this* story.

Creation is not a static, linear, determined process. This is not how evolution works; its "authority," its essence, is not centralized and passed down through a hierarchy. On the contrary, it is a ferment, experimenting here and there and everywhere, trying things out, seeing what works, then putting energy in those places. It bubbles up from below and spreads out horizontally, not vertically and from above. Evolution is an intensely dynamic process, not evolving in a straight line, but rather as a tumultuous series of events of creation and destruction.

We have arrived at a new moment in the consciousness of the human, and it is unsettling our place in the universe. But it is bubbling up all over the place and cannot be reversed. It suggests, for one thing, that creation is not here *for* us, but rather that we are of it, part of its magnificent expression. The human, it turns out, is not the reason why all this has happened. We are neither the beginning nor the end. Rather, we are right in the midst of the process of creation; it brings us into being and takes us back again; we are of it, within it; it unfolds through and around us. Much came before; much will come after.

I'm not making this up; it is what human *knowledge* has shown us and what mystics have intuited over the centuries, what the Jesuit paleontologist Pierre Teilhard de Chardin once called, "the pure majesty of the real itself."[9] It is not a story we are writing, but a story we are coming to understand. "The offering you really want, the offering you mysteriously need every day to appease your hunger, to slake your thirst is nothing less than the growth of the world borne ever onwards in the stream of universal becoming."[10]

Those words were written nearly half a century ago, and only now is science beginning to catch up with this profound spiritual insight (though the spiritual insight will always probe deeper, always place meaning beyond what science can tell us).

Now, each of these emerging stages in consciousness of our place in the universe and within the earth story is a wrenching shift that affects everything in our lives, including how we experience the presence of God within this creation story. Let's not be too hard on ourselves or others around us if this truth seems a bit overwhelming, if the first reaction is to flinch from it, or retreat back into a comfortable certainty and then cling to it with all our might. When we glimpse the photos from the Hubble Space Telescope, especially the Deep Field images, when we see galaxies forming in the first half-billion years after the Big Bang, when we realize that this light is only reaching us now and only because our ingenuity created the telescope that could capture the light, when we realize that the source of that light, those galaxies, doesn't exist anymore, that something else is out there now whose light will not reach us for billions of years, and the earth won't be here then, when we realize that those galaxies existed in a universe whose size was then a mere fraction of what it is now after thirteen billion more years of expansion . . .

Well, then . . .

What happens to the old ideas of a God who stood outside and judged us for our sins, and who has prepared a special place for us in a heaven outside the universe once we are dead? Given the leap we are making in our understanding of the earth story within the context of the cosmos, it is no wonder that many people of faith are losing fascination with this divine image.

At the same time, what happens to the meaning of the cross and resurrection? What happens to the promise of eternal life?

I don't know. I cannot know. I cannot from my vantage point see the vast panorama that is this creation. But I do know that we are beginning to get a glimmer of meaning in the trajectory of these old stories that is more profound and more "dazzling" than we were capable of perceiving until now.

But even more important, given the stakes for our earth right now, it is time for our spirituality, as some have said, to "grow up," or grow into this new awareness. It is urgent that we face the consequences of what we now know of our place within the earth's life systems, even as that affects our formative myths and beliefs; operating out of old religious constructs that no longer serve, that do not shed light on our true situation, or even block the light, has become a real problem in our search for a way out of our planetary crisis. We are not outside and "in charge" of creation. We are not a "chosen people" assigned the role of conquerors of promised lands. This orientation that puts the human above nature and not subject to it has created an alienation, a disconnect from who we truly are. It has made us suspicious of nature, made us self-conscious about our bodies and our mortality, about our vulnerability and our dependency on all that lives.

We forget that without the larger earth community we cannot live, but that that community can do quite well without us, thank you. It is not the earth that is dying right now, but rather the millions of species that evolved in the conditions that made us possible over the course of the past 500,000 years or so. Sixty-five million years ago, conditions that made dinosaurs possible changed, and they no longer exist, but the evolution of life went on in any case. The earth did not need the dinosaurs, but the dinosaurs needed certain conditions in order to go on living. Our human-centered mythology has convinced us that the story cannot go on without us, at least not with any greater meaning in it—after all, if we are made in God's image and we become extinct, what then becomes of God?

"Growing up" means coming to that point where we begin to take responsibility for our lives, when we pass the stage of narcissism, believing the world revolves around us, our problems, our needs, our desires, and then putting God at the service of those needs and desires. Now we find ourselves in a position where how we live, informed by both the religious and secular versions of that story, has put us on course to destroy the human project altogether, because we are destroying the nature that is our home, that gives us our place within the larger earth community. From this orientation, believing this is all for us to use for our benefit, whether for capitalist gain, or for our comfort, or for human redemption, we are creating a new reality on earth in which there may be no human at all.

From alienation to connection: Restoring trust in nature

Alienation from nature, abstracting the human from the earth story, has left us a bit lost now, deeply enmeshed in an ecological crisis from which we do not know how to extract ourselves. We see our original relationship with nature as somehow connected to an inherent original sinfulness on our part from which we need to be redeemed. From there we have developed a distrust of nature, and thus of our own bodies. In this version of our creation story, our bodies betray us with their needs and desires, their natural temptations to sin, their mortality and inevitable corruption. Despite twenty-some chapters in each of the Gospels that make up the story of Jesus Christ, a story of healing, forgiveness, love, and compassion, we get very focused, as in the Mel Gibson film, on the passion, the suffering, as if this is somehow the point. This is what God sent his only Son into the world to do—to suffer and die for us because we are so terrible and *he* is so good. We are not worthy of this sacrifice, of course. Why? Because of being nature, natural, a body, part of an earth community, soil, humus, dependent, mortal, subject to decay. This decay is part of the natural process that brings forth life. But, by this version of creation, what is nature bears within it this fundamental flaw—death, symbol of sin. Therefore, the driving goal is somehow to save ourselves from being subject to the nature that is our home and substance, our beginning and end.

If we are to free ourselves for the transition that is coming, that we have already entered, I believe we must heal this alienation from nature, and soon. We must *reconnect* the human body to the earth community all around us.

When the tsunami struck Indonesia, Thailand, and Sri Lanka, we all heard the stories—when the ocean was first sucked out away from the beaches, many people rushed down to watch, to see this strange phenomenon. Many stood transfixed. Meanwhile, elephants, birds, and other animals started fleeing inland. They sensed innately, in their biology, what was coming.

We are no less capable of this instinct being no less *biological.* But our alienation has cost us the connections with nature, the relationship, that makes it possible for us to hear and see and *sense* what is happening all around us.

I remember well the odd, uncomfortable feeling in the Maryland suburbs the years that every single crow disappeared by September because of West Nile virus—a 100 percent mortality rate. It was eerie, weird, and hardly something I had thought about before. Crows. Noisy, pesky, irritating, all-present in our urban and suburban worlds. Yet playing a vital role in the balance of life, robbing nests of their eggs to keep the bird population under control, helping to clean things up by eating the carcasses of dead animals.

What I noticed, then, was the absence, especially of their sound.

This was a temporary phenomenon, but a hint of our future, of many *absences* to come if we do not learn how to live differently with our fellow species.

On December 14–15, 2006, the Seattle area was hit by powerful storms packing seventy mph winds in the city and over one hundred mph in the Cascade Mountain Range. Huge hemlocks, Douglas firs, and red cedars came crashing down. Before, this would have been just another fabulous storm event in the forests, but now there are people and homes all over the place.

When the trees came down, so did power lines—millions were without electricity for days. And then there were the smashed cars, and roofs, and driveways. A lot of damage. It was a record storm, something that happens pretty rarely in those parts.

But what an inconvenience for those who now live in this fast-growing part of the country, who were attracted in part to the beautiful wooded areas around the city. Some arborists say that trees had been weakened by all that development, part of the reason for the extent of the damage. "They cite trees that toppled because their roots had been severed or shrunk by development; trees once safely flanked in a forest but left fatally exposed as remnants in housing developments; and trees with poor and hasty pruning, perhaps intended to expand a view of the Cascades or the Olympic Mountains or prevent a tree from falling."[11]

Must have the view. Must destroy nature for a view.

How did people react? Well, for many, the solution was obvious: get rid of more trees. You see, it's not that the human turned out to be dangerous for the trees, it's that the trees are now dangerous for the human. Now they are suspect, an ominous presence, because we live under them, because we have property under them, because they might fall down and smash our cars, or leave us without electricity for days. Arborists and employees of the Department of Natural Resources were making an effort to reeducate people about living with trees. The article cited above speaks of some experts carrying out a campaign "to restore trust" in the trees.

Restore trust in the trees. That's how far we have strayed from our roots in the natural world.

The article also describes "the mountainsides' worth clear-cut over a century of logging in the Pacific Northwest and the development of recent decades that has pushed people eastward from Seattle onto golf course communities carved from second- and third-growth timber farms."[12]

Really, sometimes I have to get up from writing this stuff and take a walk, because it is so heartbreaking. What in the world are we doing?

Speaking of the long-time residents of these areas who had learned long ago how to live with the wonders of nature, Doug Schindler, director of special projects for the Mountains to Sound Greenway Trust, told the author of the article: "To them, that's what happens when you have storms, and trees fall down, and you lose power. Rivers rise, and you have floods, and that's part of living in the natural world. And they're ready for that. Part of the problem you're finding now is more and more urban people are moving into rural areas."[13] Yes, and often they do not have a clue.

Here's another tidbit along these lines: timber exports from the Amazon rainforest "increased in value nearly 50 percent in 2004 over the previous year to just under $1 billion. . . . Nearly 40 percent of the wood cut in the Amazon is now being shipped overseas, compared with only 14 percent in

1999."[14] The main markets? I don't have to tell you. The United States, Europe, and China. The United States accounts for *one-third* of these shipments. Our imported wood is ravaging the Amazon rainforest.

Now, around Seattle, people are worried about the trees they *see*. After the storm, they look at a tree and see danger or property damage. Meanwhile, when we buy a piece of furniture made from imported rainforest wood, we worry not at all about the trees we *don't* see. Either way, there is something wrong with the relationship between this human biology and the biology of the forests. Trust within that relationship has broken down. Restoring mutual trust between this human species and the others with which we are in relationship, with which we share this planet, is one of the great tasks of this generation.

We need a faith, a spirituality, that can make this healing possible.

In search of a new story

The alienation embedded in our original Western Judeo-Christian creation stories reflects this human-centered orientation, this belief that it is all here for us. But the stories also reflect something else—a deep and profound search for meaning that is a unique experience of human consciousness, as far as we know. Humans of long-ago centuries didn't create these stories with the intention of bringing about the destruction of the ecosystems of the planet and eventually our extinction. Those realities did not enter into their stories because they were not in the consciousness of those who wrote them down. They were dealing with their own harsh realities in a very harsh world. These stories originated with nomadic tribal peoples whose lives were affected by the terrain, the weather, and the various warring tribes and empires all around them. They searched for a God who could liberate them from slavery, save them in battle, ensure a supply of food and water, protect them from wild creatures, be their protector and source of strength. In exchange, God asked them to enter into a covenant, one that demanded of them certain behaviors and rituals, and above all, justice.

Creation myths of all sorts—and there are so many wonderful creation stories—are about humans trying to make sense of their world and to draw meaning from it, or trying to tame it and make it less threatening, placating the forces of nature that were indeed so threatening to humans through most of our history, until brick houses, electricity, guns, locks, and police forces. Myths were created to give people a sense of identity and place, to provide cohesion, sometimes by force. Many myths are about battles among gods of different tribes and peoples vying for supremacy or allegiance. Sometimes gods were needed to rouse people to war or to strengthen them to face their enemies in battle. The repercussions of failure in these battles could be horrific, including extremely violent death, captivity, or slavery. One needed a strong god to face this kind of trauma and remain stalwart or to hold the community together through difficult times.

Myths also helped explain the cosmos, the wild creatures, the fears and the wonders experienced by our ancestors. They helped define and articulate the night skies, the shifting sun, the waxing and waning of the moon, the migration of animals needed for food, the spirits of the hunt, the creatures that dwell in the forest, the rhythms of night and day and of the seasons. They illuminated a particular geography and the challenges, wisdom, gifts, and ecstasies experienced there.

In the tribal times of the Middle East two thousand years ago and more, myths about gods consolidated chosen peoples, fed the hubris of conquerors, gave strength to the enslaved and oppressed. When Rome was powerful, so were the gods of Rome, and when the Hebrew God defeated Baal and the nature gods, there was only one God, YHWH. And when Jesus Christ rose from the dead, death itself had been conquered—we were saved from the result of our original sin. This was a powerful God, indeed.

We draw our identities from our stories. They tell us who we are, which is why they have such hold on us, why they have so much power *over* us. If you put together the story of the Garden of Eden, our banishment from nature because of our fundamental flaw, our innate sinfulness, with the secular myth of the United States' "manifest destiny," you get a sense of what we are up against in this society to try to change the story to something more appropriate to the new knowledge of our place in the earth community and within the cosmos.

When I was traveling out West, I stopped at a national park area in Idaho on ancestral lands of the Nez Perce tribe, or the Nimiipuu (the People). I parked my car at a spot marked as the birthplace of the People and walked down the path to find it. At the end was a large mound of earth surrounded by a simple wooden fence. There I pressed a button for a recording of the Creation story, narrated by an elder of the tribe.

It is very complex and wonderful, so I do it no justice by this summary. But it came about this way: The Monster covered the surrounding hills and was devouring all the animals. Coyote grew lonely and devised a plan. First, he carefully sharpened five knives. Then he drew the attention of the Monster, who then swallowed him as well. Inside the Monster, he found all the animals. Then, with the knives, he began slashing at the Monster's heart. It was very strenuous work, and the knives kept breaking. But in the chaos, the animals were able to escape through the Monster's various bodily orifices. Finally, with the very last slash of the very last knife, Coyote killed the Monster. He then cut the heart into pieces and threw them all around the Northwest. Where each chunk of heart fell, a tribe was born.

And here at this mound, he threw the last piece of the heart, and the People came into being.

The Nimiipuu know where they come from. I was sitting right there at the spot where they were created.

This is an incredibly strong bond between that part of the earth and these humans. It is part of what our "manifest destiny" tried so hard to destroy—the identity of the Native American tribes with the land that birthed them.

In our Western myth we were thrown out of a mythical garden and we don't have a clue where it was, where we were born, where we come from. Is this part of our problem—this story? We were banished from our roots, taken out of our land and given another, and we just kept going. Our manifest destiny has been to be on the move, conquering, converting, controlling the destinies of others, imposing our God on peoples and cultures. Time and again, we have left home on this restless march to—where? freedom? fame and fortune? a better life? to "civilize" others? to convert them to the one true God? Who knows anymore what originally drove this journey—yet it is from that history that we have taken our identity.

As I sat there that day in Idaho, I found myself envious of the Nez Perce.

But there's another reason why I mention this story here. Because in 1838 a Christian missionary named Henry Spalding came to the land of the Nez Perce to convert them. He set up a mission at the site of the government agency. You can visit it. It's part of the National Park Service (NPS) historic site. Now the NPS describes this contact between the Nez Perce and the Christians as "painful."

The Nez Perce tribe was well off, known especially for its horses. The Nez Perce traveled around the Northwest trading, hunting, fishing. Spalding saw this as a problem. It is hard to preach to a people on the move. So, in addition to his notable fire-and-brimstone preaching, he tried to coax the People to abandon their way of life and become farmers. He built a grist mill, and it says right on the sign that the mill helped some of the Nez Perce to abandon their way of life.

On December 9, 1838, he wrote in his diary: "May we in this house count souls flocking to Jesus as doves to their windows."[15] I'm sure Jesus would have been proud.

The mission split the Nimiipuu in two between those who converted and those who did not. It's a tragic story, really, and gave me pause to reflect on how almost every time Christianity came to the "heathen," the result was violence, division, and the upending of a relationship among a tribe, a people, and the earth where they lived. The contact was usually "painful," a legacy that Christians today might want to pause and consider.

In the Visitor Center, and I wish I had written it down, was a quotation about how the White Man came from somewhere else, but the People were born out of this earth. I found myself wondering what it will take to restore the relationship of we US Americans, steeped as we are in our own religio-cultural mythologies, with the natural world that surrounds us and the larger diverse, multicultural, burgeoning human community whose fate we now share.

We, too, were born out of this earth; we, too, are part of that community, and that's the part of the story that we need to reclaim.

Business as usual must stop

Sometimes I find profound and deeply spiritual reflections in unexpected places, like the *New York Times*:

> Like you, I've been reading dire reports of declining species for many years now. They have the value of causing us to pay attention to species in trouble, and the sad fact is that the only species likely to endure are the ones we humans manage to pay attention to. There was a time when it was better, if you were a nonhuman species, to be ignored by humans, because we trapped or shot or otherwise exploited all of the ones that got our attention. But in the past 40 years, we have killed all those millions of birds or, let us say, unintentionally caused a dramatic population loss, simply by going about business as usual.[16]

This column, written by Verlyn Klinkenborg, refers to a report from the Audubon Society showing that we are bringing some of our most beloved and ubiquitous bird species to the brink of extinction—Northern bobwhites, Eastern meadowlarks, the common tern, field sparrows, and more—25.5 million meadow birds "missing," a staggering drop in their populations. Klinkenborg continues:

> Agriculture has intensified. So has development. Open space has been sharply reduced. We have simply pursued our livelihoods. We knew it was inimical to wolves and mountain lions. But we somehow trusted that all the innocent little birds were here to stay. What they actually need to survive, it turns out, is a landscape that is less intensely human.[17]

Again, what they and other species need to survive is *a landscape that is less intensely human*.

Business as usual is killing life on this planet—not divorces, not contraception, not gay marriage, not women priests, not ordained gay men—business as usual—buying a house, driving a car, building big box stores, shopping at Wal-Mart, developing high-tech corridors on former woodlands and wetlands, building vacation homes in the mountains, on lake shores, and coastlines, buying imported wood, drinking bottled water, flying around the world, fighting wars, strip-mining for coal, mono-cropping for agriculture, spraying pesticides on fields, bulldozing the next green area for a subdivision.

"In our everyday economic behavior, we seem determined to discover whether we can live alone on earth."[18]

We know, we know, we know, we cannot.

We know this.

And now we need a story, a framework of meaning, a *faith*, if you will, that is up to this moment in our evolutionary history, that can articulate this new situation, speak to it, bring it into the light, challenge us—make *seeing* it as inescapable as *seeing* what the political and religious authorities did to Jesus because of what he preached and did. Because right now the passion of *our* times is not only the body of the suffering human God nailed to the cross; it is the suffering of the sacred earth, whose life is dying all around us. The passion of our times that we must *see* is the destruction, the death, the unraveling of the earth's life-giving systems; what we must see is our potential to end this story of life on this planet, or at least this chapter of the planet's story, when life exploded in an unprecedented burst of creativity out of which we, too, emerged.

Sadly, rather than reverence the earth, we have tried to make nature submit to us, and we see all around us the detritus, the ruin—in our personal lives, our human communities, the condition of our planet—because of something so incredibly obvious: business as usual.

Now we know that this human-centered story is not the essence of the universe story, not its central theme. The sun will burn out one day, and the earth may be lifeless long before that. The observable universe is vast beyond reckoning and is still expanding. What we see from the Hubble Space Telescope doesn't exist anymore and hasn't for billions of years. We can see what was "out there" millions of light years ago, but not what is there now. Some scientists even suggest that we may not be the only universe, whatever that means.

In this vastness of mystery and creation, it is hard sometimes to believe that so many of us think that going to the shopping mall is what gives our lives meaning, or that whether or not we can buy an SUV is a matter of our freedom. We have had the privilege in our time of being able to leave the planet and look back at its wonder, its beauty unique against the blackness of space, its atmosphere a thin veil that holds within it all life—yet we resist seeing what it is that we have the power to destroy—and the power to save, if we are willing to relinquish, well, power. We have trouble appreciating what we are part of, what is taking place in and through us.

Are we simply too small for this gift of consciousness? Because if we are, we have two choices—to remain small and continue this deadly course, or to enlarge.

We are headed for some very difficult times, no matter what we do now. That is one of the points I am trying to make in this book. Nothing will make this wrenching transition go away; we can neither avoid it nor escape it. We have nowhere to go. We will either find a way to live through it, with dignity, with integrity, with *hope* (not optimism), or we will go through it with mounting human suffering.

Gerald Barney in our interview said:

> Now you're going to ask, is there time? I think what we have to recognize is that we're all riding on a jumbo jet, and I think it's going down and we don't know exactly how much time until it hits down; but one thing about jumbo jets is that they're egalitarian. It doesn't make much difference whether you're first class or the last row of the coach section. It's bad all around.
>
> I think a lot of what is causing us to wring our hands is wanting to view that there is a way out that is not going to be really uncomfortable. And I don't think there is.

Or again, Barney offers another parable:

> The image that comes to mind is somebody in a canoe who has gotten a little too close to Niagara Falls and there comes a point where you can stop furiously paddling because you know you're going to go over, and then it comes down to thinking more about how I'm going to go over, what I am going to do.

How to get that marble to roll as gently as possible down the side of the bowl, because it's coming down in any case.

It must change, or it's going to destroy us. We must change, or we are going to destroy what we need to live. If we really embrace a faith centered on principles like the Beatitudes and Woes, laying down our lives for others, Matthew 25, the healing stories, the absolute centrality of love, the loaves and fishes, truth that sets us free, the story of the rich young man, and so on, then it is time, and even past time, to start applying these stories to the world in which we now find ourselves—as it is, not as we wish it. The Christian story is a deeply troubling and disturbing affair; it quickens the conscience. It makes us see the suffering all around us—the wounded one who falls into the hands of robbers, the poor family whose land becomes uninhabitable, the unemployed miners drinking toxic water—and tells us that these are truths from which we dare not turn away as did the priest and the Levite.

At the same time, it tells us something about how God acts in the midst of all this—and that is the point. God acts *in the midst* of all this, not apart from it, but in *it*, the whole thing, the whole story. And to me it is unmistakable that we are being called in this time to a much larger experience of faith, one large enough to embrace the ecological crises that threaten life on this one planet, large enough to embrace our new sense of who we are within the cosmos. It is time to live into this urgent, vital, vibrant, all-encompassing sense of God, intimately present within the crisis, calling us to an utterly new way of life, coming into our consciousness in a wholly new way now in our time and in the consciousness of this one species that has in its hands the possibility of bringing the marble down gently—all hands cooperating—of going over the edge of the falls with the flow instead of against it. Because if we go against it, we will surely break apart.

Our little canoes, those belief constructs that no longer hold, simply cannot withstand the force of this new creation.

8

Ecological Hope

or,

Living Beyond the "End of the World"

> *When we look back from the year 2100, I fear*
> *we will see a period when our creations—*
> *technological, social, and ecological—outstripped*
> *our understanding, and we lost control*
> *of our destiny.*
> —Thomas Homer-Dixon[1]

> *There is not only the so-called dark night of the*
> *soul but the dark night of the world. What if,*
> *by chance, our time in evolution is a dark-night*
> *time—a time of crisis and transition*
> *that must be understood if it is to be part*
> *of learning a new vision and harmony*
> *for the human species and the planet?*
> —Constance Fitzgerald, OCD[2]

We are coming to the end of the world, or at least to the end of *a* world. How it ends will be very much up to us. We have many choices in front of us, but not *this* one—that the world we know is ending. What has been familiar to us as a framework in which we have lived our lives for a very long time is ending. Assumptions that propped up that framework have proved faulty, most of all, that we humans are not subject to finitude, are not subject to nature, are not at the mercy of the earth's awe-inspiring, wondrous, and most beautiful balance of life.

More, a whole world view that has shaped our history for centuries is collapsing of its own weight, a weight we have attempted to describe, however

158

falteringly, in this book, the weight of how this one species has lived on the earth, out of balance, with a certain swagger and hubris, and belief systems that propped up our grandiose sense of ourselves, belief systems that were born when the universe known at the time was a desert land, a land of scarcity, containing a people oppressed by empires and by religious and political authorities of their time, a drama taking place on a tiny earth around which the sun revolved and the constellations moved across the night sky. God was in the heavens, and we humans looked to him for our salvation. When his mercy outweighed his judgment, he would enter into history to liberate his people, renewing a covenant of complete loyalty and fidelity in exchange for his protection. That was the centerpiece of the drama, and all the rest a stage, a drama going on between God and humans that took place just a bit outside, above, and beyond the evolutionary story of everything, under the arc of that small universe.

Jesus Christ corrected many parts of the story that we got wrong with his love and compassion, forgiveness and healing, relinquishment of power and authority, and an ethic of sharing, of community beyond boundaries of ethnic, cultural, class, religious, or imperialist identities. God had been distanced; now God was brought close, into intimacy, a relationship that needs no interlocutors, arbiters, no outside powers or authorities, no hierarchical ladder, no *over and above*, a *horizontal* relationship that is best defined by selfless love and the breaking of bread. Healing came by faith, and faith was something that came from *within*, something to which we all have access.

Come to think of it, now that we know there is no up and down in our universe, *horizontal* is right on the mark, both radical in the context of how the Western version of God has often been conceived (above and over) and completely appropriate for our new awareness. And what we know from Einstein and those that came after is that horizontal does not mean straight, since all lines bend through the curve of space and time. Such is the mystery embodied now in the beams of the cross, stretching out in all directions, a sacred symbol for many ancient religions right up to our own age.

Jesus did not speak to the ecological crises of our times because we were still a long ways from them, from the steam engine and gears churned by coal-powered electricity and private automobiles and ocean dead zones and mountaintopping and ozone holes and melting polar ice caps. Gaps between rich and poor were huge then, as they are now, along with slavery to provide the work force for those in power, as was the experience of oppression and domination—and he had a lot to say about those things. From that witness came our social justice traditions, our passion for justice, our preferential option for the poor, our concerns for structures of injustice.

So, too, did he speak of those in religious authority who used doctrine and laws to judge and oppress others, making pacts of corruption and collaboration with the empire while at the same time trying to put obstacles in the way of anything new or innovative, new insights or revelations that would undermine their authority—like Jesus himself, for example.

He did not encounter the phenomenon of global limits, of reaching and then surpassing the earth's "carrying capacity," because the earth, though suffering numerous local wounds in many places by then, often as a result of rapacious empires, was still quite able to carry 300,000,000 Homo sapiens in concert with other living creatures. We can search scripture, but we will find little in the way of chapter and verse to enlighten our predicament or accurately describe our world now. But I think we can glean something of how Jesus would have approached the ecological crisis and what he might have to say to us about these times, given those "corrections" to the original story. Given the extraordinary witness that he was in his time, it would be sad to leave his word there as if his story, too, is finished, has nothing more to say to us, as if the God whose love he revealed was not relevant for the age of transition we have entered some two thousand years later.

I believe we are being drawn by the crises and revelations of our times to a much larger setting for the narratives of our faith, not of lesser consequence than the setting in which the Gospels were first written. I believe we are being called to greatly enlarge our sense, or *experience*, of God within that setting. We are being drawn by an insight about the Divine embedded in this age of planetary crisis and scientific discovery, an insight embedded within this twenty-first century world "in which we live and move and have our being" (Acts 17:28, KJ). For this reason, our faith is being pulled and stretched as never before, asking more of us, challenging us in entirely new ways as we face entirely new realities.

Unless we think our faith too small for the world we live in now, or believe it a comforting shield to protect us from the harshness of our world, it is incumbent upon us to expand our experience of faith to embrace the full reality of our predicament and to inform the decisions we make from here on out. This *is* what Jesus did—face his world fully and honestly, not shying away from the suffering or the disquieting demands that it would make on him. We need a faith now that can help us face *this* world that we have made, one that can encompass our ecological crisis, provide it with content and meaning, and help us find a way through and beyond it.

Beyond the exigencies of a gospel of healing and justice within the human community comes need for a faith that can embrace the earth.

Because all of this can appear daunting and terrifying, we also search for an experience of God, a relationship, that is both large enough—and *intimate* enough—to counter the disorientation, dizziness, and sense of displacement we feel with these discoveries of how large our world is, the true place of the human in our planetary history, and how grave our ecological crisis is. We seek a faith that can enlighten and inform all this disturbing news by providing a framework of meaning for it, a place for an experience of the

Divine within it, a new sense of our true home, of our cherished place in the cosmos and on this planet, a *spiritual space* large enough to contain all of our fears and our hopes, our questions and our bewilderment.

We need a sense of God that can encompass and embrace with great compassion this feeling of being overwhelmed and terrified by our new knowledge and the enormity of the planetary project in front of us now, knowledge that can make us feel so small, so insignificant, so helpless.

We need a sense of God greater than our ecological grief, one that can sustain us through it and give us courage to go on.

We need a sense of God that does not invite us to grow smaller, to retreat into personal sins with the expectation of some salvation apart from and outside this larger drama of our earth and cosmos. We need a sense of God that embraces that drama fully, with urgency, with passion, with love, as did the God revealed in Jesus Christ.

From that experience, then, out of that enlarged sense of God, we begin to articulate a framework of meaning, a *spirituality*, that can help us rise to the enormity of the challenges we face. The values that shape our lives from now on need to be as broad and as profound as that experience of God. Our values need to be able to inform and give shape to all that we need now to save ourselves and the rich life of this planet. Within the context of this new framework, we rediscover the mission of the human, and in particular, in the context of this writing, *the mission of US Americans,* as we face our planetary crisis.

In the same way as those gospel stories we so cherish—the Beatitudes and Woes, the Last Judgment and Last Supper, the healing stories, the parables, the woman at the well, the stories of Martha and Mary, the Good Samaritan, the cross and resurrection—shaped meaning that gave heart and vision and strength to a religiosity and spirituality that embraced the passion of the human being for twenty centuries, now we need the stories, images, inspiration, and values that can give heart, vision, and strength to a religiosity and spirituality as big as what we know now of the universe, of the place of the human within it, of what is at stake on this one small planet. We need stories that can help us hear, receive, and respond to the invitation at this moment of crisis and vastly expanded consciousness, to respond not only to the bad news, but also to the attraction and seductiveness of an all-encompassing Creator God emerging out of the very heart of the cosmos, indeed, out of the very crisis itself.

As our knowledge of the universe and our place on the planet expands and matures, so too does our experience of something else—of *Presence,* enormous, vibrant, and immediate *Presence,* here right now, in every moment of time and space that knits together this cosmos. "Where two or three are gathered" is still true but extends now to all energy and matter, everything that binds and connects us to the real mystery. Whatever this is that is at work at the core of the creative process is closer to us than we are to ourselves. That we have become so alienated from this Presence is remarkable, given the depth of intimacy in all that relates us to the dynamism of creation all around and within us.

It has been said so many times, source of so much contemplative reflection over the past four decades: when human beings finally left the planet and then looked back, they saw something truly remarkable, a planet without maps, without borders, a magnificent blue world, white clouds swirling in a climate made by a thin layer of atmosphere, all life contained within it. The vision brought ecstasy, depression, exhilaration, crashed through old visions of our world. Many expected a tremendous breakthrough in human consciousness, with changes in behaviors to go along with it—like the end of war, a new sense of the common destiny of the human being, even a wholly new sense of identity.

The first color photo of our planet has become a virtual icon, the sacred image of our times, a new revelation.

And then we went on about our business, and most major religions were affected hardly at all. Maybe part of the problem is that the old ways of trying to channel and control the essence of the Divine were suddenly being overwhelmed by the power of this icon. How do mere humans control the way in which such an enlarged canvas for the experience of the Sacred will manifest itself in human consciousness? What doctrine, human-made institution, hierarchy, or orthodoxy can hold and control it or how it comes to us now? What becomes of the human drama on so large a canvas?

What could possibly be more threatening to those constructs?

I can feel the trembling, I can hear the foundations cracking and crumbling beneath my feet. What will happen to me, if, instead of looking around for something to grab onto to keep from falling, I simply let go?

A creation story

In May 2005 I went off for a solitary journey into the history of my evolution. It was not my intention that day. I thought I was going off to see the wonders of the Petrified Forest/Painted Desert National Park in Northern Arizona. You just never know what will happen when you venture out into creation.

If you have been there, you know what I'm talking about; it is a breathtaking expanse of desert, and it is called painted for a reason. The deep reds, roses, pinks, and shades of brown and beige, especially vivid in the late afternoon sun, create a landscape unique in the world; they speak to us, or reflect back to us, a geological history that goes back hundreds of millions of years. This land is still taking shape, sculpted by the winds and desert storms.

As the land erodes, the remains of ancient trees appear; the living matter of the wood disappeared long ago. Once upon a time, these two-hundred-foot towers of tropical life fell, sank, and were slowly dragged along the bottom of an immense river bed. Sediment got stuck in the flood plain, in the log jams and river detritus. Trees were torn from river beds by raging rapids, carried hundreds of miles, and then buried beneath the soil. Slowly, slowly, over millions of years, silica seeped through the walls of the cells that made up the living matter of the trees, for those trees were porous, as we are, as is all matter. Every cell of these ancient trees filled up with iron oxides, glassy minerals. What we see now is not wood but the magnificent colors of quartz rock formed in those cells like a mold in the perfect shape of the trees. And as the winds and rains erode the desert surface, little by little they are being uncovered, here and there, scattered all over this old flood plain, to be discovered by Homo sapiens now, tens of millions of years later. No one knows how many logs remain below ground to be revealed perhaps to some other visitors hundreds and thousands of years from now, assuming we have left the earth habitable for visitors to Arizona.

Fossil bones, patterns on rock, all speak to this ancient land once vibrant with an entirely different kind of life, and there I was walking along, stunned, being, well, enlarged. How could I not be?

And I wondered to myself how this land had become so dry, why the climate had changed, what forces were at work over those millions of years to make the rains go away and the animals become extinct and the giant trees disappear. The signs in the park gave me my answer, and this was the part that altered my perceptions of the Southwest, and this living earth, forever.

This land I was on, whose trails I walked across, was not in that spot back then. It was not *there*, in that location. It was somewhere around Panama, near the equator—which explains the tropical climate, the two-hundred-foot trees now permineralized and buried, land that slowly floated off to Arizona so that on that day, 220 million years later, I could get in my rented car, show my park pass at the gate, park my car, stroll across the footpaths, see what the winds and rain are revealing, and gasp in awe.

Now I know my basic earth science. I know about floating continents and other ancient ages of life and great extinctions. But in that space, in that moment, all that science got out of my abstract thoughts and into every part of my conscious being. I had a powerful sensation of standing on a living planet, one that still seethes, moves, trembles, floats, creates, and re-creates itself over and over again—as with those tectonic plates that suddenly gave way and slipped underneath each other in the ocean off Indonesia. I felt the earth moving beneath my feet, carrying me. I had a dizzying sensation of all the Creation that came before me and led up to me in that moment. I had an almost overwhelming sensation of what it means that, after all those eons of changes, there are creatures that park their cars, take a walk, look out at all of this, know what they are seeing, and pronounce it awesome and beautiful.

That's what we are part of.

I think we are supposed to "get" something here. I think there is a reason for consciousness. I think the planet is trying to communicate something to and through us by creating us at all, and I don't think it is about shopping or the value of our stock portfolios.

I think the story is a bit bigger than us.

Meanwhile, in 2007, a new natural-history museum opened in Petersburg, Kentucky. It is called the Creation Museum. I haven't seen it, at least as of this writing. But a reviewer for the *New York Times* did, Edward Rothstein, and he described the experience.[3] It is a museum to the creationist version of our universe story—that six thousand years ago, God pronounced a series of edicts over six days and all that ever was and is now was created. Everything that has come and gone, every species and age, every natural wonder, every galaxy and black hole in the heavens, all created then in that moment. Dioramas show human figures sharing the land with the dinosaurs, just to prove the point.

Some 45 percent of US Americans doubt the science of evolution. They believe instead in the creationist version of our story, the literal Genesis story—all creation by the command of God made in a week's time.

And I ask myself, are we able to stretch our ideas of God enough to grasp our situation, or will we use God as our blinders, even the beam in our eye? What is it about us that would make some people build a temple to an idea of God that no longer reflects what we have come to know about our world, to cling so stubbornly to a belief structure as to create a venue for a version of a story that no longer holds?

Now the Painted Desert and the permineralized wood of the Petrified Forest, now the land that moves under my feet, become a threat to a shaky foundation of religious belief. Now a museum is created, a monument, to a version of truth that can explain neither the Painted Desert nor how we have come to this point in our evolutionary history, when the fate of life as we know it on the planet is in jeopardy.

The museum was not a humble attempt. The place cost $27 million to build, testament to the fear of embracing a reality that is causing old meaning structures to collapse. The framework of meaning belonging to a creation story in which the planet would take 220 million years to create a landscape, move it to Arizona, and bring me to the wonder I experienced that day seems too inscrutable, too uncomprehending—I cannot get my head around that idea of God or find the simple rules of life that will get me to heaven, that define righteousness and truth.

When the new revelation seems too hard, it is easier to retreat back to the old smaller gods and worship there. We build temples and walls around that "truth" and then defend it against all comers.

We become tribal once again. And God becomes head of the tribe.

Why tell this story? Because it says something about how our stories, our metaphors, shape our meaning constructs, our values, how we live. I started this book with the Katrina metaphor. That is one way to look at our relationship with the earth. Standing in the vastness of space and time there in the Petrified Forest, I experienced a very different kind of relationship, as sacred as any other I have known.

My "God," my sense of the Sacred, enlarged that day. I will never forget it. How can God get small again? How can I ever again look at this earth as something other than alive, dynamic, the location of my life, my being? How do we care for our "home" and the family that resides there?

Why tell this story? Because maybe it will help us see the earth a little differently. Maybe it makes it just a bit harder to see the planet as a "resource" for our human uses, but instead as an unfolding creation, and the human within it. Maybe it helps us see the larger canvas on which the story of creation is still being written, the unfolding revelation of whatever it is that burst forth fourteen billion years ago into this vast explosive creative wonder that is our cosmos. Maybe it helps us see the uniqueness of this planet, and then the uniqueness of consciousness, this ability to know that we know, and how amazing and incredible is this gift of life.

I mean, thank goodness that these places belong to the National Park Service or we might see people resting their feet on some ancient permineralized logs in front of the porches of a desert vacation home.

Looking back on the earth from outer space—this, too, suggests another kind of relationship, one we thought might bond human beings in a new way as we glanced collectively back at our home planet. Maybe it is just taking us some time to adjust. Maybe there is still time to live the consequences of that collective moment in human consciousness. And maybe this is what can save us.

If we can begin to see what we are a part of, this one species on a magnificent planet floating in space, and start to gather up these moments of revelation of our place, our real story, from all the corners of the earth where they are happening—and they are happening everywhere—we might also begin to see the way through what is going to be a profoundly difficult transition. In this common bond of revelation and awareness of our shared fate occurring now within our species, perhaps we can begin to find the courage we need to get through this "uncomfortable" time that is coming, courage and faith enough to arrive at and then live through and beyond the "end of the world."

Enlarging our sense of God

Why does this matter, this business of our experience of God? Why does it matter to the fate of life on earth? It matters because for most humans, spirit-religion-faith is still how we attempt to articulate and to live *meaning*, what gives life purpose and from that the values by which we live. Our human experience of meaning must grow now, just as our consciousness of the planet's reality, and our role within it, has grown. This is what will give shape and direction to our response to the crisis.

As the revelation of our place within the cosmos has enlarged our conception of the Divine, so, too, does it enlarge the meaning of the human journey on this earth and within the cosmos. It enlarges and expands our sense of place and identity beyond nationalisms, religions, ethnicities, or other tribal identities. Indeed, it must. Our survival depends upon it, so riven is this world by these very things. On this common ground of our shared humanity in this moment of crisis, rather than in our assertions of singular and only truth, competing for the depleted "resources" of the planet or for economic and political hegemony, we can begin to move out of our competitive, distrustful, selfish, and fear-based approach to our problems toward a sense of solidarity among humans and the larger earth community.

Here in this shared space, with each contributing from his or her own unique story and tradition, insight and experience, we can begin to find the common wisdom and the strength for what many now call the great turning, the turning from one age and way of life to another. Because this is the challenge of our generation, and the next, and the one after that—to live through the "end of the world," to ease how that end comes about, to find strength to do what we need to do to bring the marble down gently, knowing that we may have to endure a great deal of difficulty in the process.

If I could communicate one thing in all these pages, it would be to share with you this sense of how significant we are right now in the living story of our planet, how large our *ecological meaning* is—larger than the economic meaning of a consumer society and the private personalized religion assigned to us as the constructs of our lives in these times in which we live.

Enlarging our sense of God is not some radical new thing, not unprecedented in the human journey, nor does it make God purely a human invention. Rather, God becomes that intimate connection and bond, that powerful force, energy, dynamism that keeps inviting this evolutionary process to open more, and then more. This force just keeps urging it, us, on.

The Bible is based on stories in which the sense of God is being enlarged over and over again, or something new in the consciousness of the human being enlarges the experience of God. In the biblical journey we go from one tribal God among many vying for survival, power, or loyalty, to the one

God of a liberated chosen people being declared as the "only" God, bonded with his people through a covenant. We journey from a God who condones war and oppression to a God who says we must love our enemies, from a God who turns on the nations of unbelievers and spits the unfaithful out of his mouth to a God who shows us that every human being is to be treated as a child of God and is equal and precious in God's eyes. Later, we discover a God who no longer sees Gentile or Jew, woman or man, but all are one and equal, a God who no longer prefers a chosen people for an exclusive salvation. That was enormous change in the consciousness of the Jewish and Gentile communities of the time.

In the Old Testament story of Abraham and his son Isaac, YHWH announces something new—that human sacrifice is no longer acceptable as a mode of worship. Later in the prophets we find a God who has become concerned about the oppression of others, even when his chosen are the perpetrators, a God who suddenly cares passionately about justice, about slavery, about wealth and corruption. In later episodes of the Old Testament story, we find a God very involved in the passion of a people whose betrayals constantly cause them to be conquered, punished, but in whose history God will soon be getting deeply involved and who will one day, one more time, liberate them from their oppressors.

Centuries later, many of the people who clung to this eschatological hope came to realize that God was not coming back to free his people in a political, historical project, though this version of historical hope would surface over and over again in following centuries, in Jesus's time and in our own.

Then a new story emerges: With Jesus of Nazareth, God unfolds or manifests in spaces unheard of before—not in power and glory, not in battles and judgment, not in historical liberations, but in the Beatitudes, in Matthew 25, in the sharing of loaves and fishes, in breaking down barriers among people along tribal and racial lines, in forgiveness and love of enemies, in the recognition that even slaves and Roman soldiers are *persons*, are equals in the eyes of God, that power is to be eschewed and we are to share all things in common so that all needs for dignified life can be met—until no one is in want.

We have a hard time seeing this from our perspective two thousand years later, but this represented an extraordinary breakthrough in human consciousness, this value placed on the life of the human being and the inherent rights and dignity of each person—values it has taken two thousand years to appreciate and to encode in national and international law, and still we struggle with living out the full ramifications of this "revelation."

Jesus challenged his followers to move beyond their historical understandings of God, often by contradicting his own religious traditions, breaking out of the confines of religious authorities and orthodoxies, abrogating old laws, violating them at times, contradicting them and moving beyond them

("You have heard it said . . . but *I* say . . . "). To follow Jesus does not mean to live within the confines of the religious traditions of the time; his example is to break through boundaries that close off or obstruct access to the Sacred, to the Divine.

The human experience of God has enlarged over and over again, a reflection of the evolution of our consciousness, or our awareness of our story.

Evolution did not end with the Jesus story, and it did not end with us; we are not the conclusion of the story of creation. The evolution of consciousness has not ended with the capacity of the human mind at this moment, much less two thousand years ago. God is always greater than what we know, than the stories we create in our attempts to approach *meaning*, especially the meaning of the human, always calling us, pulling us forward to more—and then more.

Earth theologian, or geologian, as some call him, Passionist Father Thomas Berry has used the phrase "re-inventing the human presence on the Earth."[4] I believe our task is no less than that. We learned in the previous chapter that this earth needs *less* human presence if all its species, including us, are to have a chance at survival in this altered world. That we have altered it, this one species, in so short a time, is the surest sign that we have come to a new understanding of the human and its place within the fabric of life. Meanwhile, it is also *through* us that this consciousness of our planetary predicament is being realized. That says something about our unique role as well as our unique responsibility.

We have a planetary crisis on our hands. We need a faith that is big enough to encompass that crisis, one that can move us toward a way of life that makes possible *ecological hope*.

Turning toward what?

Enlarging our sense of God and finding a framework of meaning that can carry us now will require, as we said above, a great turning. Turning from what toward what? From all we've read up to this point, we get a sense of the content of this turning. We are turning away from a way of life, a life "style," that is killing the planet, but we are also turning from a framework of meaning, a certain narrow religiosity, and a Western capitalist culture that have allowed that lifestyle to flourish.

That framework of meaning has been centered on what is to the benefit of the human, and, in this culture, of the *individual* human, an economic system that has been rigged for the enrichment of the few and for a while in this country the comfort of the many (that old American Dream), the earth at the service of that enrichment, comfort, and convenience. The economic model that has proved so vibrant and resilient over many generations is founded on the belief in endless growth and wealth generation, and based on a concept of the human as innately competitive and aggressive (and so also our gods and religions). It doesn't work anymore, and the solution to our crises cannot be found within that framework

In this society, in particular, we are turning away from a view of our nation as somehow innately better than others, superior, the "City on the Hill" version of national religiosity. We are discovering that we don't know everything, or know "better," and that to get out of our predicament we need to start seeing ourselves as part of a species that's in a whole lot of biological and ecological trouble. We are turning away from narrow patriotism to a new experience of planetary identity, one we share with all other humans.

We are turning our heads, our eyes, our whole orientation, *away from one all-encompassing view to another*—nothing less significant than that. We are closing the book on the Cartesian, mechanistic view of our world, an Age of Enlightenment that put the world at the service of the rational, thinking human, that separated us from our planetary story, and turning toward, or re-turning toward, our true roots in the evolutionary story of the earth. We are turning away from "I think, therefore I am" to "I live in this biosphere, I breathe its air, I share its humus—therefore I am." We are turning from the God inside our heads, contained in our thinking and yet "outside" the universe, to the God who is the Creation happening all around and in and through all living beings, all galaxies, the creative energy of the cosmos.

The Creation Museum is one example of what we are turning *from*, a dramatic one. Here's another striking but revealing example:

In spring 2007, the Associated Press covered the story of a group of religious leaders who traveled to Kentucky to bear witness to mountaintopping and to offer a word of protest and a prayer over the wounded Appalachian Mountains.[5] As I mentioned in Chapter 3, coal companies are not exactly thrilled to have these visitors in their neighborhood. Brian Patton, president of James River Coal Company, was among the unhappy ones. His company is involved in mountaintopping and strip mining—a lot of wounds ripped into the earth.

Patton is also a deacon at the Calvary Baptist Church in Lexington.

Now, the religious leaders are looking out at the expanse of the oldest mountain range in North America and the damage that human beings have done to it in order to get power to run the engine of our enormous economy. They are reconnecting to something primal in the human spirit, a reconnection that is vital if we are to heal the wounds of the earth. Yet it is Patton who is quoted as saying that the protesters have "a narrow view of things."

My first thought was, what could be narrower than viewing these mountains as mere detritus to remove to get to the coal veins, making big profits in the process? Economic self-interest is certainly a narrow view, one shared widely in this society. And fitting the reality of these mountains into the small space of that self-interest takes some doing. But then he articulates perfectly our "religious" problem:

"As a Christian, I've been taught to worry about saving souls, *as opposed to* environmental issues" (my emphasis).[6] Saving souls as opposed to caring about the destruction of the mountains. Environmental issues, by this account, are not part of the Christian mandate, and saving souls is something that goes on quite outside the economic and ecological realities of our daily lives.

This is a particularly striking example of the tension between the "personal salvation" version of Christianity and a spirituality that embraces the world. And unless we think that the breakdown of ecosystems and the possibility of the end of human life on the planet have no bearing on the Christian story, this very small, very narrow religiosity has little to offer us. In fact, it can justify, excuse, or ignore the enormous damage we are inflicting on our "home," along with all the human suffering that accompanies it, because these things have no bearing on whether or not we are "saved." It can approach our planetary crisis with a shrug of the shoulders.

Which "Christian" witness offers us the best hope of ensuring a habitable planet for the next generations? Where do we think our priorities ought to be? Unless we don't think the planet matters.

But even then, even praying over the mountains and protesting these egregious wounds, we need to turn more, stretch farther. Another example: In June 2007 the Episcopal Church Presiding Bishop Katharine Jefferts Schori, who is also an oceanographer, testified before the Senate Committee on Environment and Public Works on behalf of the National Council of Churches about the connections between poverty and climate change. "All living things are deeply interconnected, and all life depends on the life of others. . . . This interconnectedness is one of the central narratives of Scripture. God creates all people and living things to live in relationship with one another and the world around them." She stressed that "climate change will exacerbate poverty" while poverty "will hasten climate change." They are inextricably linked. "Those living in poverty . . . will suffer a disproportionate share of the effects of climate change." She called on the US government to increase foreign aid to fight poverty, cancel debts of poor countries, and change international trade rules in a way that empowers poor people to find their own path out of poverty.[7]

Then she called on our leaders to "take seriously our share in the global responsibility for reducing carbon emissions," and to help provide the technology that poor countries need to meet their energy needs without "hasten[ing] the rate of climate change." This was powerful testimony reflecting the organic reality of creation, and humans as part of it. But the tension is revealed in the contrast between the urgency of the language about the crisis expressed in her testimony and the language used when calling for change on the part of this affluent society. As an example, submitted with her testimony was a list of principles on global warming endorsed by at least sixteen religious organizations, including the National Council of Churches USA, which sponsored the initiative, several denominations, and Pax Christi USA. Among the principles was "*Sufficiency*: In a world of finite resources, for all to have enough requires that those among us who have more than enough will need to address our patterns of acquisition and consumption. We cannot achieve significant reductions in global warming emissions unless we make changes in our lifestyles and particularly in our energy consumption."[8]

This is good; this is a partial turning in the right direction. And many denominational leaders are saying these things. But the turning required of us in this society involves something more, because for all the concerns about global climate change and its impact on the poor, we are still largely ignoring that other elephant in the room—*the crisis of ecological overshoot.* We need not only to reduce emissions of greenhouse gases in order to save the planet for future generations, but also *to consume less*, a lot less. And we cannot ask this of the poor.

The statement of faith principles uses very careful language here—"address patterns of acquisition and consumption." It doesn't sound so scary or life-changing. But the reality is that addressing these "patterns" in a way that can bring our ecological footprint back into balance with the earth's life-giving ecosystems will require some pretty drastic changes.

It seems to me that what is really needed here is a call from religious leaders around the world to their communities and congregations, on ethical and moral grounds, to stop living beyond the means of our planet, and to begin that project immediately. Since this will involve some pretty significant economic jolts, we had better get to work soon figuring out how we're going to do this—with as much *ease* as possible, which doesn't mean easy or without some considerable discomfort.

It seems to me that the clarion call that needs to go out, to this society in particular, is to turn *away from the age of the economic being to the age of the ecological being.* What is required now, and this must be the content of the call, is that this nation and other rich countries—and our religious and pastoral leaders as well—be summoned to turn toward a new way of life, to begin creating that new way of life, one that puts our consumption and waste back into balance with nature, into a relationship with the earth that allows the earth to heal, restore, regenerate what is needed to continue the story of life, while *at the same time* making it possible for poor people to no longer be poor.

And this is going to be hard; it is going to be for us who are so used to so much, who take so much convenience for granted, the hardest thing we have ever done. But *not* making this turn will also be the hardest thing we have ever done, because we will be handing over to the next generation and the one after that a planet in terrible shape where all the crises we have outlined in this book will be manifesting themselves at the same time.

Religious leaders must help this cause by becoming witnesses to this new way of life through relinquishment of personal and institutional privilege and, yes, comfort and convenience. It will require more than "greening" our buildings and offsetting carbon emissions produced by our lifestyle habits, however necessary those habits seem to be in *our* case. The most important witness religious leaders and congregations can make in the face of our crisis is to turn themselves away from a nonviable, unsustainable way of life to a downwardly mobile, ecologically healing way of life. They must do this because it is incumbent upon them to offer *hope*, and there is no other way to offer it. If we don't show that the turning is possible, then we cannot expect people to turn. Instead, we just offer a very bleak view of the future and a witness of helplessness, selfishness, and despair.

What are we turning from? We are turning away from a way of life that has created a vast store of knowledge, technological and scientific advance, creativity and ingenuity, personal comfort and convenience, but also enormous suffering in our world, vast ecological destruction, great chasms between rich and poor, wars and terrorism across the planet, threats to our future and the future of our children. We are turning from a way of life that has used knowledge and technology to "overcome" nature and turning toward a way of life that uses knowledge and technology as sources of wisdom about how to live appropriately on the planet.

What are we turning toward? A way of life that stops the destruction, creates the possibility of healing these gaping wounds on our planet, and brings the human project back down into the balance of life.

A dark night, a deep dying

We are also turning from older, narrower versions of our religious story, our faith traditions, in search of one that can encompass that hope. This will mean a spiritual *turning* as well, letting go of ideas and values that no longer serve, that keep us *small*, and turning toward a greatly enlarged sense of the Sacred, the Divine. If we can no longer wrap our minds around God or make God fit neatly into our world views, since those world views are being shattered or have become destructive, we have to do something difficult— live into what we do not understand, what we cannot quite see, what we cannot hold in our hands, what doesn't lay out a neat predictable map for how to behave in order to be saved. We will need to walk into a kind of spiritual darkness, feeling our way through, not controlling the transition but letting go and allowing it to happen through us, trusting that *it* knows what *it* is doing.

Constance Fitzgerald, OCD, whom I quoted at the beginning of this chapter, is a contemplative Carmelite nun living in Maryland, so her spirituality has deep roots in St. John of the Cross and a spirituality of "dark night." Her 1984 essay "Impasse and Dark Night" speaks to the spiritual crisis in which we find ourselves:

> We are citizens of a dominant nation, and I think that as a nation we have come to an experience of deep impasse and profound limitation. . . . As Americans we are not educated for impasse, for the experience of human limitation and darkness will not yield to hard work, studies, statistics, rational analysis, and well-planned programs. We stand helpless and confused, and guilty before the insurmountable problems of our world. We dare not let the full import of the impasse even come to complete consciousness. It is just too painful and too destructive of national esteem. We cannot let ourselves be totally challenged by the poor, the elderly, the unemployed, refugees, the oppressed; by the unjust, unequal situation of women in a patriarchal, sexist culture; by those tortured and imprisoned and murdered in the name of national security; by the possibility of the destruction of humanity.
>
> We see only signs of death. Because we do not know how to read these kinds of signs in our own inner lives and interpersonal relationships, we do not understand them in our societal or national life, either. Is it possible these insoluble crises are signs of a passage or transition in our national development and in the evolution of humanity? Is it possible we are going through a fundamental evolutionary change and transcendence, and crisis is the birthplace and learning process for a new consciousness and harmony?[9]

Twenty-some years after this essay was written, hasn't it become clear that this is what is happening?

Fitzgerald notes the troubled signs of the times that manifest our predicament: "Is it any wonder we witness the impacts of impasse among us— anger, confusion, violence—since real impasse or dark night highlights destructive tendencies? Frustrated desire fights back."[10]

As we enter into a dark night for humanity, when we find ourselves on the brink without any easy way out, would we expect the world to be calm and peaceful, to think we can get the tensions under control with wars and bloated defense budgets and economic sanctions imposed on others and secret detention centers and covert intelligence operations and authoritarian government? Do we think we can create a Department of Homeland Security that is capable of warding off the forces of change by sticking its thumb in the hole in the dike while the dam is collapsing all around us?

Is there a technological quick fix for our situation?

Of course the world is going to be turbulent, violent, terrified, and terrify-ing—just as the Earth will move and buildings shake and ocean waves wash over us. Such are the forces of creation. The question for us is, how do we live through such a time?

Again, Fitzgerald: "We dare not believe that a creative revisioning of our world is possible. Everything is just too complex, too beyond our reach. . . . Death is involved here—a dying in order to see how to be and to act on behalf of God in the world."[11]

Embracing the dying, the dark night, the impasse, crisis, limits. Letting go of our American can-do attitude and our belief that we are the center of the world. Acknowledging and accepting the end of our way of life. Living with insecurity and risk in a turbulent world. Becoming downwardly mo-bile.

These are not exactly traits that come naturally to US Americans.

And yet, ecological hope depends upon those traits. There is no other way out.

The role of US Americans

Things are pretty bad, so what are we going to do? How do we proceed? Once we know that we are "in a pickle," so to speak, how do we get out of it?

First, of course, is that we have to stop doing the things that got us into the pickle to begin with. If we can see now how our predicament was cre-ated, then it would be crazy to just keep going on like this, wouldn't it?

Once again, we need to be clear about how dramatic a shift is called for here. Thomas Berry wrote an essay many years ago now that articulates it pretty well:

The violence done to the Earth is on a scale beyond all understanding. It can only be considered as the consequence of a deep cultural pathol-ogy. The change required by the ecologist is a drastic reduction in the plundering processes of the commercial industrial economy.

Never before has the human community been confronted with a situation that required such a sudden and total change in life style un-der the threat of a comprehensive degradation of the planet.[12]

What Berry describes in this short essay is the nature of what is now the really basic conflict among humans in terms of ecological crises—those who favor continuation of the destruction, whose self-interests lie there (devel-opers), and "ecologists," whose "orientation [is] towards the natural world."[13]

We will either save the fabric of life on the earth, or we won't. In many ways, humans now have more power over the fate of the planet than ever before—and yet part of our fundamental response to the threat posed to the earth must be *that we use our power to relinquish power,* especially here in the West, and especially here in the United States.

Only a deep cultural pathology could explain how we can keep on destroying what we need in order to live. That pathology is defined more than anything by the manner in which our modern industrial and technological way of life has separated us from nature, broken our awareness of our intimate connections with the natural world.

Again, Berry: "A special poignancy is experienced in a realization that future generations will be living amid the ruins, not simply amid the ruined infrastructures of the industrial world, but amid the ruins of the natural world itself."[14]

When I was a kid, we used to catch little frogs on our walks to school. They were prancing around yards and up tree trunks. Fifty years later, after all that development in Wauwatosa, I was walking along the old trails, the very same ones of my childhood, with my godson Aidan, right along the banks of the Menomonee River, and despite our searching, in all those many walks, we managed to find one frog—one. I remember his joy. It was the most exciting moment of his day—and therefore of mine.

"The profoundly degraded ecological situation reveals a deadening of some parts of human intelligence, and also the paralysis of human sensitivities," writes Berry. "Developers have lost the capacity for experiencing the loss of beauty and magnificence as we devastate the woodlands and ruin the habitat of birds and butterflies and so many other living creatures."[15]

And in this capitalist culture, we believe they can do this by "right," and we have set up a legal system to protect those rights. The earth and its creatures have no voice, for the most part, in our economic decisions—ask the spirits that reside in the Appalachian Mountains in coal country. Some of those enriching themselves on that business have actually said that they "improved" the mountains by building golf courses and retail business on the flattened land. This creates jobs, a local economy.

Every mountain shall fall, and every valley be filled in. Eschatological future of our Western faith traditions. All the coal companies are doing is what God pronounced as sign of his presence within our history.

We need, desperately, a new spirituality, a new story.

For the consumer society, the consequences of our choices now give us a role that is both grave and crucial, whether or not we welcome it. As Thomas Homer-Dixon says:

> We need to move away from what I call strictly utilitarian values which focus on simple likes and dislikes that emphasize consumption of material goods, towards moral values, and even what I call existential values. These relate to what we consider the good life, what brings meaning

into our lives, what kind of world do we really want for our children and our children's children.[16]

Sadly, and I agree with Homer-Dixon here, given the evidence so far:

I don't think we're going to really begin those conversations in a proper way until we face some crises or breakdowns. . . . I believe there is a spectrum of forms of collapse. At one end is the ideal, optimistic future where we solve all our problems and we live happily ever after. At the other end is catastrophic collapse. We have tended not to fill in the spaces in between, but that's actually where things might be very interesting. There may be some form of disruption and crisis that will actually stimulate us to be really creative. Most importantly, they may allow us to get the deep vested interests that are blocking change out of the way. . . .

The key thing . . . is that we have to keep the breakdown from being catastrophic. There has to be enough resilience in the system, enough information, enough adaptive capacity that things can be regenerated. With catastrophic breakdown, recovery is often impossible.[17]

I included this long quotation in order to pose this question as clearly as possible—*what is the role of the US American, the world's biggest consumer society, in preventing catastrophic breakdown that would make recovery impossible?* Because that more than anything defines our mission, our task, in helping our world get out of this predicament. Ecological hope depends upon how we answer that question; it depends upon making the right decisions regarding that role.

George Monbiot writes:

Capitalism is a millenarian cult, raised to the status of a world religion. Like communism, it is built upon the myth of endless exploitation. Just as Christians imagine their God will deliver them from death, capitalists believe that theirs will deliver them from finitude. The world's resources, they assert, have been granted eternal life. . . .

Now, despite the endless denials, it is clear that the wall towards which we are accelerating is not very far away. . . .

One reason why we fail to understand a concept as simple as finitude is that our religion [the millenarian cult of capitalism] was founded upon the use of other people's resources: the gold, rubber, timber of Latin America; the spices, cotton, and dyes of the East Indies; the labor and land of Africa. The frontier of exploitation seemed, to the early colonists, infinitely expandable. Now that geographical expansion has reached its limits, capitalism has moved the frontier from space to time: seizing resources from an infinite future.[18]

Now, political systems of the West have also been built on this economic system. Unless politicians promise this infinite future, more purchasing power for individual voters, more guarantees for investors and businesses, they do not win office. And, especially in the United States, if candidates cannot attract major funds from the corporate world, they are unable to compete successfully. They cannot even get noticed by our corporate-owned media.

Again, Monbiot:

> Everyone who holds power today knows that her political survival depends upon stealing from the future to give to the present. Overturning this calculation is the greatest challenge humanity has ever faced. We need to reverse not only the fundamental presumptions of political and economic life, but also the polarity of our moral compass. Everything we thought was good—giving more exciting presents to our children, flying to a friend's wedding, even buying newspapers—turns out also to be bad. It is, perhaps, hardly surprising that so many deny the problem with such religious zeal. But to live in these times without striving to change them is like watching, with serenity, the oncoming truck in your path.[19]

Are we up to the challenge?

What do you think? Are we up to this?

Let's lay out the challenge clearly—human beings must drastically lower, overall, our levels of consumption and waste to live within the means of the earth's carrying capacity. That means we must cut consumption and waste by that 40 percent of that capacity beyond which we are living right now, and we must do this as we add two to three billion more humans to the planet.

Now, justice demands that we who have so much more than we need do this to the amount, to levels, that allow five billion people who are and will be living in abject poverty to no longer live in abject poverty. They must be allowed, as it were, to *increase* their consumption and waste to levels that allow that to happen without continuing to steal more from the future of the planet.

That's it. That's the inescapable moral challenge of our time. Right there, in that location, reside both the source of ecological hope and what blocks it, depending on how we rise to the challenge.

In the last chapter I critiqued the social justice framework, but we haven't done away with it. Now it falls *within* the framework of our ecological reality rather than *being* the framework. Because, as we begin to reinvent the human presence on the earth, it is the responsibility of those who created the ecological crisis, who have benefitted from it, to downscale their consumption and emissions to the point where the poor can upscale and emit more in order to live dignified lives.

At the same time, the human community is part of an *earth* community, a community of living beings and creatures of all sorts who depend upon one another and the living systems of the planet for the continuing unfolding of *life*. This is why our sense of justice must also enlarge, respecting all other beings with whom we share this planet and the ecosystems that support their existence, respecting not only other humans with whom we share the earth, but also the forests, the oceans, the wetlands, the deserts, and all that reside within them, all that makes this a living planet.

Jane Blewett, founder of the EarthCommunity Center in Laurel, Maryland, and an associate of the Medical Mission Sisters, has spent the past twenty years advocating among religious congregations, especially women religious, for a spirituality that puts the earth story at its center. In an interview for this book conducted in May 2007, she said to me:

> We grew up with this thing of examining our conscience, or looking at your life in a moral framework. More and more it seems to me that the questions that come to the human are, what do we put, or what does our breath put, into the air of creation every day; what do I bring of life from within me that is life-giving to the rest of the community? How does my life contribute—my life, my breath, my spirit—how does that enhance the community? *That's* the question at the end of the day.
>
> The times demand a much larger context than what I have said to my neighbor [for example]. I don't want to dismiss that, but it's too small a context for our times. The times demand a much larger context, a context larger than we've ever incorporated in our consciousness. To get to the context of the human, to get to other peoples, other countries, other nations, that was an expansion. It wasn't just me, my family, my neighbor, my country. Expanding beyond our human community, the community we identify with, to other humans was certainly an advancement, and it continues.
>
> But expanding that context now to this larger community of all creation—that is the setting within which we make our moral judgments today. That's the setting. Anything smaller than that is too small.[20]

What is our role, then, as US Americans in addressing our planetary crisis? Nothing smaller than that—making moral judgments each and every day about how the choices we make, however large or small, affect that setting that has now enlarged to the community of all creation. Our role is to start ratcheting down the ecological footprint of the human species on the planet by drastically reducing our exorbitant, inordinate contribution to its destructive impacts. We have to scale down and begin reducing quickly our consumption toward the basics of what we need for a dignified, meaningful life—and no more.

Since it is very late and since we cannot expect that overnight we will be able to live without our cars or the produce shipped from faraway places—that is part of the world we must reinvent—we need to begin re-creating how we live at the same time as we must strengthen ourselves for the difficulties this world will endure because of the harm that has already been done. This is called adaptation, and it ain't going to be easy.

Do we have what we need to do this? Do we have what we need *within*? Is our faith or religion big enough to hold us on this journey and give us what we need to make the great turning? Ecological hope rests in how we answer those questions in the day-to-day living out of our lives. If we can find what we need *within* to do this, than that ecological hope will carry us through this difficult transition to living beyond the "end of the world."

9

And in Conclusion

or,

What Kind of Human Beings Will We Be as We Go Through the Crisis?

> *In time of crisis, we summon up our*
> *strength.*
> *Then, if we are lucky, we are able*
> *to call every resource, every forgotten image*
> *that can leap to our quickening, every*
> *memory that can make us know our power.*
> *And this luck is more than it seems to be: it*
> *depends on the long preparation of the self to*
> *be used.*
> *In time of the crises of the spirit, we*
> *are aware of all our need, our need for each*
> *other and our need for our selves. We call*
> *up, with all the strength of summoning we*
> *have, our fullness. And then we turn; for it*
> *is a turning that we have prepared; and act.*
> —MURIEL RUKEYSER[1]

We must reinvent the human presence on the earth. We must face the reality of our planetary crisis. We must take up the work of bringing the human project back down to scale. We must restore the balance of this one species with the rest of nature. We must do this respecting the lives, dignity, and integrity of every person on the planet, whose right to life is as valid as ours. We must wrest our spiritual values from an economic system that has endangered our planet and greatly cheapened the meaning of our lives.

What could be a more worthy task for people of faith? For everything we do now is weighted with meaning and responsibility, with moral and ethical content related to this crisis. Our lives have taken on new importance, and how we articulate and live out our faith within this context will play a crucial role in determining how that importance affects the fate of life on this earth—whether for its healing or its destruction.

We can hardly waste another day. We know now that we cannot save ourselves from more turbulence, even catastrophes, as Katrina and 9/11 have already shown us. But neither do we have to see these events as signs of an "end time" in which there is nothing we can do to "save" the world. We have to see these events not as signs of defeat and despair but opportunities for awakening and for hope.

Thomas Homer-Dixon writes that "we're unlikely to prevent all forms of breakdown and that sometimes breakdown can open up opportunities for deep and beneficial progress . . . if men and women of courage and good sense are prepared to act." He continues: "We're entering a crucial time in our history. In coming decades we'll come upon one critical junction after another in rapid succession. The choices we make and the paths we choose at each junction will be irreversible."[2] That is a whole lot of moral weight resting in those choices, but there it is. It is the world we have made, the one we actually live in. There is no escaping it.

When Muriel Rukeyser, one of the great poets and literary figures of the twentieth century, wrote the words in the epigraph above, the world was passing through a very dark time—the rise of fascism, World War II, the rise of the Soviet state. She was recalling a fearful flight, a journey out of Spain just as that country was descending into civil war. A shadow was falling on that nation, and in the end those struggling for freedom did not win. Dictatorship and repression followed for a generation. These words came out of a very fearful time, a turbulent time, a time when despair could easily have overwhelmed hope as the darkness of fascism spread across Europe.

We call up our strength. We call on all the resources we will need to get through and beyond the "end of the world"—including, and most of all, our faith, our values, what gives shape and meaning to our lives and the decisions we will make from here on out.

We begin "the long preparation of the self to be used," as Rukeyser put it, in this most important journey of our lives.

I want to conclude this conversation with one more question, really, the important one that lies latent in everything written so far: What kind of human beings are we going to be as we go through the crisis time, the time of transition? That is the question that ought to greet our every waking moment now, the one we pray into each morning, meditate with through the day, ponder as we go to sleep at night. That is the question for our examination of conscience. That is the moral question that presents itself to us before the lives of our young and those to come after them.

There are many things we can *do* or advocate for as we begin the reinvention of the human and how we live on the planet. There are economic, political, and policy choices that are already being discussed in many places around the world and have been for some time. We are not helpless to get this process under way if we can wrest our political culture away from the domination of corporations and the politicians whose careers they own, and start getting our families, friends, colleagues, and church communities to rally behind some of the needed changes.

But the wresting we must do—and that will not be easy.

I can think of all sorts of policy changes, new laws, a change in economic thinking, that could make huge differences in how deep the crisis will be. Take tax policy as one example. We could return to the days of heavily taxing excessive wealth and locking those monies into programs that would ease the transition to a new economy: providing social supports for the urban and rural poor; funding programs to re-create the entire food-production system, moving away from industrial agriculture to locally appropriate farming, especially organic farming; revamping education to address the ecological crisis and prepare students for this new world; and the list goes on, a long one.

I think of things like cutting the defense budget in half, for starters, and putting that money toward new technologies for clean, ecologically appropriate energy, or toward financing the shift from a growth economy based on consumption to an economy based on the balance of life, or toward transformation of the infrastructure away from individual automobiles toward clean and accessible mass transit. I think about not only a steep carbon tax on our fossil-fuel burning but also pricing energy by its actual costs to the environment—like putting a value on the Appalachian Mountains, the land, the streams and rivers, the pollution and permanent destruction for future generations—and making the coal industry and consumers actually pay for that—which would put the costs of coal out of reach pretty quickly.

I think about turning the US political culture away from its hubristic approach to foreign policy to one based on the urgency of international cooperation on these critical issues.

I think of prohibiting the manufacture of cars and other personal vehicles that get less than fifty to sixty mpg (the technology exists for this) and offering tax incentives to turn in our gas-guzzlers, with plans to recycle the metal and other materials. I think of taxing second, third, and fourth homes at an ever-rising rate—a big one, based on energy usage and the real costs to the planet. Make the wealthy pay for their exorbitant ecological footprint, and then use that money to put more land out of the reach of developers. I think of changing laws to put sharp constraints on developers on where and how they can build. I think of building codes that would mandate the construction of "green" buildings, and green buildings only.

I think of stripping the constitutional "right of persons" from corporations, one of the greatest follies in all our history, and turning them into what they ought to be—institutions at the service of human needs, not human greed. Gerald Barney calls them "fictitious persons,"[3] and we need to end this fiction.

I think about re-creating human communities so that more of the vital activities of life—going to school, to worship, to parks, to get groceries—can be done without getting in our cars. I think about the need to start planning for the relocation of coastal communities, including the dismantling of buildings and infrastructure safely away from future flood zones.

I think about increasing international aid with a focus on helping poor nations cope with the impacts of climate change and environmental degradation, while providing recompense for the damage we have done through generations of capitalist exploitation.

I think of some things more controversial from the perspective of some of our churches, perhaps, but equally urgent, like international family-planning programs, and especially the education and empowerment of women around the world along with the availability of reproductive services—the most proven path thus far for lowering birth rates (abortion rates, too).

However, this chapter is not about policy changes. I only mention them here to give us a sense that we are not helpless; there is work we can do now to begin moving toward this new culture of the "ecological citizen." And that work needs to be part of how we see our mission as humans within this society, part of the answer to the question of what kind of human beings we will be. The choices we make must also inform our *political* choices, and this political culture is in great need of alteration—from its roots. Making the wholesale changes implied in our long, and still only partial, list of necessary policy changes will require a wholesale change in that culture, in how we perceive ourselves as US Americans, in what defines us as a nation and a people, indeed, what gives meaning and content to the notion of being a US American.

So what I want to focus on here is less about what we do and more about what kind of humans beings we in this most affluent of societies will be as we go through this crisis. Because how we answer this question will determine how the planetary story unfolds and the prospects for easing the marble down the side of the bowl. It is in our answer to this question that the true content and values of the faith we profess will be witnessed and proclaimed.

As Brother David Steindl-Rast said not long ago: "True contemplatives are not dreamers. Their eyes hold a vision, while their hands translate that vision into action."[4] It is time for us all to become "true contemplatives," people who can translate the vision of a new human presence on the earth into action.

First, restoring a primary relationship

It should be obvious at this point that among the most critical "turnings" that we must make for the healing of our planet is that we renew, rediscover, reconcile, and begin to heal our relationship with our "home community." This is the primary relationship of our lives, the one on which all others are based. And it is very broken, profoundly damaged. In many ways, it is paradigmatic of all the other broken relationships of our lives.

Jane Blewett says:

> If in the human arena you've broken a relationship, or have not established a relationship, the only way to correct that is that you have to spend time, you have to invest in building a relationship, or rebuilding it. If you've destroyed something, you have to go back, re-create and try to rebuild what you've destroyed. Or, if you've never established a relationship, how do you establish one? You invest time and energy in the enterprise.
>
> We have to invest ourselves in learning again, or learning for the first time, who is this community within which we live. Who are the members of this community? I have to learn, I have to invest time in establishing a new relationship between me, the birds, the trees, and the squirrels. And that means study, that means work, that means time and energy in that enterprise.[5]

As we "study" our ecological being and our location within the earth community, we relearn our sense of place, who we really are within it, what are the very surroundings within which we live and move and have our being. Dust we are—humus, cells and molecules, energy and matter—and unto dust we shall return—what forms us, creates us, takes us back again. Our surroundings, this natural world, is us, the womb that births us and holds us. It would be pretty crazy to kill the very stuff of which we are made.

That we don't feel ourselves part of that "stuff" speaks not to our being separate from it, but to the creation of a way of life and thinking and worship that has caused us to feel separated. The relationship is broken, and to heal any relationship takes time and energy and compassion and love. Sometimes we must ask forgiveness, be reconciled, before we can bring our gifts to the altar, before the relationship can be restored.

Relationships cannot be healed by hubris, by airs of superiority, by lies or distortions, by avoiding truth, by being unwilling to face up to things, what we've done, the sources and causes of the brokenness. They can only be healed by facing the truth about ourselves and each other. They can only be healed through mutual respect, honoring the truth and reality of the other, by not trying to steal from the spirit of another something we want selfishly for ourselves.

And so of our planet earth and all its living reality.

So also the importance of taking a walk in the woods, listening to the birds, breathing in the air of the forests, the scent of the oceans, taking our children by the hand and letting their wonder help us rediscover our own.

Restoring these relationships may do far more than we realize. Our alienation from our true roots, our primary community, is part of our contemporary pathology. US Americans spend a lot of money going to see psychotherapists, and the psychotherapeutic world tends to keep us focused on our individual stories and broken relationships. This puts a lot of pressure on individuals, couples, and families to deal with their "inner wounds," or avoid them, within the context of an ecologically damaged and broken world. But, as we have seen, many of the pressures on these relationships are directly related to the torn fabric of our planet and our societies caused by the pathological mode of living that makes up so much of the contemporary world. We seek something in these personal relationships that can heal the alienation, which can only be healed by healing the alienation.

A book that offered a very different view of this, and that has influenced my own thinking, is *Ecopsychology: Restoring the Earth, Healing the Mind*. It consists of essays by psychologists and ecologists who examine the links between our individual pathologies and broken personal relationships, and our broken relationships with the earth. An example of what I mean:

> An ecologically responsible construction of the self will require what Arne Naess calls the "ecological self," which includes not only growth in human relationships with family and community, but a broadening of the self through identification with all beings, even with the biosphere as a whole. This broadened identification with all beings is the basis for the mutuality and passionate engagement, the direct experience of interconnectedness, called for by the ecological crisis of our time. When we are able to experience this interconnectedness, we need no moral exhortation to adjust our behaviors and our policies in the direction of ecological responsibility. As Naess points out, if we "broaden and deepen" our sense of self, then the earth flows through us and we act naturally to care for it.[6]

If we invest the time in the relationship, if we know one another and love and respect one another, we will act "naturally" to care for the relationship. How can we not? In the truth of the relationship, in the investment of time in it, we will find, not by edict or exhortation, but through what comes naturally, what it is we need to do.

So that's the first thing—invest in the relationship.

Kinship

What kind of relationship? In recent generations, our relationship with the earth has been marked by exploitation, greed, and self-interest. The result is reflected all around us. Sister Miriam Therese McGillis, OP, founder of Genesis Farm in New Jersey, where programs in the "new universe story" and earth literacy have been going on for more than three decades, describes the relationship as "a human material culture walking on a dead, material planet."[7] Her project has been a counter-witness to this "dead" connection between the human and the earth, and thousands of people have participated in her programs, reconnecting with the natural world, learning skills for ecologically whole and healing ways to live within the earth community, restoring a human relationship with a living, organic planet.

Another kind of relationship is that of stewardship, of earth put into the care of humans as garden to be tilled and nurtured, what some call creation care. In this relationship, we are indeed appalled by what we have done to this wondrous garden, and it is our responsibility to tend it with greater care, with an attitude of gratitude for the gifts of nature given to the human by a loving God and with a sense of responsibility to future generations.

Now this is clearly an advance, a major step forward from seeing the earth as a resource to be exploited for human gain. But there remains a tension here, a somewhat patronizing tone in the face of nature, an "over and above" approach to it that is already part of our problem. This kind of relationship still has the earth given to humans for our benefit. Lacking is a sense of our horizontal interrelatedness, relationships among equals, and we humans still have a hard time thinking of other life forms as equals. We are not talking here about equals in the sense of intellectual achievements or levels of consciousness—we are not the same as the worms. We are talking instead about how each participant playing a role in holding together the fabric of life, maintaining ecosystems and bioregions, is deserving of our respect, has its own integrity within the whole.

We are talking about the *integrity* of creation, all of it. Worms may not write books or build cities, but humans cannot live without them.

In these relationships we realize that we do not have all wisdom and knowledge, and that in order to receive the wisdom of the other we need to stop and listen and learn and see what the other has to teach us (which is how science can become a profoundly contemplative act). When something gets out of balance, or a life form emerges that could threaten the whole—and this does happen in nature all the time, like now, for instance—everything else reacts to it, and often nature must make the correction, restore the balance, reknit the fabric. Sometimes nature is able to adapt and integrate, put the new thing into a new balance, but sometimes not and a time of turbulence ensues. Even from the things that go "wrong," we learn something about how all life is related in an organic whole.

We humans already play a role in healing imbalances, often, as in our search for a cure for AIDS or Alzheimer's disease, our earth restoration projects, our Endangered Species Act, our growing fears about global climate change. We are also nature trying to restore balance, recover from things that go awry.

Consciousness is, of course, a great advance of (not *from*) nature, providing an astounding capacity to know our world and to reflect on it and also giving us what we need to protect and enhance the prospects for abundant life unto the seventh generation—if we use it with wisdom and a good dose of humility.

At the same time, this one species, mistaken perhaps about the role of consciousness, could bring about the kind of collapse that destroys the natural resilience that makes recovery, healing, and regeneration possible. Instead of enhancing the resilience of the system, we could, by our relentless assault on the earth's ecosystems, take nature past the point where recovery is possible. We could become one of those species that earth must recover from, rather than a tool in its healing, a species the earth can no longer support.

So "caring for" is crucial, no doubt. But I believe we need to go deeper, to move beyond a "caring" approach to the natural world, for this too pretends a vantage point of the human standing just outside nature rather than within it. We need to overcome this sense of hierarchy among living beings, remembering—as we have said before in this book—the earth and living creatures can get along fine without us, as they did for millions and millions of years, but we cannot get along without them. We, too, need to be cared for and nurtured by nature. The caring must be, as Thomas Berry would say, mutually enhancing.

At this point in our evolution, when this species threatens life in a manner unprecedented in hundreds of thousands of years, it may behoove us to remember what nature can do, and has done in the past, when life has gone out of balance. Eons of time have passed, and geological records show us the many times the earth has destroyed one version of life in order to create another. We are no more or less subject to that earth story. But how do we want that story to continue for Homo sapiens?

So we seek a different kind of relationship, from *within* this community rather than from without.

Jane Blewett tells the story of a village in the Dominican Republic where a logging company had taken down eighteen giant ceiba trees, trees that were part of the community. "The people's reaction was to toll the church bells that announced the deaths of members of the community when that happened. It was spontaneous, it wasn't planned."[8]

I remember when it became necessary to cut down a century-old oak tree just outside the back of my old house in Takoma Park, Maryland, because it was diseased and had become a real hazard. Making that decision had been wrenching, but an arborist assured us that it was necessary, that trees, too, have a life span. The night before they came with the crane and the chain saws, I spent some solitary time with that tree, thanked it for its beauty and its shade, told it that I loved it and was sorry for what we had to do. I leaned against it and took in its strength.

When the workers cut at last through the trunk, we found the tree to be hollow inside. We had made the right decision, but I can fully understand the grief that might lead one to run over to the nearby church tower to toll a lament. At least this act had been done with respect, with appreciation and gratitude, we humans playing a necessary role in that neighborhood fabric of life.

Sister Elizabeth Johnson, CSJ, who teaches theology at Fordham University, speaks of the importance of the connections between ecology and theology. She notes that coming to a stewardship model is definitely an advance, "but once you start to work with this issue, and begin to love the Earth, then your spirit moves to kinship. It happens on the level of spirituality."[9]

"From stewardship to partnership to friendship," said Blewett, "that seems to me the evolutionary journey that we're on. We begin to see ourselves as partner in the enterprise, and then we're friends. We become friends with the rest of creation now in a very different context. There is a progression [in the relationship] that also registers a change in time."[10]

A change in time, in *our* time. A change in our experience and our knowledge of the place of the human, as well as what binds us with the sacred. Where two or three are gathered, in the connections within and among all the different aspects and life forms of this planet earth and from the earth within the cosmos, the interrelationships through which life continues to evolve and unfold and manifest itself, there *I am* in the midst of you.

How do we bring this relationship into our daily lives, into our overcrowded urban communities, our monocultural suburbs? How do we make it possible for us to see the damage, knowing that awareness will bring grief and the necessity of change, a sense of how deeply we have wounded these primary relationships? How do we return love to the community?

Well, we do the work. We take the time. We remember that of which we are a part, and we reverence our place within it. We let go our need to control the relationship, to understand everything, to figure everything out. We *be* in the relationship. We restore our connection with that which is deepest within ourselves, and beyond ourselves, that binds us to everything, that is the Creator and Creation happening all the time everywhere. And from there, out of that relationship, we begin to take up a new way of life.

Here's how Thomas Merton once put it:

> I must learn . . . to let go of the familiar and the usual and consent to what is new and unknown to me. I must learn to "leave myself" in order to find myself by yielding to the love of God. If I were looking for God, every event and every moment would sow, in my will, grains of His life that would spring up one day in a tremendous harvest.
>
> For it is God's love that warms me in the sun and God's love that sends the cold rain. It is God's love that feeds me the bread I eat and God that feeds me also by hunger and fasting. It is the love of God that sends the winter days when I am cold and sick, and the hot summer when I labor and my clothes are full of sweat: but it is also God Who breathes on me with light winds off the river and in the breezes out of the wood. His love spreads the shade of the sycamore over my head and sends the water-boy along the edge of the wheat field with a bucket from the spring, while the laborers are resting and the mules stand under the tree.
>
> It is God's love that speaks to me in the birds and streams; but also behind the clamor of the city God speaks to me in His judgments, and all these things are seeds sent to me from His will.
>
> If these seeds would take root in my liberty, and if His will would grow from my freedom, I would become the love that He is, and my harvest would be His glory and my own joy.[11]

As beautiful as the psalms—the experience of God filling every point, every moment, every interconnection of life and matter, in all of creation. Pierre Teilhard de Chardin wrote:

> But now . . . a swift reversal is making us aware that your main purpose in this revealing to us of your heart was to enable our love to escape from the constrictions of the too narrow, too precise, too limited image of you which we have fashioned for ourselves. What I discern in your breast is simply a furnace of fire; and the more I fix my gaze on its ardency the more it seems to me that all around it the contours of your body melt away and become enlarged beyond all measure, till the only features I can distinguish in you are those of the face of a world which has burst into flame.[12]

And Rosemary Radford Ruether:

Consciousness is one type of highly intense experience of life, but there are other forms present in other species, sometimes with capacities that humans lack. . . . Human consciousness . . . should not be what utterly separates us from the rest of 'nature.' Rather, consciousness is where this dance of energy organizes itself in increasingly unified ways, until it reflects back on itself in self-awareness. Consciousness is and must be where we recognize our kinship with all other beings. The dancing void from which the tiniest energy events of atomic structure flicker in and out of existence and self-aware thought are kin along a continuum of organized life energy.[13]

In the face of this glory, if you will, there is the reality of how we humans have mis-thought our place in the creation story, how profoundly we mis-understood, and the damage that has been done accordingly. In a section of her book *The Body of God* entitled "Sin: The Refusal to Accept Our Place," theologian Sallie McFague writes:

Our particular form of grandeur is in relation to the earth and derived from it—we are the self-conscious, responsible creatures . . . in the common creation story, we are not sinners because we rebel against God or are unable to be sufficiently spiritual: our particular failing (closely related to our particular form of grandeur) is our unwilling-ness to stay in our place, to accept our proper limits so that other indi-viduals of our species as well as other species can also have needed space. . . . Our grandeur is our role as responsible partners helping our planet prosper, and our sin is plain old selfishness—wanting to have everything for ourselves.[14]

This "sin" is what we must come to terms with now. Religion, faith, must address it—*fundamentally*, from its very roots. This is one of the central chal-lenges to our faith traditions, and indeed I believe they will be judged a generation from now by how they measure up to that challenge. Do they help restore our kinship with nature? Do they help us right our egregiously wronged relationships with the community of living beings on our planet? Do they reorient our priorities accordingly? Do they help us envision a way through the crisis? Do they provide a vision for the human presence on the earth that is commensurate with the crisis? Do they give us a framework of meaning and values that can shape our days, our life choices, the way we go on about our lives now? Do they provide us the real and tangible commu-nity supports that will make it possible for us to create this new way of life, because this is going to be hard and we will need all the friendship and shared community we can get to do this great turning?

Selfishness is our greatest failing in regard to how we have lived on this planet. We have done terrible harm because of it. It is a bad habit, one deeply embedded in the culture in which we live until it feels almost instinctive. It will be hard to give it up.

It will be hard as well to face up to the wounds we have inflicted, though the pain of those wounds is manifested all across our planet. It is hard to acknowledge the damage we have done to something so near, so intimate, so wondrous. But there is something else we need to know about this earth—it can be very forgiving. Over and over again, it has re-created, regenerated life. We can be part of the process—if we want to be. Our faith must invite us into that process and begin to cooperate fully with it.

The role of religion

In our era we have seen religion used to justify war, suicide bombings, the blowing up of mountains for electricity, disengagement from responsibility for the planet, who wins elections or even the Super Bowl, and all manner of indifference to the cultural, political, and economic values that have created our crisis. Even when religious institutions and leaders have been critical of these values, they have been very timid in the face of the controversy that such criticisms can stir up, including among the faithful. Often they write good statements—on climate change or poverty, for example—but are fearful of offering the prophetic voice that reaches down to the pews. Rarely do we see a vision proffered that lifts our spirits to the dimensions of the crisis, much less a direction and sense of purpose that can help us through and beyond it.

This is important on two counts. On the one hand, this world is going to be going through a wrenching time, as we have outlined in this book. Katrina and 9/11 are sadly portentous events, and they are matched, or even outmatched, by similar calamities already around the globe, again, as we have seen in our survey. If we are honest, we know things could get a lot worse in the near future.

Will we leave people without the framework of meaning to understand why these events occur—as pretty much happened with 9/11, for example? Will we leave people shocked, traumatized, and paralyzed, or can faith be a source of courage, strength, compassion, understanding, what can pull people together in difficult times, rather than tear them apart, or leave them feeling hopeless, angry, and bereft? We saw both the best and the worst of this after 9/11. (Remember Rev. Jerry Falwell blaming feminists, gays and lesbians, and abortionists for why God let those planes crash into the World Trade Center? At the same time, remember the voices that refused war and vengeance as moral and ethical responses to the attacks?)

On the other hand, we need faith and religion to offer vision and meaning, an enlarged sense of evolutionary and ecological purpose, to provide a unifying sense of God and a framework of values that can inspire humans as they face one difficulty after another as a result of ecosystem breakdowns and stresses.

Mary Evelyn Tucker and John Grim, research scholars and senior lecturers in religion and environment in the Divinity School and School of Forestry and Environmental Studies at Yale, spoke to this need for a greatly enlarged religious vision:

> Our challenge now is to identify the vision and values that will spark a transformation toward creating such a planetary civilization. A sustainable future requires not just managerial or legislative approaches—the saving of forests or fisheries—but a vision of that future, evoking depths of empathy, compassion, and sacrifice for the welfare of future generations. . . . We need a serious wake-up call from our slumbers. The environmental crisis presents itself as the catalyst pressing individual religious traditions to awaken to their ecological role.[15]

What they must awaken to is the unifying nature of the crisis we face. They must awaken to the necessary role they must play to help inspire humanity to the great turning required of us now. This becomes their primary task in the context of our great predicament. If anything can bring the various faith traditions and indigenous cosmologies together around one table, it should be this sense of the common story we share—of both creation, how we got to be here, and the potential of imminent catastrophe, how we could soon end this story.

Tucker and Grim write:

> Currently the dreaming meets an impasse. There's a puzzling disconnection between our growing awareness of environmental problems and our ability to change our present direction. We have failed to translate facts about the environmental crisis into effective action in the United States. We are discovering that the human heart is not changed by facts alone but by engaging visions and empowering values. Humans need to see the large picture and feel they can act to make a difference.[16]

Tucker and Grim note that in many ways this dreaming past the impasse has already begun, as more and more theologians and religious leaders around the world come to realize the gravity of the crisis and to cooperative ecumenically, with NGOs, the United Nations, and many other groups to speak out about the planetary crisis.

A many-faceted alliance of religion and ecology along with a new global ethics is awakening around the planet. Attitudes are being reexam-
ined with alertness to the future of the whole community of life, not
just humans. This is a new moment for the world's religions, and they
have a vital role to play in the emergence of a more comprehensive
environmental ethics. The urgency cannot be underestimated. Indeed,
the flourishing of the Earth community many depend on it.[17]

Because I believe this is true, that living beyond the "end of the world"
depends upon the awakening, visionary leadership, and cooperation of religions across boundaries of traditions and orthodoxies, it is also urgent and
necessary that this awakening be translated down with similar urgency to
the communities inspired by, or dwelling within, those traditions. This disconnect of which Tucker and Grim speak is not only between our awareness
of the crisis and our ability to change direction, but also between what many
religious institutions and leaders know and write about the crisis and what is
actually communicated in sermons, teachings, schools, bible classes, cat-
echisms, and more, among their faithful. The language of "patterns of acquisition and consumption"[18] needs to become concrete in the daily living
out of our lives, in the choices we make about how we live, in how we reshape the politics of the country in keeping with the exigencies of the crisis,
and how the community of faith takes up the challenge set in the last chapter in the concrete witness of that community—to bring the ecological footprint of the human species back into balance with the life systems of the
planet while allowing billions of poor people to no longer be poor. Whatever one's religious tradition, this should be at the very heart of the project
of faith from here on out.

Turning

So, how do we begin the turning? First, lest this all feel impossible and
overwhelming, let's acknowledge that we are not starting from scratch here.
This is not a lonely struggle to which we are being called. The awakening to
our planetary crisis is happening all around the world, bubbling up from
local communities everywhere. Already, communities, centers, projects, aca-
demic programs, and more have been and are being created to begin the
process of reinventing the human presence on the planet. Already, people of
faith have gone to their traditions to find what is there that can help us now.
Already, earth spiritualities are surfacing as many people move past the constraints of traditions and the values of an alienated culture to articulate this
"something new" in our consciousness about the place of the human within
the earth and the earth within the cosmos, within this one act of creation

ongoing since the Big Bang. Already, people are finding within that act of creation the *Presence* of the Sacred and the Divine.

For some, it begins in meditation and spiritual renewal. For others, it begins with a loving glance around the immediacy of our local community to see not only the beauty around us but the threats on all sides to that beauty from pollution, overuse, and abuse, from exploitation, greed, and indifference. As I traveled around the country in recent years, there was hardly a location that did not have some local environmental group trying to defend some aspect of the earth community. If you look around your world, you will find them, and this is certainly one place to get started.

Still others look at the global view and, seeing the melting glaciers, the shrinking Arctic Sea ice, the warming oceans, the endangered species, the lands becoming uninhabitable, the threats to human communities across the world as a result, get involved with organizations seeking to protect the planet in the many aspects of the crisis, including an overhaul of US policies and practices in regard to the environment.

Part of our new spiritual practice, whether in our quiet meditation or in our actions and projects, must be the *practice of listening*, the *practice of wonder*, the *practice of seeing*. This is an essential aspect of that investment of time described by Blewett and others. For example, stop for a moment to be very conscious of your breathing. With each breath, you are taking in the oxygen created by the living planet and breathing back out the carbon dioxide that, in balance, greens the forests and fields. You are integral to, a participant in, the living processes that make the earth unique in the observable universe. You are enveloped in living relationships that made you and keep you alive.

When you sit at meals, be very conscious of your food, not just where it came from and the hands that made it, but how every molecule within that food was created from the moment of creation some fourteen billion years ago, as are our own. By the work of creation over those billions of years, some stardust settled into this planet, into this body, into this food, into those hands that produced the food, into the table where we sit, and into the other hands we hold in our blessing. It got organized over time, with a little help from us, and here we are sharing this repast together.

As we become more aware of the interlocking dynamisms of our beings-in-connection, we are likely also to become more aware of the role we play in the living rhythms of our biosphere. It is a crucial role, one that can now work for healing or destruction. We begin to get a sense of what we might be breaking apart by how we live and why it is important to live in such a way that we honor those connections.

It is a form of conscious, or mindful living, of contemplation and even mysticism. Our senses and spirits are awakened to every aspect of our being, inside and out; we are in relationship, inside and out, spiritually and physically, living now in a state of heightened awareness. We bring to each day, each breath we take, each decision we make, this awareness of how our decisions and actions will affect all the other beings around us, the air we all breathe, the soil from which comes our food, the ecosystems that maintain and nurture life in our bioregion, the tensions among the human community.

We try to lower the impact of our ecological footprint; we try to minimize the damage; we seek ways to promote the healing. We begin to turn.

Feels daunting, doesn't it, when you're stuck in rush-hour traffic, or you're under pressure to spend vast amounts of money on consumer goods for Christmas, or you have to keep working in a job that exploits the planet but that you can't quit because you need the salary and the health insurance for your family.

Sometimes this version of living in communion with nature sounds very romantic, but not very real, right? The world has been organized differently, not with the earth in mind, and now we have to begin, step by step, to reorganize it based on quite different priorities, with the well-being of the planet at the very center of our concerns. The turning will not happen all at once, but it can begin today, right now, in the choices we make.

Living in a world of trouble

I want to say just a word about the turbulence of this transition at the risk of articulating too much fear, but I think we need to be brave about this— life on this earth, human beings on this earth, are going to go through a very difficult, painful transition. It has already begun, as we have seen in this book. The evidence of breakdown is everywhere, though, as we have said before, those with the means can ward off the full impact for a while longer.

In our new spiritual praxis we will need to learn how to embrace upheaval rather than fear it, along with a lot of inconvenience that will come with it. We will need to do this with patience, with calm, with balance within ourselves, holding steady as the turbulence increases, not responding to violence with more violence, holding in check that knee-jerk response that demands vengeance and the justice of the God who surfaces so often in the Old Testament, the one who seems bent on the utter defeat and humiliation of the "enemy."

We have seen way too much of this in recent years, and the human community can hardly stand much more of it. In these years since the attacks of 9/11, we have seen what violent responses do, how much success they have in healing the wounds of our world, what success they have in beating back hatred. Wars, human rights violations, incendiary policies and rhetoric have brought us closer to a cliff's edge that is steeper and more dangerous than anything since the United States dropped the atomic bombs on Japan, with the possibility of truly irreversible, catastrophic results for all living creatures on the earth. Mix hatred with nuclear, chemical, and biological weapons technology and you have a mix more volatile than the most powerful explosives ever invented.

We have to stop bashing the heads of the babies and children of our enemies against stones. We have to stop bombing their villages, their homes, whether or not the insurgents take cover there. It is wrong, and the hatred is fed a generous portion.

This is what we are to do instead—love our enemies and pray for our persecutors now more than ever before, with passion and compassion, as hard as this is now and is going to be in a world in which this nation has drawn so much hatred to itself, in a world of great upheaval where everything, everything, is undergoing deep and wrenching change. We must end war as an acceptable response to a world of trouble.

I was reading again the context of that passage from the prophet Joel that is traditionally read on Ash Wednesday—the one about rending your hearts not your garments (2:13). It's pretty grim. The armies of the enemy are invading. The trumpet is sounded. "A day of darkness and gloom, day of cloud and blackness" descends upon the people. It is "the day of YHWH," and it ain't going to be pretty.

"The country is like a garden of Eden ahead of them and a desert waste behind them. Nothing escapes them" (2:3)—a vision far too close for comfort, given our world right now. A terrible battle ensues. And who is at the head of the army? None other than YHWH! (2:11).

But wait, now YHWH speaks. God pulls back. "Come back to me with all your heart, fasting, weeping, mourning." Now God is "all tenderness and compassion, slow to anger, rich in graciousness, and ready to relent" (2:13).

How do we bring about this "turn" in God? We call the assembly. We gather the community. We assemble the religious leaders, the elders, the children among us. "Do not make your heritage a thing of shame, a byword for the nations" (2:17).

Do not leave to generations that come after you a mess of shame and violence, a degraded world, a world where misery is the lot of the human.

Okay, I still rebel against the war-making image of God, but it does present, does it not, a sense of what is needed from the community of faith to stop in its tracks this course toward more war, more violent upheaval, more ecological chaos.

And in this world, what is the role of the US American?

I did not ask this question lightly: *what kind of human beings are we going to be as we go through the crisis?* What kind of human beings here in the United States? Will we be kind, generous, compassionate, forgiving, willing to share burdens, to help alleviate the suffering that is coming? Will we be willing to let go of our privileged places, relinquish possessions and the desire to possess them, scale down our lives and live far more simply, or will we try to hang on to what we have, and even more?

Will we trust forever in our military might? Will we double again our military budget or begin to turn our swords into plowshares? Will we hate our enemies or love them? Will we respond to violence with compassion and understanding? Will we relinquish our contribution to it or keep adding our measure?

Will we give up our inordinate control of the world's wealth? Will we cling to the belief that life owes us an ever-increasing standard of living—can we surrender this as a life's goal? Will we put up walls against the realities of our world until the catastrophes finally overwhelm them, as in our Katrina metaphor, or can we begin to tear them down in order to embrace a sense of common humanity facing a common predicament? Instead of trying to hold back the forces of nature, can we move out of the way and let the flood waters wash over the earth to restore, or regenerate, the flow and balance of life?

Will we break and share our bread or hide the loaf in a safe place, guarded by security systems?

It has come down to this, it really has. We will have to answer this question at every level of our lives—personal, economic, social, political, and religious. Which is why we need a deep faith, an abiding trust in what is at work here, a hope in what we cannot see, but intuit in the deepest part of our being.

And this is what I believe—that this new mission of the human, to reinvent the human presence on this planet, has the capacity to fill our lives with such meaning that we will begin living differently because *we want to.*

You see, it's not that we have to make some big sacrifice and stop shopping—oh, it hurts, it hurts!—no, rather, it's that we just don't care about shopping anymore, it's not important whether we have the new iPhone or a plasma screen. Those aren't the concerns that fill our days anymore. They just fall away—we don't *give up*, rather, we *enter into*. Consumer goods—we begin to feel the offense to the earth and our spirits. We begin to *feel* the alienation and emptiness, the void where meaning should be. We begin to simply lose interest.

What could possibly be more threatening to business-as-usual than that? What greater contribution could we make to lowering the temperature of our overheated, depleted, violent world?

Getting to work, the *great work*, that is

Back in 2004 I referenced the planetary crisis for the first time in a presentation I delivered at Marquette University in Milwaukee. The event was sponsored by the Central America Awareness Committee, and it was part of their annual commemoration of the deaths of four US missioners in El Salvador on December 2, 1980—Maura Clarke, Ita Ford, Dorothy Kazel, and Jean Donovan. I had spoken at such events many times over my twenty-five years with the Religious Task Force on Central America and Mexico but had never before put that event in the context of the ecological crisis and the challenge it poses to our way of life in this country, the need to downscale and alter how we live. Frankly, I was nervous about how it would be received.

Using the example of the martyrs, I spoke of the challenge to people of faith that such crises present, how in moments like the one faced by the women as El Salvador was sinking into civil war we have to decide what kind of human beings we are going to be, what our response will be, our witness, our role in that crisis. The four women made a heroic decision, one that has inspired people of faith around the world, especially in this country, for going on three decades. They stayed, despite violence and death threats all around them. They stayed, accompanied the people in that terrifying time, and then shared, as was so often reiterated over the years until it was like a mantra, "the same fate as the poor."[19]

As part of my talk, I presented the realities of the world's inequities—nothing new for this audience—but then spoke of how our consumption had gone beyond the carrying capacity of the earth and that we were headed for some very difficult times. In that context we would have to ask ourselves, as the women did, how we will respond to that reality, what kind of people we will be, what kind of faith we will witness. And then I closed with a much-quoted excerpt from Thomas Berry's *The Great Work*:

> Perhaps the most valuable heritage we can provide for future generations is some sense of the Great Work that is before them of moving the human project from its devastating exploitation to a benign presence. We need to give them some indication of how the next generation can fulfill this work in an effective manner. For the success or failure of any historical age is the extent to which those living at that time have fulfilled the special role that history has imposed on them. . . .
>
> The Great Work before us, the task of moving modern industrial civilization from its present devastating influence on the Earth to a more benign mode of presence, is not a role that we have chosen. It is a role given to us, beyond any consultation with ourselves. We did not choose. We were chosen by some power beyond ourselves for this historical task . . . We are, as it were, thrown into existence with a challenge and a role that is beyond any personal choice. The nobility of our lives, however, depends upon the manner in which we come to understand and fulfill our assigned role.[20]

And then I concluded by saying that, as Berry suggests, if we have been given that role, we must believe we have everything we need to fulfill it. We must trust that if we have evolved a consciousness that knows we are arriving at the brink, if we have evolved a consciousness that is now trying to pull us back from the brink, then we can trust that same process to help us find what we need to go through the transition from one age to another, to find what we need to reinvent the human presence on the Earth in a way that is mutually enhancing for all living creatures within the sacred biosphere. In Berry's words, "we must believe that those powers that assign our role must in that same act bestow upon us the ability to fulfill that role. We must believe we are cared for and guided by these same powers that bring us into being."[21]

When I finished I didn't know what to expect. What happened was not on the list—a sustained standing ovation. I was completely taken aback. Why? Why after all this bad news, indeed, for people of this society, would I be greeted so enthusiastically? I was really stunned. And then I realized that that response came out of an awareness, a fear, largely neglected in this society but already buried in the hearts of many people. They already know we are in big trouble. Clearly, I had addressed those fears, and done it in a public forum where people could see there were others sharing the fear. But more, using the witness of the four women as example, the witness of a quarter century of faith-based solidarity work in this country, along with the words of Thomas Berry, put hope on the radar screen. We were calling in that moment on the best in ourselves. We were offering to one another in a time of fear and great uncertainty about the future a call to a deeper faith, a more profound framework of meaning, a reason to get out of bed in the morning.

I will never forget it—not my surprise, not the little chill that went down my spine at the response, not the conversation that followed, not the passion that was in that auditorium that day.

As things turned out, it was not the only time I would receive this kind of response. What I had found was the pulse of a great number of people in the justice-and-peace community, in the solidarity community, in aware and struggling congregations around the country, seeking a way through the crisis, a path for the great turning, and a sense of connection with others on the journey.

Loaves and fishes: A spirituality for the coming times

So, now what? Now that we have some idea of where this world is headed, what do we do? Well, a few concluding thoughts. Obviously I don't have the comprehensive game plan for how we get out of our predicament, but I do have an idea about the path, how to get started on the journey through and beyond the "end of the world." Obviously, we need to alter the *culture*, the way we think, the values that undergird the system that has such a hold on our lives. We have to begin moving out of that system while we advocate for what can and must replace it.

This will not be easy, and what it requires is a *movement*, if you will, a critical mass of people prepared to do the switch. Remember, it has never taken a majority of a population to make big changes, as we know from the antiwar movement of the 1960s and 1970s, the civil rights movement, the women's rights movement, the labor movement, and more. And, as we saw above, the little seedlings of this ecological movement have been poking out of the earth all around this world in the past three decades, and they are growing like crazy. Our dandelions are cracking through all sorts of pavement.

But as we are wrestling with this from the vantage point of faith, we need to find within our traditions and beyond them what can help provide the spiritual sustenance and vision for the work we need to do. The United States remains a deeply religious society, and much of that religiosity still has a fundamentalist, conservative bent. Another discourse is needed now, one that reclaims the place of the human within this grand scheme of creation, including our role and responsibility toward the life systems from which we emerged and that sustain us and all living creatures. So I went looking for an image that could help inform the moment and inspire us as a model or metaphor for the times.

I turned again to the story of the loaves and fishes, an apt reflection for living in a world of scarcity, for a spirituality that can begin to shape our response to such a world. The people are hungry, and they have not brought food with them. The day is ending. The disciples cannot expect these folks to walk miles on foot back to their homes. They are tired. They need calories.

They have among them five loaves and a couple of fish, "but what are these among so many?"

Well, they are everything.

Now, this story could have gone another way. Jesus and the disciples could have said that there isn't enough for everyone, so let's keep information about the availability of this food from the people, let's keep the food for ourselves, and then we will be sure that *we* at least have enough to eat. This is the incarnate God and his followers, after all. They should come first.

Of course, had it gone that way, we would not be reading the Gospels at all two thousand years later.

Okay, I won't torture the obvious. Jesus blessed the loaves and fishes and the disciples distributed them among the crowd, each receiving a portion, and it turned out there was enough for everyone and even more than enough.

Out of the sharing came the abundance.

The loaves and fishes—taking from the scarcity of the moment to provide what is needed by all—can suggest a great deal for us in a world where food, water, and energy are becoming crucial issues for much of humanity, where we must find a way to share these things without depleting what will be necessary so that future generations have food, water, and energy.

We have to remember when we worry that there will not be enough to go around that we in the rich developed countries control and consume an overwhelming majority of all that is consumed on this earth, that 1.5 billion well-off people consume far more than the other five billion people on the earth, and that if we would stop doing this we could begin to have our own loaves-and-fishes stories. And we need to believe—for one thing because it is true—that we could reorganize the way in which the world does its business so that we in this society would indeed begin to have less so that others could have more.

What is lacking is the moral and ethical will to create such a world.

From all that we have learned in this book, we also know that we cannot do that, even *with* the moral and ethical will, if we deplete the life-sustaining gifts of the earth beyond its capacity to support this burgeoning human population. We have to reduce our consumption and waste below these critical carrying-capacity thresholds and reinvent a human economy that mimics the balance of nature and the workings of the biosphere.

In other words, in large measure, like it or not, the onus is on *us* to make this loaves-and-fishes world possible.

So here's my fantasy—that all around this country, pastoral workers, teachers, religious leaders (come on, you can do it and we need you to do it), parents, cultural workers come together wherever they are—in churches, schools, community centers, neighborhood organizations, around the family dinner table, on radio and TV talk shows—to "sound the trumpet," to "proclaim a solemn assembly," to "call the people together, assemble the elders, gather the children, even the infants at the breast" (Jl 2:15–16) to talk about our planetary crisis, how it came about and what we need to do.

I have this fantasy that we come together to proclaim a fast, not a fast of repentance and mourning, of punishment for sin, of miserable faces and growling stomachs that make us feel good in the moment but change very little in regard to our predicament. Rather, this would be a permanent fast from a way of life that has compromised our spirits and the biosphere in which we live and move and have our being, a fast from our overconsumption, our credit-card bills, our wasteful lifestyles. We proclaim the fast of the loaves and fishes, one that involves a scaling down to a simplicity in which it is possible to feel our bodies again as part of the earth, to feel our spirits alive and vibrant, part of this great act of creation begun fourteen billion years ago. We begin to take time, that time made available to us when we stop shopping and consuming and trying to make payments on those credit-card bills, to look around us at the people we love, the community we care about, including the earth community in our bioregion, and begin to spend time living into these relationships.

As we assemble, we are called not just to fast from this way of life, but to ask together, to really discuss and wrestle with, how we—as individuals, families, parishes, neighborhoods—can begin to do the turning, what commitment we are willing to make not just to lifestyle changes but to alterations in the political and economic culture of this nation. We ask ourselves in the context of our various communities how we can build the resilience required both within and without that we will need to get through the hard times that are coming, the difficult transitions. As we do this, we seek to create within these many layers of our lives the way of life that can carry us through, that can sustain us and help create the new human presence on the planet beyond the world that is now ending.

Community becomes essential in this permanent fast. Sharing implies community. Sharing is necessary if we are to ratchet down our consumption. Can you imagine people in your neighborhood or parishes joining together to carpool for grocery shopping to save energy and reduce carbon emissions? Can you imagine things like shared cars and trucks? Can you imagine the community building that might come from meeting with neighborhood groups to talk about how to make your town or city "green," environmentally sustainable, what energy sources might exist locally (solar, wind, geothermal, etc.), and then how to alter the tax structure and local economy to create these systems? Can you imagine the fun of making connections with farmers' markets and local farmers, developing community garden space right in your neighborhood, and helping to re-create your own local food system?

Can you imagine organizing your family and community to work together to influence local and national government policy, to attend candidates' forums and get-out-the vote efforts centered on an earth agenda?

There are so many possibilities and all of them take place in the context of community. Remember, community mimics something that comes naturally to the life processes of our earth. All life acts in community, interacting with what surrounds it. No life form exists on its own, which is one reason that our philosophy of individualism, of the individual in charge of his or her own destiny, is such a lie. The entire life story of the universe is based upon the interacting of all its different parts. The cosmos, nature, *is* community. Our insistence on the independence and autonomy of the individual is part of our cultural pathology—it does not exist in nature.

At the same time, a gospel-centered way of life is built upon community—where our possessions are held in common and we ensure that no one is in want (Acts 4:32–35). Would that we had ever lived anything like this vision of the early Christian community. It would be a very different world indeed.

Must we be reminded that in the Christian tradition not only is God present in community, where two or three are gathered, but that God *is* community, as revealed in the doctrine of the Trinity? Our individualistic approach to life in this culture has separated us not only from the nature that is our womb and life source but also from this very idea and experience of God.

Now, as we gather around our ritual meals, our bread and wine, as we offer up a prayer of blessing, we also recall that other foundational meal, the Last Supper. In this meal, in the sharing of something so basic as food and wine in a very difficult, heartfelt moment, a time of fear and confusion, the Divine became present. The bread and shared cup became for the disciples the stuff of life, the food of our bodies, nourishment for the journey, hope past the fear, infused with the Presence of all that is.

So our faith offers an insight into the way forward, a vision that can help us feel our way toward the new world we must create. We reach into its depths not for something spiritually superior, not for a holier way of life than others. It was never really meant to be that in any case. But now, relinquishment, simplicity, sharing things in common, becoming downwardly mobile, these things are no longer just admirable traits for the spiritually wise and advanced, *they have become necessities for the future of life.*

What kind of human beings will we become? As we embrace this difficult passage in our earth story, these shared stories and rituals will be important to expressing our fears and hopes, our sense of purpose, our visions for a new world, for healing, regeneration, hope beyond the "end of the world." They offer us a place to draw strength, build community, and find sustenance for the long haul as we make the necessary transformations. We are not carried outside faith, but deeper into it.

I want to close with these last thoughts. Our universe, as our understanding of it unfolds with the new cosmology and the new physics, is one indivisible all-encompassing explosion of energy and matter, creating and re-creating all that is, including space and time—kind of like our ages-old insight about God. We have learned that the source of creation exists at every point in spacetime, every point filled with the potential, the source of creation, for the bursting forth of life. Every point in the universe is a center from which the universe is expanding. Every place we look or touch, in every image that comes to us from the Hubble Space Telescope to the tiniest blade of grass, we are viewing a center of the universe.

All this matter and energy is interconnected, and science is telling us that there is some self-organizing principle at work, that mere randomness does not explain how the universe has unfolded.

This is pretty big stuff, and I can't get my head around it. However, embedded within this enormous creation from the very beginning were the conditions that created life on this one small planet in one of billions of galaxies in a solar system anchored by a fairly ordinary star.

Here is what we are part of: conscious human life emerged on that planet, and now we have the potential of snuffing it out. That's the drama. That is our stage. We know the role we played getting here, and now we have an idea of the role we need to play to bring this drama to a better conclusion than the one presented by our ecological crises.

This will take the fundamental transformation of that conscious life form. And whether or not that transformation takes place depends upon our answer to the question posed in this chapter—what kind of human beings will we be as we go through the crisis? How we answer that question will determine whether or not we live beyond the "end of the world."

I choose hope. I have to. I remember the many people who went down to Central America and changed their lives forever because of it, out of fidelity to the people they encountered, who welcomed them into their simple homes, shared their heart-rending stories of violence, war, and poverty. I remember how so many of us could never again look at our affluent lifestyles here in the United States and not feel emptiness and sorrow as we realized our interconnectedness with that suffering. I remember how, when people gathered to break bread, or tortillas and a piece of a chicken, it felt like the gospel had come alive now in our time—there was Jesus walking again in the streets of Nazareth.

Faith helped inspire and nurture that experience that so many US Americans described as conversion. And so it must again as we face this greatest challenge of our generation. We will do the great work, or there will be a depleted planet and much catastrophe in the coming generations. We need to believe that this great work is possible—within *us* and through *us*. We must believe we have what we need to do this turning.

Despite the bleak picture of the world presented in these pages, I choose hope here, crazy as it may seem. I choose hope because I have to, because despair and indifference cannot be the response of this species to the planetary crisis we have created. I choose hope because of what it would mean not to make that choice.

I choose hope because, before the children and young people in my life, before the mountains and forests, the oceans, lakes, and rivers, before that yellow-bellied marmot, the polar bears of the Arctic, before the meadow birds, the frogs, and the butterflies, I cannot, cannot accept the alternative.

Notes

Preface

1. I do feel some guilt about the carbon emissions, though flying would have been far worse. I assuage my conscience a bit by owning a high-fuel-efficiency Honda Civic—because I can't afford a hybrid yet—that uses forty-two miles per gallon. An efficiency rating at this level or better should be mandatory by now, because we have the technology.

Introduction

1. Cathy Lynn Grossman and Dan Vergano, "The Whole World, from Whose Hands?" *USA Today*, Science and Space section, October 10, 2005. Available online.

1. Of Earthquakes and Hurricanes

1. Muriel Rukeyser, *The Life of Poetry* (Ashfield, MA: Paris Press, 1996), 1.
2. US Army Corps of Engineers, "The Mississippi River and Tributaries Project," mission statement. http://www.mvn.usace.army.mil/pao/bro/misstrib.htm.
3. Daniel Zwerdling, "Sinking into the Sea," September 2002. http://www.americanradioworks.org/features/wetlands/index.html.
4. Brian Handwerk, "Louisiana Coast Threatened by Wetland Loss," News Archive, *National Geographic News*, February 9, 2005.
5. Cited in "Louisiana Marshes Fight for Their Lives," *New York Times*, November 15, 2005.
6. Anna Quindlen, "Don't Mess with Mother," *Newsweek*, September 19, 2005.
7. Daniel Zwerdling, "Hurricane Risk to New Orleans," September 2002. http://www.americanradioworks.org/features/wetlands/index.html.
8. "Louisiana's Marshes Fight for Their Lives."
9. Zwerdling, "Hurricane Risk to New Orleans."
10. Clifford Krauss et al., "As Polar Ice Turns to Water, Dreams of Treasure Abound," *New York Times*, October 10, 2005.
11. Andrew Bridges, "Development Raises Flood Risks Across U.S.," Associated Press, February 18, 2006.
12. See, for example, "Storm Puts Focus on Other Disasters in Waiting," *New York Times*, November 15, 2005.
13. Bridges, "Development Raises Flood Risks Across U.S."
14. Quindlen, "Don't Mess with Mother."
15. Nicholas Pinter, quoted in Bridges, "Development Raises Flood Risks Across U.S."

205

2. Climate Change

1. Cited in David Ignatius, "Is It Warm in Here? We Could Be Ignoring the Biggest Story in Our History," *Washington Post*, January 18, 2006. Lovejoy is head of the John Heinz III Center for Science, Economics, and the Environment.

2. Geoffrey Lean, "Global Warming Approaching Point of No Return, Warns Leading Climate Expert," *The Independent UK*, January 23, 2005.

3. Ibid. Another good article on this topic is Mark Hertsgaard, "It's Much Too Late to Sweat Global Warming: Time to Prepare for Inevitable Effects of Our Ill-fated Future," February 13, 2005. SFGate.com.

4. For a scary article about what is likely to happen in Boston, see Susan Milligan, "Study Predicts City Flood Threat Due to Warming," *The Boston Globe*, February 15, 2005.

5. Chip Ward, "It's Not Just Eskimos in Bikinis, Climate Helter-Skelter in the Lower 48," June 6, 2005. TomDispatch.com.

6. Andrea Minarcek, "Mount Kilimanjaro's Glacier Is Crumbling," *National Geographic Adventure*, September 23, 2003.

7. Ibid.

8. Michael McCarthy, "Global Warming Takes Its Toll on the World's Highest Mountain as Everest Shrinks by 4ft," *Belfast Telegraph*, January 26, 2005.

9. Jonathan Watts, "Highest Icefields Will Not Last 100 Years, Study Finds," *The Guardian*, September 24, 2004.

10. Andrew Buncombe, "Is This Proof of Global Warming?" *The Independent UK*, October 21, 2005.

11. Mike Aamodt, in ibid.

12. Ibid.

13. Sheila Watt-Cloutier, cited in Tom Engelhardt, "Xtreme Weather Meets Xtreme Media Bubble." http://www.tomdispatch.com/index/mhtml?pid=1851.

14. Ian Sample (science correspondent), "Warming Hits Tipping Point: Siberia Feels the Heat," *The Guardian*, August 11, 2005. The research was reported in *New Scientist Today* (August 2005).

15. Andrew Revkin, "The Big Melt—No Escape: Thaw Gains Momentum," *New York Times*, October 25, 2005.

16. Ibid.

17. Study cited in Andrew Revkin, "Climate Study Warns of Warming and Losses of Arctic Tundra," *New York Times*, November 2, 2005.

18. Ibid.

19. Kenneth Cladeira, cited in ibid.

20. Gerald A. Meehl (climate modeler), quoted in Revkin, "Climate Study Warns of Warming and Losses of Arctic Tundra."

21. Larry Rohter, "A Record Amazon Drought, and Fear of Wider Ills," December 11, 2005.

22. Ibid.

23. Joel Gay, "Climate Change Will Push Wildlife Northward and Upward," *The Anchorage Daily News*, January 3, 2005.

24. Steve Connor, "Warmer Seas Will Wipe Out Plankton, Source of Ocean Life," *The Independent UK*, January 19, 2006.

25. Doug Struck, "'Rapid Warming' Spreads Havoc in Canada's Forest, Tiny Beetles Destroying Pines," *Washington Post*, March 1, 2006.

26. Ibid.

27. Ibid.

28. Cited in Sandi Doughton, "The Truth About Global Warming," *The Seattle Times*, October 9, 2005.

29. Ibid.

30. James Randerson, "Deep Inside an Arctic Mountain, the Noah's Ark of Seeds That Will Survive a Catastrophe," *The Guardian*, January 12, 2006.

31. Eugene Linden, "Cloudy with a Chance of Chaos," *Fortune Magazine*, January 17, 2006.

3. The End of "Cheap Oil"

1. Michael Klare, "Global Warming: It's All About Energy," *Foreign Policy in Focus*, February 15, 2007.

2. James Howard Kunstler, "Globalization Is an Anomaly and Its Time Is Running Out," *The Guardian*, August 4, 2005.

3. Peak oil is based on the theory that the amount of oil buried in the earth is finite and that the rate of production follows a bell curve. On the way up, oil is abundant through discovery and recovery technology. At the peak, oil is in maximum production, after which it begins a steady decline. The theory was first developed by American geophysicist Marion King Hubbert and is often called the Hubbert Peak.

4. Klare, "Global Warming."

5. Gerald O. Barney, with Jane Blewett and Kristen R. Barney, *Threshold 2000: Critical Issue and Spiritual Values for a Global Age* (Arlington, VA: Millennium Institute; Grand Rapids, MI: CoNexus Press, 1999).

6. Jad Mouawad and Matthew L. Wald, "The Oil Uproar That Isn't, Despite Rising Fuel Prices," *New York Times*, July 12, 2005.

7. Daniel Yergin, "Energy Independence," *Wall Street Journal*, January 23, 2007.

8. Matt Simmons, "Energy in the New Economy: The Limits to Growth," speech, Energy in the New Century Conference, Energy Institute of the Americas, October 2, 2000.

9. Brian J. Fleahy, "USA's Triple Energy Whammy in Electric Power, Natural Gas, and Oil," iNet News Service, January 12, 2001.

10. Jeff Goodell, *Big Coal: The Dirty Secret Behind America's Energy Future* (New York: Houghton-Mifflin, 2006).

11. Corey S. Powell, "Black Cloud," *New York Times Book Review*, June 25, 2006.

12. Erik Reece, "Death of a Mountain: Radical Strip Mining and the Leveling of Appalachia," *Harper's Magazine* (April 2005).

13. John Holdren, quoted in Tim Folger, "Can Coal Come Clean?" *Discover*, December 18, 2006.

14. Ibid.

15. Ibid.

16. The easiest way to present this reality is to invite you to visit a website such as mountainjusticesummer.org or www.ilovemountains.org. Take a look at the photo galleries. Here you will see what is being done to the Appalachian Mountains in Kentucky and West Virginia in order to extract coal. Read some of the reflections from the people who live in these communities. Hold these pictures in mind as you continue to read this book.

17. Erik Reece, "Moving Mountains," February 16, 2006. Grist.org. Originally published in *Orion Magazine*.

18. Ibid.

19. Ibid.

20. Paul B. Brown, "What's Offline: How Many Miles to the Bushel," *New York Times*, May 27, 2006.

21. David Pimentel, quoted in Roger Segelken, "CU Scientist Terms Corn-based Ethanol 'Subsidized Food Burning,'" *Cornell Chronicle* 33, no. 2 (August 23, 2001).

22. Ibid.

23. Lester Brown, quoted in Rick Barrett, "Fuel for Car May Be Food for Trouble," *Milwaukee Journal-Sentinel*, January 5, 2007.

24. David Tilman and Jason Hill, "Corn Can't Solve Our Problem," *Washington Post*, March 25, 2007.

25. Ibid.

26. Sasha Lilley, "Green Fuel's Dirty Secret," *CorpWatch*, June 1, 2006.

27. Ibid.

28. Tilman and Hill, "Corn Can't Solve Our Problem."

29. Ibid.

30. Elisabeth Rosenthal, "Once a Dream Fuel, Palm Oil May Be an Eco-Nightmare," *New York Times Business Day*, January 31, 2007.

31. Ibid.

32. George Monbiot, "The Most Destructive Crop on Earth Is No Solution to the Energy Crisis," *The Guardian*, December 6, 2005.

33. Andrew Pollack, "Redesigning Crops to Harvest Fuel," *New York Times*, September 8, 2006.

34. Tilman and Hill, "Corn Can't Solve Our Problem."

35. Lester Brown, quoted in Barrett, "Fuel for Car May Be Food for Trouble."

36. Clifford Krauss, "Drivers Shrug as Gasoline Prices Soar," *New York Times*, March 30, 2007.

37. Clifford Krauss, "In Canada's Wilderness, Measuring the Cost of Oil Profits," *New York Times*, October 9, 2005.

38. Cat Lazaroff, "Oil Will Dominate Growing Energy Demand," Environment News Service, March 23, 2002.

39. Donella H. Meadows, Jorgen Randers, and Dennis L. Meadows, *Limits to Growth: The Thirty-Year Update* (White River Junction, VT: Chelsea Green Publishing, 2004), 88.

40. The report is available online at numerous websites.

41. Rt. Rev. Richard Chartres, quoted in Simon Baker, "Roads Group Slaps Down Bishop Who Called Gas Guzzler Cars Sinful," *The Guardian*, July 24, 2006.

42. Jad Mouawad, "Oil Innovations Pump New Life into Old Wells," *New York Times*, March 5, 2007.

43. Robert Heilbroner, *An Inquiry into the Human Prospect* (New York: W. W. Norton, 1974), 183.

4. Living Beyond Our Means

1. Lester Brown, *Plan B 2.0: Rescuing a Planet Under Stress and a Civilization in Trouble*, Earth Policy Institute (New York: W. W. Norton, 2006), 3.

2. Donella Meadows, Jorgen Randers, and Dennis Meadows, *Limits to Growth: The Thirty-Year Update* (White River Junction, VT: Chelsea Green Publishing, 2004), xiv, xxi.

3. Ibid., 138–39.

4. Ibid., 1.

5. Sven Burmeister, "Can the Twilight of the Gods Be Prevented?" *Friday Morning Reflections at the World Bank: Essays on Values and Development* (Santa Ana, CA: Seven Locks Press, 1991), 41–42, 46.

6. Brown, *Plan B 2.0*, 5.

7. David Brooks, "A Nation of Villages," *New York Times*, January 19, 2006.

8. Ibid.

9. Naomi Lubick, "Western Aquifers Under Stress," *Geotimes*, May 2004.

10. Meadows, Randers, and Meadows, *Limits to Growth*, 137.

11. *Ecosystems and Human Well-Being, Our Human Planet: Summary for Decision Makers*, Millennium Ecosystem Assessment series (Washington DC: Island Press, 2005). Unless otherwise noted, all quotations in this section are from this volume.

12. Steve Connor, "The State of the World? It Is on the Brink of Disaster," *The Independent UK*, March 30, 2005.

13. Walt Reid, quoted in ibid.

14. *Ecosystems and Human Well-Being, Our Human Planet: Summary for Decision Makers*, 3.

15. Ibid., 16.

16. Stephen Carpenter, quoted in Usha Lee McFarling, "'Green' Measures Key to Earth's Future, Report Says," *The Los Angeles Times*, January 20, 2006. Carpenter is one of the Millennium Ecosystems Assessment authors.

17. Brown, *Plan B 2.0*, 95.

18. Stephen Leahy, "World Stands at a Crossroads," Interpress Service, January 19, 2006.

19. International Water Management Institute (Colombo, Sri Lanka), *Water for Good, Water for Life: Insights from the Comprehensive Assessment of Water Management in Agriculture*, ed. David Molden (London: Earthscan Publications, 2006), 1.

20. Ibid.

21. Ibid.

22. *Ecosystems and Human Well-Being, Our Human Planet: Summary for Decision Makers*, 18.

23. Meadows, Randers, and Meadows, *Limits to Growth*, 41.

24. Thomas Homer-Dixon, *The Upside of Down: Catastrophe, Creativity, and the Renewal of Civilization* (Washington DC: Island Press, 2006), 64.

25. Ibid., 65.

26. Meadows, Randers, and Meadows, *Limits to Growth*, 124.

27. UNEP, *Global Environmental Outlook 2000*, quoted in Meadows, Randers, and Meadows, *Limits to Growth*, 124.

28. According to the National Oceanic Atmospheric Administration (NOAA).

29. Meadows, Randers, and Meadows, *Limits to Growth*, xv.

30. Ibid., 123. *Throughputs* are "flows of material and energy from the supporting environment, through the economy, and back to the enviroment" (Donella H. Meadows, Dennis L. Meadows, and Jorgen Randers, "Beyond the Limits, Executive Summary"). Available online.

31. Meadows, Randers, and Meadows, *Limits to Growth*, 124.

32. Burmeister, "Can the Twilight of the Gods Be Prevented?"

33. Brown, *Plan B 2.0*, 98.

5. A World of Trouble

1. Lester Brown, *Plan B 2.0: Rescuing a Planet Under Stress and a Civilization in Trouble*, Earth Policy Institute (New York: W. W. Norton, 2006), 110.

2. Thomas Homer-Dixon, *The Upside of Down: Catastrophe, Creativity, and the Renewal of Civilization* (Washington DC: Island Press, 2006), 17.

3. James Howard Kunstler, "The Long Emergency," *Rolling Stone*, March 24, 2005. www.rollingstone.com/news/story/7203633/the_long_emergency.

4. Lydia Polgreen, "Nigerian Oil Production Falls after a Pipeline Hub Is Overrun," *New York Times*, May 16, 2007.

5. Homer-Dixon, *The Upside of Down*, 81.

6. Chalmers Johnson, "America's Empire of Bases," *Common Dreams*, January 15, 2004.

7. Brown, *Plan B 2.0*, 78.

8. Homer-Dixon, *The Upside of Down*, 55.

9. Ilan Greenberg, "Russia to Get Central Asian Pipeline," *New York Times*, May 13, 2007.

10. Flynt Leverett, "The Race for Iran," *New York Times*, June 20, 2006.

11. Ibid.

12. Homer-Dixon, *The Upside of Down*, 55.

13. World Bank, Nigeria Country Brief. http://go.worldbank.org/F110T240K0.

14. World Bank, cited in Christian Allen Purefoy, "Oil Inflames Nigeria's Ethnic Tensions," *Christian Science Monitor*, July 26, 2005.

15. Jeremy Keenan, quoted in Jason Motlaugh, "US Takes Terror Fight to Africa's 'Wild West,'" *San Francisco Chronicle*, December 27, 2005.

16. Homer-Dixon, *The Upside of Down*, 125.

17. Luke Burgess, "Insider Information: What the Military Doesn't Want You to Know About Its Oil Consumption," *Energy and Capital*, July 11, 2006.

18. Sohbet Karbuz, "The US Military Oil Consumption," *Energy Bulletin*, February 26, 2006.

19. Eileen Westervelt and Donald Fournier, "Energy Trends and Implications for US Army Installations," US Army Engineer Research and Development Center (September 2005), 4. The report is available online.

20. Ibid.

21. Thom Shanker, "Military Plans Tests in Search for an Alternative to Oil-Based Fuel," *New York Times*, May 14, 2006.

22. Michael Aimone, in ibid.

23. Adam Fenderson and Bart Anderson, "US Army: Peak Oil and the Army's Future," *Energy Bulletin*, March 12, 2006.

24. Michael T. Klare, "The Post-Abundance Era," *Foreign Policy in Focus*, November 30, 2006.

25. Terrence McNally, interview with Thomas Homer-Dixon, "Is the Deadly Crash of Our Civilization Inevitable?" Alternet, February 13, 2007.

26. Richard Heinberg, "Threats of Peak Oil to the Global Food Supply," *Museletter/Energy Bulletin*, July 3, 2005.

27. Ibid.

28. José Antonio Rodríguez, quoted in Tim Gaynor, "Countries Increasingly at Odds over Water Sharing," *Reuters*, March 16, 2006.

29. Kevin Watkins and Anders Berntell, "How to Avoid War over Water," *International Herald Tribune*, August 23, 2006.

30. Ibid.

31. Ben Russell and Nigel Morris, "The Water Wars," *The Independent*, March 1, 2006.

32. Paul Rogers, quoted in Mark Trevelyan, "Climate Change Seen Fanning Conflict and Terrorism," Reuters, January 24, 2007.

6. The End of the American Dream

1. Thomas Homer-Dixon, *The Upside of Down: Catastrophe, Creativity, and the Renewal of Civilization* (Washington DC: Island Press, 2006), 186.

2. "Is Humanity Suicidal?" *New York Times Magazine*, May 30, 1993.

3. "In our every deliberation, we must consider the impact of our decisions on the next seven generations" (declaration of the Iroquois people).

4. Eduardo Porter, "Study Finds Wealth Inequality Is Widening Worldwide," *New York Times*, December 2, 2006.

5. Homer-Dixon, *The Upside of Down*, 187.

6. David Cay Johnston, "Income Gap Is Widening, Data Shows," *New York Times*, March 29, 2007.

7. Ibid.

8. Ibid.

9. Tony Pugh, "US Economy Leaving Record Numbers in Severe Poverty," McClatchy Washington Bureau, February 22, 2007.

10. "SEC to Tighten Reporting Rules for Executive Pay," *New York Times*, January 18, 2006.

11. US Census Bureau, 2005.

12. Sheila R. Zedlewski and Sandi Nelson, "Many Families Turn to Food Pantries for Help," November 25, 2003. Urban Institute website.

13. David Ellis, "Making Less Than Dad Did," May 25, 2007. Money.CNN.com.

14. Niall Ferguson, "Reasons to Worry," *New York Times Magazine*, June 11, 2006.

15. Ibid.

16. US National Debt Clock. http://www.brillig.com/debt_clock/.

17. Paul L. Wachtel, *The Poverty of Affluence: A Psychological Portrait of the American Way of Life* (Philadelphia: New Society Publishers, 1989).

18. Alan Thein During, "Are We Happy Yet?" in *Ecopsychology: Restoring the Earth, Healing the Mind*, ed. Theodore Roszak, Mary E. Gomes, and Allen D. Kanner (San Francisco: Sierra Club Books, 1995).

19. Homer-Dixon, *The Upside of Down*, 197.

20. Shankar Vedantam, "Social Isolation Growing in US, Study Says," *Washington Post*, June 23, 2006.

21. Greg Critser, quoted in Michiko Kakutani, "Tense? Lonely? There's Promise in a Pill," *New York Times Book Review*, September 30, 2005.

22. "Study Suggests Most in U.S. Will Be Fat," Associated Press, October 4, 2005.

23. Shankar Vedantam, "Science Confirms: You Really Can't Buy Happiness," *Washington Post*, July 3, 2006.

24. Daniel Kahneman et al., "Would You Be Happier if You Were Richer? A Focusing Illusion," *Science* 312, no. 5782 (June 30, 2007): 1908–10.

25. Robert A. McDermott, "The Spiritual Mission of America 1," Philosophy, Cosmology, and Consciousness at the California Institute of Integral Studies (March 2003). Available online.

26. Ibid.

7. Alienation from Nature

1. Rosemary Radford Ruether, "The Biblical Vision of the Ecological Crisis," in *Readings in Ecology and Feminist Theology*, ed. Mary Heather MacKinnon and Moni McIntyre (Kansas City, MO: Sheed and Ward, 1995), 75.

2. Ibid., 76.

3. Ivone Gebara, "Cosmic Theology: Ecofeminism and Panentheism," in MacKinnon and McIntyre, *Readings in Ecology and Feminist Theology*, 209.

4. Ibid., 210.

5. Ibid., 210–11.

6. Ibid., 211.

7. Thomas Merton, *Life and Holiness* (New York: Image Books, 1964), 101.

8. Bible quotations in this chapter are from *The Jerusalem Bible* (New York: Doubleday, 1966). Translations, of course, vary.

9. Pierre Teilhard de Chardin, *Hymn of the Universe* (New York: Harper and Row, 1961), 19.

10. Ibid., 20.

11. William Yardley, "Some Northwest Residents See Trees Differently After Storm," *New York Times*, January 8, 2007.

12. Ibid.

13. Ibid.

14. Larry Rohter, "Loggers, Scorning the Law, Ravage the Amazon Jungle," *New York Times*, October 16, 2005.

15. From a display at the historical site.

16. Verlyn Klinkenborg, "Millions of Missing Birds, Vanishing in Plain Sight," *New York Times*, June 19, 2007.

17. Ibid.

18. Ibid.

8. Ecological Hope

1. Thomas Homer-Dixon, *The Ingenuity Gap* (New York: Vintage Books, 2000), 8.

2. Constance Fitzgerald, OCD, "Impasse and Dark Night," in *Living with Apocalypse, Spiritual Resources for Social Compassion*, ed. Tilden H. Edwards (San Francisco: Harper and Row, 1984), 94.

3. Edward Rothstein, "Adam and Eve in the Land of Dinosaurs," *New York Times*, May 24, 2007.

4. Thomas Berry, "Reinventing the Human," in *The Great Work: Our Way into the Future* (New York: Bell Tower, 1999), 159–65.

5. "Religious Leaders Tour US Coal Mining Sites, Praying for End to Mountaintop Removal," Associated Press, May 3, 2007.

6. Brian Patton, quoted in ibid.

7. Katharine Jefferts Schori, testimony to the Senate Environment and Public Works Committee. www.episcopalchurch.org/78703_86656_ENG_HTM.htm.

8. For the "Faith Principles on Global Warming," including a list of institutional endorsers, see the Friends Committee on National Legislation website. www.fcnl.org/issues/item.php?item_id=2693&issue_id=102.

9. Fitzgerald, "Impasse and Dark Night," 93–116.

10. Ibid.

11. Ibid.

12. Thomas Berry, "Ecologist vs. Developer Conflict Replaces Liberal vs. Conservative," *Earthkeeping News* 3, no. 4 (March-April 1994). Available on the nacce.org website.

13. Ibid.

14. Ibid.

15. Ibid.

16. Thomas Homer-Dixon, in interview with Terrence McNally, "Is the Deadly Crash of Our Civilization Inevitable?" February 13, 2007. www.alternet.org/story/47963.

17. Ibid.

18. George Monbiot, "Our Quality of Life Peaked in 1974. It's All Downhill Now," *The Guardian*, December 21, 2002.

19. Ibid.

20. Jane Blewett, interview with author.

9. And in Conclusion

1. Muriel Rukeyser, *The Life of Poetry* (Ashfield, MA: Paris Press, 1996), 1.

2. Thomas Homer-Dixon, *The Upside of Down: Catastrophe, Creativity, and the Renewal of Civilization* (Washington DC: Island Press, 2006), 30.

3. Gerald Barney, interview, May 2007.

4. David Steindl-Rast, quoted in Rich Heffern, "A School for Engaged Wisdom," *National Catholic Reporter*, September 7, 2007.

5. Jane Blewett, interview, May 2007.

6. Sarah A. Conn, "When the Earth Hurts, Who Responds?" in *Ecopsychology: Restoring the Earth, Healing the Mind*, ed. Theodore Roszak, Mary E. Gomes, and Allen D. Kanner (San Francisco: Sierra Club Books, 1995), 163–64.

7. Sister Miriam Therese McGillis, OP, quoted in Jeffrey J. Guhin, "Where Are the Catholic Environmentalists?" *America* 194, no. 5 (February 13, 2006).

8. Blewett, interview.

9. Sister Elizabeth Johnson, quoted in Guhin, "Where Are the Catholic Environmentalists?"

10. Blewett, interview.

11. Thomas Merton, *New Seeds of Contemplation* (New York: New Direction Books, 1961), 16–17.

12. Pierre Teilhard de Chardin, *Hymn of the Universe* (New York: Harper and Row, 1961), 34.

13. Rosemary Radford Ruether, *Gaia and God: An Ecofeminist Theology of Earth Healing* (San Francisco: HarperCollins, 1992), 250.

14. Sallie McFague, *The Body of God: An Ecological Theology* (Minneapolis: Fortress Press, 1993), 113–14. The phrase "common creation story" refers to the Big Bang and evolution, the creation story shared by all human beings, however varied our religio-cultural traditions.

15. Mary Evelyn Tucker and John Grim, "Daring to Dream: Religion and the Future of the Earth," in "God's Green Earth: Creation, Faith, Crisis," special issue, *Reflections: A Magazine of Theological and Ethical Inquiry* [Yale Divinity School] (Spring 2007).

16. Ibid., 6.

17. Ibid., 9.

18. "Faith Principles on Global Warming." www.fcnl.org/issues/item.php?item_id=2693&issue_id=102.

19. A book by this title tells the story of Maryknoll Sisters Maura Clarke, Ita Ford, and Carla Piette, who gave their lives in El Salvador. See Judith Noone, MM, *The Same Fate as the Poor* (Maryknoll, NY: Orbis Books, 1995).

20. Thomas Berry, *The Great Work: Our Way into the Future* (New York: Bell Tower, 1999), 7.

21. Ibid., 7.

Index